## DATE DUE

| | | | |
|---|---|---|---|
| | | | |
| | | | |
| | | | |
| | | | |
| | | | |
| | | | |
| | | | |
| | | | |
| | | | |
| | | | |
| | | | |
| | | | |
| | | | |
| | | | |
| | | | |
| | | | |
| | | | |
| | | | |

# Global Capital and
# National Politics

K

# Global Capital and National Politics

## Reforming Mexico's Financial System

*Timothy P. Kessler*

PRAEGER

**Westport, Connecticut**
**London**

**Library of Congress Cataloging-in-Publication Data**

Kessler, Timothy P., 1965–
    Global capital and national politics : reforming Mexico's
financial system / Timothy P. Kessler.
        p.    cm.
    Includes bibliographical references (p.      ) and index.
    ISBN 0–275–96568–6 (alk. paper).
    ISBN 0–275–96569–4 (pbk. : alk. paper)
    1. Finance—Mexico.   2. Financial institutions—Mexico.
3. Finance, Public—Mexico.    I. Title.
HG185.M6K47   1999
336.72—dc21        99–22111

British Library Cataloguing in Publication Data is available.

Library of Congress Catalog Card Number: 99–22111
ISBN:   0–275–96568–6
        0–275–96569–4 (pbk.)

First published in 1999

Praeger Publishers, 88 Post Road West, Westport, CT 06881
An imprint of Greenwood Publishing Group, Inc.
www.praeger.com

Printed in the United States of America

The paper used in this book complies with the
Permanent Paper Standard issued by the National
Information Standards Organization (Z39.48–1984).

10 9 8 7 6 5 4 3 2 1

**Copyright Acknowledgments**

The author and publisher gratefully acknowledge permission for use of the
following material:

Excerpts from Tim Kessler, "Political Capital: Mexican Finance Policy under Salinas,"
*World Politics* 51.1 (October 1998): 36–66. © 1998. Center of International Studies,
Princeton University. Reprinted by permission of the Johns Hopkins University Press.

*Para Luzma*

# Contents

# Acknowledgments

Many people contributed to this book, the idea for which began at U.C. Berkeley before the term "emerging market" was in fashion. The most enduring contributions were made by political science professors Ruth Collier and Jonah Levy, who guided me through the formation of the research question, and helped me situate the work within political economy debates on liberalization. Each offered extensive criticism on early drafts which refined the emerging argument.

I benefited from participating in a 1996 dissertation seminar with a number of Berkeley colleagues working on Latin America. Special thanks go to David Collier, Carol Medlin, Ken Shadlen, Marcus Kurtz, Jeff Sluyter, Jim Mahoney, Rich Snyder, Pierre Ostiguey and Peter Houtziger for their willingness to offer ideas, criticism and suggestions. Other colleagues from the United States and Canada who gave me valuable advice for the final manuscript include Max Gordon, Carol Wise, Riordan Roett, Maureen Molot, and Judith Teichman.

Mexico's open and vibrant academic community made my field work possible. I am indebted to the Facultad de Ciencias Sociales at the Instituto Tecnológico Autónomo de México (ITAM). Department director Federico Estevez kindly provided me not only with his political insights, but also—and no less critically—a desk, computer and phone. Mexican scholars and officials were extraordinarily generous in sharing their time and knowledge with me. Special thanks go to Yemile Mizrahe, Alonso Lujambio, and Luis de la Calle. I am also grateful to several U.S. colleagues that I met in Mexico City, Catherine Mansell, Kristin Johnson, Joy Langston, and Jeff Weldon.

My research was made possible by financial support from several organizations. The Mexico-U.S. Binational Commission awarded me a Fulbright-García Robles fellowship in 1994, which was indispensible for conducting field work. The following year a fellowship from the Center for U.S.-Mexican Studies, at U.C. San Diego, allowed me to concentrate on writing a preliminary draft. In 1996 a U.C. Mexus travel grant enabled me to return to Mexico to gather data and conduct interviews that were still needed.

Finishing the book was made possible by the Carnegie Endowment for International Peace in Washington, D.C. I especially want to thank Tom Carothers, head of the Global Policy Division, who invited me to be a resident associate in 1998. Several colleagues at the Carnegie Endowment supported and improved my work, particularly Dan Morrow, Virginia Haufler, David Lipton, Ann Florini, and Robin Markowitz.

My deepest debt is to Luz María de la Mora. This *chilanga* made her initial contributions to the project as a colleague in San Diego. She was later forced to become more deeply involved with virtually every aspect of the book—from theory to Spanish accent marks—the high price of becoming more deeply involved with the author. Reading, commenting, debating and correcting several hundred pages of someone else's work takes more than academic commitment. The book should find its way into print around our first anniversary. *Gracias.*

# 1

# Introduction: Bringing Finance and Politics Together

One of the central arguments for undertaking market reform in developing countries is to improve economic efficiency and prevent privileged groups from obtaining rents from the policy-making process. Yet this prescription fails to address the complex political process that governments are likely to confront when moving toward the market. This study shows how political considerations distorted the reform process in the Mexican financial sector.

Mexican financial policy offers an ideal case to explore the extent to which the liberalization process may be politically manipulated. The finance sector is often considered to be a natural refuge for the economic bureaucracy. Policy analysts believe that the highly technical nature and arcane jargon of financial policy help insulate an elite group of technocrats from typical social pressures (Helleiner 1994; Vogel 1996). The complexity of finance makes it difficult for interest groups to understand how policy reform may affect their economic welfare, much less to make well-focused regulatory demands.

In addition, political scientists have argued that the Mexican state enjoys an unusual degree of "autonomy." When the country's political leaders adopted a neoliberal economic strategy beginning in the 1980s, the dominant Institutional Revolutionary Party (PRI) was able to marginalize social opposition to market reform. The "strong state" provided Mexican technocrats considerable freedom to impose painful market solutions (Centeno 1994; Heredia 1994; Reding 1989). In short, if economic liberalization can be consistently implemented anywhere in the developing world, we have good reason to expect it to be in Mexico, particularly in the area of finance.

However, this study shows that Mexican finance policy not only provided rent-seeking opportunities to the private sector, but also increased the state's capacity to finance public sector obligations. Moreover these were often incurred to pursue political goals. While the PRI's extensive linkages with social and economic organizations guaranteed political victory for most of the century, the viability of Mexican corporatism depended on satisfactory social relations. When political challenges threatened the PRI's ability to rule, either in the form of social mobilization or electoral opposition, the party responded by using financial policy to provide economic benefits in exchange for renewed support.

The strategic allocation of benefits is nothing new in Mexican politics. During the economically bleak 1930s, following the devastation of the Revolution, Mexican leaders had limited material resources to distribute. Under such circumstances, political recognition represented an important component of patronage. The PRI supplemented symbolic and political goods with tangible economic benefits. It managed its corporatist alliance through clientelism, "a relationship based on political subordination in exchange for material rewards" (Fox 1994a: 153).

The PRI became the consummate political machine, offering loyal supporters money, jobs, favors, and helping them circumvent bureaucratic obstacles. At the same time, it also wielded coercive powers to discourage the formation of political opposition. The ability of party chiefs to target the withdrawal of economic resources, hire and fire individuals, circulate negative information, and ultimately to repress represented an equally important resource in the maintenance of political domination.

President Lázaro Cárdenas became an "anti-system" reformer and solidified the leadership of what would soon become the ruling party by mobilizing social groups whose support strengthened his mandate to rule. Indeed, he encouraged strikes and land seizures among workers and peasants, responding to social confrontation and violence with permissiveness (Cornelius 1973). The incorporation of organized labor in particular became the cornerstone of the PRI's domination of the political system (Collier and Collier 1991). In some cases, such as the nationalization of the petroleum industry or the creation of communal *ejidos*, the party expropriated and redistributed private resources. For the most part, however, the business of state building depended on the mobilization of popular sector associations and their official linkage to the ruling party. In short, early patronage politics in Mexico consisted of co-optation.

This strategy enabled the PRI to minimize the influence of social pressures on policy making. While the Mexican government has occasionally met the economic demands of particular groups, since the 1940s, it has tended to reject redistribution based on independent social mobilization. As Evelyn Stevens argues in her analysis of three major protest episodes in Mexico, "The determination to limit participation in decision making seems to be the product of the regime's conviction that to do otherwise would endanger its economic program by putting too great a burden on the available resources. Limited plurality is seen as a necessary condition for political stability, which in itself is regarded as a prerequisite of economic growth" (1974: 280).

The maintenance of a stable corporatist alliance precluded aggressive social mobilization. The state refused to satisfy demands for progress or equality, which originated in societal groups. To do so would risk the unleashing of competition for scarce economic resources among social sectors whose political support and unity were required for the PRI's continued dominance. Just as Cárdenas openly encouraged what Wayne Cornelius described as "changes in the demand structure" of popular sectors, so have subsequent party leaders taken the initiative in implementing the country's redistributive policies. Mexican patronage was thus a political project led by the state.

## THE ARGUMENT

While the PRI's distribution of economic benefits has been the subject of extensive research, that work has not focused on the generation of resources required to make patronage possible in the first place. To address this question, the present study represents an effort to build a bridge between research on political clientelism and financial policy making.

From the 1940s to the early 1970s, during which the Mexican economy grew at an annual rate of over 6 percent, the source of government income was easy to identify. Virtually the entire federal budget during this period came directly from tax revenue and parastatal income. Fiscal deficits were relatively low. The vast bulk of government spending went toward industrialization and urban subsidies, such as food, fuel, transportation, and education. Aggressive industrialization increased the size of the union sector, the main pillar of PRI support, while subsidies improved the living standards in the growing cities. At the same time, conservative monetary and fiscal policy ensured a degree of economic stability unmatched in the rest of Latin America.

Unfortunately for the ruling party, the social cohesion provided by this happy state of affairs was not to last. The main argument of this book is that the Mexican state pursued financial policy changes in order to generate capital that the ruling party required to address several political crises. These critical moments were the result of social and economic turmoil that threatened the PRI's undisputed control over the Mexican political system. In response, the party implemented a wide range of financial policies—some strengthening and others weakening market forces—which offered economic benefits to specific groups whose support was essential for maintaining legitimacy.

Economic factors and ideology clearly influenced the evolution of Mexican financial regulation. Policies were shaped by economic opportunities and constraints within the domestic economy and abroad. The availability of credit, stability and growth levels, and the impact of exogenous shocks directly affected the government's willingness and ability to implement changes in the financial system.

Moreover, economic strategy and changing bureaucratic ideology also influenced the direction of financial policy. The statist model of the 1970s, based largely on "structuralist" economic theory, required an increased level of government credit and created institutions to facilitate the growth of public debt. After the collapse of debt-led growth in 1982, populism was discredited, and a new breed of administrators, committed to reversing excesses of the past, filled the economic ministries. These technocrats implemented a comprehensive neoliberal model based on deregulation and reprivatization.

Notwithstanding the role of these factors, financial regulation in Mexico lacks economic and ideological coherence. Populist and neo-orthodox presidents alike implemented policy changes that directly undermined their declared priorities of growth and stability. In addition, while each administration advanced a well-defined developmental model—typically as a response to the failure of an earlier growth strategy—the financial policies they pursued frequently contradicted the prevailing ideology about the proper role of the state and market in economic activity.

While most observers have perceived a clear trend toward increased liberalization from the 1970s to the 1990s, this characterization of the evolution of Mexican finance policy ignores important evidence. These omissions belie a much more complex and contradictory policy process. In arguing that this supposed trend toward liberalization is misleading, I describe and explain a number of unexpected policy outcomes:

- The populist administrations of Echeverría and López Portillo implemented a highly interventionist development model, which gave the state the primary role in economic activity. Yet they also promoted and modernized markets for debt and equity, strengthening the regulatory and institutional infrastructure required for greater private sector participation in the financial system.

- The de la Madrid administration inherited the bank nationalization, a period during which the financial system was under the highest level of government control. Yet it also deregulated the banks and liberalized the securities market. At the same time, a government heavily committed to recovering economic stability provided incentives for volatile financial speculation and unsustainable increases in the public debt.

- The Salinas administration, the most aggressive promoter of economic liberalization in Mexican history, implemented policies that distorted financial services markets and the currency valuation. Notwithstanding their embrace of economic orthodoxy, during the 1990s PRI policy makers protected the banking sector and used state intervention to over-value the exchange rate. A government that fully committed its resources and reputation to strengthening investor confidence directly undermined stability.

To make sense of these paradoxes, it is necessary to place economic policy making in a political context. This study addresses the changing political and economic environment within which Mexico's ruling party struggled to maintain power from the 1970s through the 1990s. The PRI, which controlled the bureaucratic machinery of the state, used finance policy not only to address fiscal necessities, but also to overcome a series of challenges arising from the opposition of important social sectors. Moreover, because both structural constraints on spending and the sources of social opposition changed over time, the task of achieving political and economic objectives became a moving target. This changing environment led the PRI to implement a disjointed and seemingly irrational series of financial policies.

I argue that a central component of the PRI's strategy to maintain political power was to channel material benefits to groups whose civic, economic, or electoral behavior threatened the party's dominance. I divide the analysis into four periods, which correspond to presidential *sexenios* since 1970.[1]

## Legitimacy Crisis: Appeasing the Left (1970–1982)

During the Echeverría administration, the PRI confronted a serious threat from highly mobilized social opposition, including intellectuals, students, and workers. These groups demanded not only economic redistribution, but also political opening and an end to electoral fraud. At the same time, the high growth rates that had characterized the last two decades were coming to an end. In the context of these political and economic challenges, the PRI's political project was to legitimize the continuation of authoritarianism through social redistribution and development.

Echeverría's solution to leftist mobilization, which was intensified by successor President José López Portillo in the second half of the decade, was a new political project based on economic populism and state-led development. In attempting to overcome opposition by stimulating employment and income levels, the PRI's strategy now depended on a tremendous expansion of the state's role in the economy. To procure the necessary capital both presidents forced domestic banks to lend heavily to the public sector. Luis Echeverría began to borrow abroad to finance this government expansion. In the context of an unprecedented global capital glut, the product of recycled petro-dollars, in addition to Mexico's own oil wealth, José López Portillo accelerated foreign borrowing. As a result the budget deficit exploded. When global interest rates went up in the early 1980s, the government was left insolvent and devalued and nationalized the banks as revenge for capital flight.

However, even as the state expropriated an increasing proportion of capital resources and asserted itself as the central economic actor, it also established key financial markets. Ironically, two highly statist presidents were responsible for the regulatory infrastructure that would be the foundation of future financial reform. Echeverría sought to compensate large businesses that it had squeezed out of credit markets by modernizing and deepening the stock market. López Portillo created the treasury bill, a debt instrument that not only increased the state's access to private capital, but also put in place the basis for a modern money market.

These regulatory reforms can best be understood as state initiatives to both expand public sector spending and ameliorate the economic distortions it caused. On one hand, the government gobbled up both international and domestic savings to direct fiscal resources toward dissatisfied social groups in the effort to deflect mounting opposition to its control over the political system. On the other hand, the credit crunch and inflation caused by excessive social spending also led the state to implement far-reaching modernizing regulation, which was ultimately required for the development of the markets for equities and debt.

### Economic Crisis: Regaining the Right (1982–1988)

As a result of the debt crisis and bank nationalization, the de la Madrid administration confronted the business community's virulent opposition to populism, presidentialism, and the PRI's continued hegemony. Its main economic mission was to recover fiscal solvency and prevent the collapse of large firms. For most of the decade, the PRI was thus committed to regaining both the political support and capital of the private sector.

Big business was economically critical. Confronting a virtual cut-off of foreign capital, the government still generated massive budget deficits throughout the first half of the decade. Domestic capital remained the only steady source of public financing. Moreover, since the financial crisis was largely the result of capital flight, the state desperately sought to bring scarce economic resources back within national borders.

Large firms were also politically important. Their social prestige conferred legitimacy to their demands for limitations on presidential authority. They also generated their own economic resources, enjoying the greatest degree of autonomy among economic groups. The leaders of the independent business associations shaped the political positions of the national business community, influencing the opinions of much of the Mexican middle class.

The de la Madrid administration responded to business opposition and public sector financing needs by transforming the financial sector into a lucrative vehicle for private investment. It sold huge quantities of treasury bills on the open market, internalizing much of the public debt. The marketization and expansion of treasury bills dramatically increased not only how much the government could borrow domestically, but also the interest rates it paid on that debt. These reforms stimulated the money market, enriched investors, and helped transform brokerage houses into the dominant force in Mexican finance. The state also made significant reforms in the stock market, such as prudential regulation and the privatization of clearinghouse activities. It also stabilized stock prices through the direct purchase of equity shares. Finally, fiscal incentives made equity financing more attractive.

In addition to developing new financial instruments, the state liberalized the brokerage industry, enabling the private sector to take full advantage of opportunities in debt and equity markets. More institutions were now allowed to trade stocks and manage money. Smaller, middle-class savers participated heavily in the lucrative stock market, helping to fuel a spectacularly profitable boom. Finally, financial liberalization was supplemented by an exchange rate adjustment program to provide foreign debt relief for the largest corporations, which had been on the brink of collapse following the 1982 devaluations.

Yet throughout the administration, the government also exercised an unprecedented degree of control over the economy through proprietorship of the banking sector. Because of the need for fiscal discipline and the political importance of recovering macroeconomic stability, covering the deficit and foreign interest obligations became priorities. Accordingly, the state absorbed the vast majority of bank resources. Indeed, at the same time that de la Madrid liberalized and expanded the securities market, he kept the banks under a tight regulatory harness: high reserve requirements, interest rate controls, and other restrictions caused the banks to stagnate relative to the brokerage sector and largely removed them from the role of productive or social investment.

### Electoral Crisis: Recasting the Social Bases of the PRI (1988–1994)

By 1988, the PRI's electoral invincibility had been shattered. Although austerity finally brought stability to the Mexican economy, six years of recession and falling wages had taken its political toll. The Salinas administration faced massive defection from diverse social groups whose support was indispensable for the PRI's continued dominance. The poor and middle class had voted in large numbers for opposition parties on both the left and right. Yet given the priority of macroeconomic discipline, traditional fiscal stimulation was no longer a viable option for recovering popularity.

Salinas maintained that the transformation of the Mexican economy was the key to sustained growth. The government continued to cut public spending, turning a huge budget deficit into a moderate surplus and reducing inflation dramatically. The state also eliminated barriers to foreign trade, sold off parastatals, and pursued regional integration.

A modernized financial system was the central element to the new growth strategy. To attract global investors, the Salinas administration deregulated and internationalized the securities sector, opening up the market for government debt to foreigners. It also liberalized foreign investment regulations to encourage overseas institutions to participate in the Mexican stock market. In addition, Salinas deregulated the (still nationalized) banks to improve their access to global capital. The 1991–1992 bank reprivatization represented the zenith of financial liberalization.

However, banking liberalization was accompanied by protectionism. The administration effectively shielded the banks from competition. Protection served a number of the PRI's political purposes. It sealed the party's alliance with the new bank owners, the country's most powerful capitalists. More indirectly, it helped the PRI recover popularity among the poor. Protection enabled the government to receive extremely high bids from prospective owners, providing the state with extra revenue that it strategically allocated to impoverished communities under widely publicized social development programs. Unfortunately, bank protection made credit costlier for domestic borrowers and contributed directly to the destabilization of the banking system.

Salinas also undermined free markets in foreign exchange markets. By fixing the peso to a "crawling peg," the government inflated the currency's real value over time. Financing the growing trade deficit depended largely on massive foreign purchases of government securities, which were denominated in pesos. Foreign investment in treasury bills, however, could only be sustained as long as the Mexican currency was artificially over-valued, a highly unstable economic model that exposed the country to the danger of capital flight.

The government refused to allow necessary adjustments in the currency's value because a strong peso helped secure numerous political objectives. While it made foreign debt cheaper for big business, the inflated currency subsidized import consumption of luxury goods for the middle class. In addition, the crawling peg represented an important anchor on inflation. It became instrumental in maintaining the viability of the social "pacts" between labor unions and employers that underlay price and wage restraint. Because of political obstacles to exchange rate adjustment, the neoliberal transformation ironically precluded the option to float the currency on open markets. As a result, Mexico's dependence on massive inflows of short-term foreign capital turned into an economic trap that ultimately led to the peso's collapse.

### Negotiating Reform: Policy Making and Competitive Politics (1995–1999)

The administration of Ernesto Zedillo began on a positive note. In spite of the Chiapas uprisings and the assassination of two high-profile PRI politicians, the party proved in 1994 that it could retain control of Congress and win the presidency in a legitimate election. Carlos Salinas's ability to get the economy in order was clearly a major factor in that achievement. Opposition parties were now viable. Yet having orchestrated such successful transition to open markets, the PRI appeared well situated to continue its political dominance.

Less than two weeks into the term, however, the peso devaluation dragged Mexico into yet another financial crisis. As the economy went into a freefall, borrowers defaulted on a massive scale, leaving banks with high levels of foreign debt on the verge of insolvency. The Zedillo administration became mired in a series of bail-out schemes. It launched a number of debt restructuring policies designed to provide relief for farmers, credit card users, homeowners, and businesses. Of greatest political consequence, however, was the bank rescue, in which the government's deposit protection fund relieved the banks of billions of dollars of non-performing loans and appeared to absolve many wealthy debtors of their obligations at the taxpayers' expense.

In 1997, under assault from highly critical and well-organized opposition parties, the PRI lost control of Congress for the first time. The event marked a watershed in Mexico's policy-making process and led to a protracted and acrimonious debate between the PRI and opposition legislators over Zedillo's proposed finance reform package. The president conceded to replacing government guarantees for large corporate loans with politically popular guarantees for smaller consumer debts proposed by the opposition. Although the government eventually won most of what it asked for, its victory merely reflected the absence of realistic alternatives.

### ALTERNATIVE EXPLANATIONS OF FINANCE POLICY OUTCOMES

The political hypothesis advanced in this study stands in contrast to conventional explanations emphasizing institutional ideology, interest group pressure, and international change. While taken together these approaches help us refine an understanding of policy change, none of them can be reconciled with policy outcomes in Mexico.

A number of scholars have explained finance policy outcomes, particularly in developing countries, as the result of technocratic change. In this approach, changes in national economic policy direction can be traced to the ideological orientation of personnel in top government positions and the shifts in power of the institutions they control (Sikkink 1991).

In the case of Mexico, following the failure of the statist model, a new generation of policy makers was formed intellectually abroad within the world's premier academic institutions and groomed for high-level public service appointments. These *técnicos* emerged as highly skilled, insulated economic bureaucrats who took over the policy-making process from old guard *políticos* (Smith 1986; Centano and Maxfield 1992). Since the 1980s, "individuals with postgraduate degrees from foreign universities, typically in economics, who have spent the bulk, if not all, of their careers in the financial sector of the government, have occupied an ever larger share of top posts in the regime" (Lindau 1992: 217).

The technocratic revolution goes a long way toward explaining economic liberalization in Latin America. Moreover, the approach is very useful for explaining the placement of liberal economists in positions of political and policy-making power. However, it cannot account for ideological contradictions from this elite group. Although Mexican policy is largely controlled by a young generation of liberal ivy league scholars, in practice these administrators have frequently rejected market-oriented principals in the critical financial policy areas explored in this study.

A second group of scholars has argued that financial globalization, made possible by technological advances in computerization and communication, led a wide range of countries to liberalize capital markets from the 1970s to the 1990s. They maintain that structural forces of internationalization and technology are relentlessly driving the world's financial systems toward integration. While global firms seek financing from a limited pool of international savings, increased corporate multinationality enables firms to exit national borders more easily. Similarly, governments compete among themselves to obtain sufficient capital to satisfy domestic demands for social services, promote investment, and sustain a stable economic environment (Goodman and Pauly 1993: 57–58; Helleiner 1994: 160).

A World Bank economist concludes that because of the importance of ensuring adequate public and private sector financing, the most important function of the central bank in developing countries is "to promote financial innovations that widen and deepen the credit or capital market through the introduction of new processes and products" (Bhatt 1989: 16). In his elaboration of the "competition state," Philip Cerny explains the wave of financial opening during the 1980s as a "defensive" response to the scarcity of global capital. The move toward free financial markets and reform is thus initiated by the state. For example, when the United States innovated short-term debt securities to finance its deficit in the 1980s, countries all over the world followed suit to remain attractive to global investors (Cerny 1988: 43–46).

While compelling, the globalization paradigm suffers from its theoretical elegance. Because it explains the uniform outcome of deregulation, the theory does not account for those markets that continue to restrict capital movements or the different levels of openness among countries that have liberalized them. The model is also limited by its narrow definition of finance regulation; it only addresses the (admittedly important) policy dimension of capital mobility and cannot even address variations in other financial policy areas, such as banking sector openness and exchange rates.

What is missing from both the technocratic and globalization models is politics. A third, and more satisfying, approach to explaining finance policy focuses on the struggle among diverse economic groups. In this analysis, political leaders are influenced by the demands of competing organized interests, which support or oppose the liberalization of capital markets according to their ability to capture benefits or their vulnerability to increased competitive pressure (e.g., Haggard and Maxfield 1993).

Borrowing the concept of asset specificity from transaction cost economics, political scientist Jeffrey Frieden predicts that those capitalists with the most redeployable assets—finance capital—should support capital market liberalization, while those whose assets are tied to a specific use, particularly heavy industry, are expected to oppose it (Frieden 1991: 440–441). This research agenda represents an advance in the political study of finance policy because it takes seriously the power organized domestic groups.

Once again, the range of this approach is limited. Focusing on interest group assets is not likely to explain outcomes in banking and currency policy. While traditional economic demands, such as tax, wage, and social spending levels are relatively easy to identify, the *financial* interests of different economic actors are difficult to determine *ex ante*. Moreover, Frieden's model fails to capture the nature of economic structures within a typical developing country. When banks and manufacturers are linked by cross-ownership and even run by the same families, the interests of large industrial firms cannot be neatly separated from those of financial firms. Indeed, even the traditional struggle between domestic and international producers over exchange rate valuation can become meaningless within an industrial structure in which the firms that sell the most abroad also buy the most foreign goods. In such an economy, when weak national currency stimulates exports only at the expense of more costly imported inputs, an interest group policy preference is not obvious. Moreover, to the extent that major manufacturers are financed with foreign capital, a weaker currency increases the debt burden.

Notwithstanding these limitations, both the globalization and interest group models provide a foundation upon which to build an empirically informed explanation of policy making. However, because financial regulation among liberalizing countries varies greatly, we must avoid the temptation to find a universal causal variable. The argument that follows suggests that in order to understand the nature of financial reforms in developing countries, we must first understand the particular political challenges facing their leaders. Rather than an inevitable outcome of ideological shifts or global capitalism, finance policy represents a resource that the state can manipulate to address the interests of domestic groups that it depends on for political survival.

## FOCUS ON STATE POLITICS

I have argued that Mexican finance policies cannot be explained without an understanding of the political objectives of the national government. A state-centered approach preserves the valuable insights from several approaches described above: political and bureaucratic leaders can make their own agenda; the international economic system creates both opportunities and constraints for policy makers; and social groups exert pressure on the government. Focusing on the state allows us to examine the policy-making process as the interaction of government leaders' political incentives, the institutional resources available to them, as well as the constraints of the domestic and international economy.

Until the 1990s, it was virtually impossible to make a meaningful distinction between the ruling party and the government in the Mexican political system. Since the 1930s, the PRI enjoyed almost exclusive access to the country's political resources. The official party exercised control over popular organizations, as well as official linkages to academic, professional, and business associations (Purcell and Purcell 1980; Camp 1989: ch. 7). In addition, the PRI exercised extensive control over the content and distribution of information, primarily through entrenched personal and economic relations with Televisa, the privately owned television monopoly whose political broadcasts are almost exclusively pro-government propaganda (Mejía Barquera 1985; *Proceso,* July 4, 1994: 6–11). Because of its virtual monopoly over patronage and symbolic resources, and the assurance of electoral victory, the PRI enjoyed uninterrupted control over the country's policy-making apparatus until its loss of Congress in 1997.

Policy power in Mexico has been highly concentrated in the office of the president. Cabinet positions and virtually all mid-level administrative posts were occupied by PRI officials. For most of the century, congressional approval of legislation was a mere formality. It is therefore difficult to separate the policy preferences of the chief executive from those of the politicians and bureaucrats who served under him.

Because Mexican presidents traditionally employed the *dedazo* to personally appoint their successors, high level administrators promoted their own political ambitions by efficiently implementing policies decided by the president. While this does not mean that significant differences did not exist within the cabinet during the process of policy formation, once the president made his decision, it was enacted and implemented without further internal debate.

Given that presidential re-election is not permitted in Mexico, how can we best describe the motives of a politician with virtually unlimited policy discretion who will promptly lose all formal authority within six years? Presidents have personal goals. While they may seek to enrich themselves personally and preserve their political influence, they also want history to remember them as effective and just leaders. In some instances, a post-presidential future at the international level may also be at stake.[2] Whatever the case, to paraphrase an American auto company executive, what was good for the Mexican president was good for the PRI. Until Ernesto Zedillo supported political reforms and economic policies which directly threatened PRI members, the Mexican president was not only the undisputed leader of the party, he was synonymous with it.

While the post-revolutionary rhetoric of social equality and autonomous development provided the PRI with an extremely powerful symbolic tool, the party's actual policy initiatives were characterized more by the changing political objectives of its presidents than by a continuous long-term ideological commitment. Between 1970 and 1994, the PRI's lock on power provided the political system with considerable continuity, even as the economic model shifted from unapologetic statism to neoliberalism. Although a president may break sharply with the programs of his predecessor, the evaluation of his economic performance is closely linked with popular perception of the party.

For these reasons, the conflation of state, party, and presidential interests is largely justified—at least until the Zedillo administration. To the extent that a president successfully fulfilled the objectives that earned him the approval of the major organized interests, the PRI gained legitimacy as the state's *de facto* policy-making institution. The degree of the party's political dominance has typically been interpreted as a function of Mexican society's evaluation of its economic policy choices. As one scholar wrote, the 1988 election, which the PRI salvaged largely through fraud, was a vote of punishment "that did not question the deep structure of the regime, but rather its recent [economic] action. . . . It is thought, then, that if the regime recovered its capacity to provide economic goods through new economic policies, the demand for democracy could be reduced, and the authoritarian structure could in some manner be preserved—as well as its legitimacy" (Crespo 1992: 25).

Another important reason to focus on the state in the present analysis is the depoliticized character of financial regulation as a public policy issue. Major domestic political interests are often absent from participation in the finance policy process. The complexity of financial systems and the indirect way in which they affect economic welfare effectively neutralizes the potential for mobilization. The issues are complex, the vocabulary obscure. Compared to bread-and-butter policy issues—taxation, wages, social services—finance policy tends to have little political salience among most citizens. While major business interests often were key participants in discussions over the shape of finance policy, Mexican economic authorities did not encounter interest group pressure and class conflict that often fills the political arena.

However, this does not mean that state leaders did not take politics into account. On the contrary, freedom to shape finance policies and even create financial institutions with minimal public scrutiny gave them an important resource for self-promoting goals. The main contribution of this study is to show that Mexican finance policy, whether liberalizing or anti-market, represented the state's effort to carry out political initiatives for which it lacked sufficient economic resources.

## BEYOND MEXICO

The Mexican experience suggests broader implications for the relationship between political and economic change in developing countries. Most importantly, the impact that Mexico's incipient political opening had on financial policy making in the 1990s suggests that it is unwise to analyze marketization and democratization as isolated events.

There has been considerable interest in the optimal sequencing of this "dual" transition. The growth records of countries such as China and Chile have convinced many observers that painful market reforms should probably precede democratic opening. However, research into this question has tended to ask only whether or not political constraints prevent governments from successfully adopting liberalization measures, which are identified as balancing the budget, privatization, and the elimination of barriers to trade and investment. Until the shock of East Asia's collapse, the mere implementation of such policies was widely regarded as evidence of the triumph of sensible economic management over politics.

Today, liberalization is being questioned by the same mainstream economists who once promoted it. The epidemic of financial collapse in emerging markets during the 1990s has provided some legitimacy for those once lonely critics who railed against the Washington Consensus and warned of the evils of global economic integration.

While opening up markets has hardly led to uniform success, it has led to sustained economic improvements in many developing countries. Moreover, given that the international tendency toward marketization is unlikely to be reversed, what the policy-making community requires is an analytical approach to reform that does not measure success in terms of implementation but rather in terms of coherence and performance. Rather than focusing on the political obstacles to adopting market reforms, the present study explores how political challenges can distort them and lead to crises that the world's finest economic minds consistently fail to anticipate.

## NOTES

1. A *sexenio* refers to the Mexican president's six-year term. The periodization reflects the fact that over the last three decades new Mexican administrations have broken sharply with or dramatically accelerated the policies of their predecessors largely because of the necessity of confronting social and economic crisis.

2. Luis Echeverría, with the support of the nonaligned Group of 77, tried to position himself to become the secretary general of the United Nations in 1976. Before his virtual political exile following the peso crisis, Carlos Salinas was a frontrunner to become the first president of the World Trade Organization.

# 2

# Crisis from the Left (1970–1982): Populist Presidents and the Creation of Financial Markets

Mexican finance policy during the administrations of Luis Echeverría and José López Portillo was characterized by two contrasting patterns. On one hand, the state increased its borrowing capacity through foreign borrowing and extraction from the banking sector. On the other hand, it modernized and developed markets for both debt and equity. While influenced by changing economic conditions, these divergent policy choices are best understood as a coherent response to social instability and Mexico's changing political environment.

The turmoil of the 1970s stands in stark contrast to the tranquil decades that came before. Dating from the late 1940s, an understanding among the state, the banks and industry helped stabilize the economy and minimize political conflict. During this highly successful period, known as "Stabilizing Development," the Mexican state achieved a level of social harmony unrivaled anywhere in Latin America.

As part of its strategy to realize that goal, the Institutional Revolutionary Party (PRI) pursued two seemingly contradictory finance policies: strengthening the banks and forced credit allocation. The state promoted the growth of the banking system in the effort to establish large and stable sources of capital for large-scale industries (Maxfield 1990: 99; Fitzgerald 1985). Even as it officially discouraged banking concentration by limiting the range of activities in which different financial institutions could participate, in order to ensure high profit levels the government restricted competition (Brannon 1986: 27–28). Equally importantly, banks were permitted to develop extensive linkages with major manufacturing firms: "Belonging to a financial-industrial group came to be a necessary condition for profit maximization. Banks became borrowing windows of economic-financial groups" (Solís 1981: 18).[1]

The security of lending to large, established firms, as well as the availability of profitable investments elsewhere, made the banks generally unwilling to invest in smaller industrial and agricultural enterprises. Given the riskiness of productive ventures in an underdeveloped economy, they tended to prefer speculation and short-term opportunities over long-term investment (Quijano 1981: 152–180; Villegas and Ortega 1991: 327).

Accordingly, financial allocation to most domestic firms was determined more by political fiat than by market forces. Even as the government sought to strengthen the country's financial institutions, it also subjected them to myriad controls and channeled private banking resources to its numerous development banks and parastatal industries. The state strictly regulated banks through interest rate ceilings and the obligatory purchase of low-interest government bonds, which provided low-cost credit for small enterprises. In addition, the government imposed "selective credit quotas" targeted to politically valuable small manufacturers and farmers (Aspe 1993: 66; Brannon 1986: 30–31). It also relied on "moral" persuasion and used central bank rediscounting to channel capital to priority sectors (Márquez 1987: 172–173). Underlying all state controls were reserve requirements, which enabled the government to control the expansion of credit and contain inflation.

In short, in order to offer selective benefits to both small entrepreneurs and public sector interests, the state sought more control over the same financial sector that it was helping to accumulate greater capital resources. Ironically, it was the remarkable growth of private banks that "enabled the state to underwrite capitalist accumulation and transfer surplus value between various social and economic sectors" (White 1992: 71).

Yet financial intervention did not mean financial irresponsibility. As its name suggested, the main goal of Stabilizing Development was economic discipline. Although the state utilized the financial system to promote both big business and smaller entrepreneurs, it also shunned inflation and kept budget deficits minimal. While it is fashionable to call the economic administrators of the 1990s "technocrats," the heyday of socially insulated, technically administered finance policy was actually the 1960s. Underlying the peaceful coexistence between business and government during stabilizing development lay a fundamentally conservative macroeconomic orientation. From 1958 to 1970, Mexican finances were directed from the virtual policy czardom of finance minister Antonio Ortíz Mena and central bank governor Rodrigo Gómez. Control over public credit expansion and the containment of inflation were undisputed economic priorities. In addition, external debt was dramatically reduced from almost half of GDP at the end of the Depression to just over 10 percent by the mid-1950s, where it remained stable until the early 1970s (Gil Díaz 1984: 340).

The implementation of quasi-monetarist, restrictive credit policies during the 1960s accompanied extremely robust economic growth and relative calm among the major social sectors. Therefore tight money was not painful to administer and at no time became subject to serious political discussion. As we will see later, the economic strain caused by the end of the "easy phase" of import substitution, in conjunction with unprecedented civic opposition to economic policy, took finance policy completely out of the hands of technical administrators and into those of political strategists.

## ECHEVERRÍA AND THE RECOVERY OF LEGITIMACY

At the end of the 1960s, Mexico was shattered by protest and violence. Like much of the rest of the Western world, the Mexican government confronted widespread student and labor radicalization. The contradictions of Mexico's uneven pattern of economic development brought the benefits of progress to many, but left millions more behind. Critics of Stabilizing Development argued that social equality and full employment remained distant even after two decades of impressive growth.

In the context of global unrest, leftist intellectuals and populists spearheaded a wave of protest and social strife that challenged the PRI's authority. They used their demands for greater social equity as a springboard for greater democratic participation, jeopardizing what had been the ruling party's uncontested domination of the political system.

The PRI's response to leftist opposition and economic stagnation was fiscal expansion. The new growth model was called "Shared Development." Rather than risk meaningful political reform, the ruling party dramatically expanded the state's role in redistribution and production. Its goals included greater social equality and a more capital-intensive stage of industrialization. The new strategy presupposed massive new public spending outlays, which in turn required radically new financial policies.

### Reviving the "Revolutionary Family"

According to the sociologist Max Weber, political legitimacy is a social attribute without which the state can rule only by using excessive physical coercion. In their analysis of the Mexican crisis of the 1970s, Robert Newell and Luís Rubio argue that a dynasty of PRI leaders, dubbed the "Revolutionary Family," had long managed to maintain political legitimacy by orchestrating policy consensus among disparate social actors. Mexican legitimacy was based on a pattern of conciliation, formal inclusion, political co-optation, and economic incentives. Direct control of popular organization was essential for this task: "Mexico's continued stability has thus been a direct function of the government's ability . . . to organize changing alliances and institutions that could sustain and develop that original consensus" (Newell and Rubio 1984: 4).

Skilled as the PRI politicians were, their political success rested upon a foundation of spectacular economic growth, which between 1950 and 1970 averaged better than 6 percent. Although some sectors fared better than others, all major organized groups saw their standard of living improve; at the same time, their political voice seemed to be heard within official associations linked directly to the ruling party. Economic success contributed significantly to Mexican social stability, which in turn was essential to broad acceptance of the PRI's continued political supremacy.

For well over two decades, Mexico was characterized by the PRI's uncontested domination of the political system, the complete marginalization of the opposition, and the orderly transfer of power from one president to the next. Social conflict was generally pre-empted by astute bargaining between the leaders of popular organizations and the PRI, while the rare outbreak of protest or violence ended quickly under a barrage of conciliatory governmental negotiation and strategic concessions designed to bring organizational leaders back into line.[2]

However, during the Díaz Ordaz administration (1964–1970), both the economic and social fabric of Mexico's political consensus began to tear. On the economic front, Mexico's insulated model of growth began to show signs of deterioration; the so-called easy stage of Mexico's import substitution strategy was coming to an end (Rámirez 1989: ch. 4; Gil Díaz 1984). As a historian of the Echeverría administration explains: "The impulse toward industrialization at all costs [during the 1960s] created a large industrial capacity that was underutilized and consequently resulted in high unemployment." Although import substitution was designed for a "large scale economy," in Mexico the domestic market represented about one-fifth of the population. By the 1970s, "Most enterprises could not afford to expand because the market for the output of many industries was only about 50 percent of capacity" (Schmidt 1991: 25–26). The seemingly effortless expansion Mexico had enjoyed since the 1940s slowed and was replaced by inflationary pressures.

To make matters worse, in August 1971, just eight months into the Echeverría *sexenio*, the Nixon administration unilaterally dismantled the Bretton Woods exchange rate system, ending nearly thirty years of stable and predictable international currency convertibility. In addition, in an effort to transfer the costs of its own macroeconomic adjustment onto international trading partners, the United States imposed a 10 percent surcharge on all imports. From the perspective of Mexico's economic policy makers, just as growth in Mexican domestic demand approached its limit and the internal market began to show signs of saturation, global power politics made the country's prospects for growth in the external sector doubtful.

Mexico's economic problems were not confined to growth. In spite of the importance of the Revolution as a symbol of social justice, Mexico's economic distribution remained among the most skewed in Latin America. As the country rapidly industrialized during the post-war period, the imbalance became quite stark by the 1960s. The benefits of modernization went to those able to obtain manufacturing jobs and the growing but relatively modest middle class. As agriculture was neglected, millions of peasants streamed into the cities in search of urban opportunities. Most ended up on the outskirts of the capital in the informal economy and in severe poverty. A reserve army of social discontents had been in the making since the 1950s. In short, although the economy was still expanding briskly at the end of the 1960s, critics successfully made their case that "growth" was not the equivalent of "development" (Schmidt 1991: 25).

The intellectuals led the way. In 1966, a series of university movements for political democracy and economic equality threatened the social peace that had prevailed throughout the period of Stabilizing Development. Echoing the wave of social discontent expressed throughout the Americas and Europe, student and teacher strikes ripped through the country's public universities. Led by activists criticizing Mexico's closed political system and brandishing books written by Che Gueverra, students sparked public sympathy by focusing on the amount of resources Mexican authorities were devoting to preparation for the 1968 Olympics. While the PRI managed to contain the movement for two years, largely through its domination of the mass media, a few days before the beginning of the Olympics disaster struck. On October 2, 1968, the state troops opened fire on a large student protest staged in one of Mexico City's most important cultural landmarks, Plaza Tlatelolco.[3]

Whether or not official estimates of several hundred deaths were closer to the truth than the protesters' figure of several thousand, the "Tlatelolco Massacre" changed Mexican politics forever: "The bankruptcy of Stabilizing Development was laid bare for the whole world to see, and the legitimacy of the Mexican state was severely shaken" (Rámirez 1989: 81). As Roberto Newell and Luis Rubio put it: "1968 was a turning point in that the former hegemony of the Revolutionary Family in that civil society began to vanish" (1984: 122).

Echeverría began his term confronting more than academics struggling for social justice. The PRI was also under pressure from a wide array of popular groups that had traditionally benefited from the party's clientelist policies and that now argued that their welfare depended on still greater state activism in the economy. Sharply distinguishing themselves from the "traitorous" transnational firms, small industrialists were supported by nationalist worker and peasant organizations. They urged the ruling party to expand the internal market, deepen import substitution by promoting capital goods, and reduce the country's dependence on foreign capital and technology (Dávila Aldás 1995: 126).

Finally, by the end of the 1960s, the PRI's main labor union ally, the Confederación de Trabajadores de México (CTM), no longer controlled all labor organization. Independent unions in both the public and private sector conducted rallies and openly criticized the government. The PRI was able to use these groups to its political advantage. By negotiating openly with independent labor organizations and showing sensitivity to their demands, the ruling party was able to present itself as both democratic and supportive of popular struggles (Schmidt 1991: 29–30, 77–82). Nonetheless, the mere existence of independent unions was another factor influencing Echeverría to adopt a more populist stance.

### Demise of Stabilizing Development

President Echeverría began his *sexenio* from a position of weakness. Chosen by outgoing president Gustavo Díaz Ordaz to succeed him, Echeverría was a relative outsider to the PRI and represented a compromise among party leaders who could not decide upon a career politician to carry on. However, as Díaz Ordaz's minister of government during the student uprisings, Echeverría was directly implicated in the order to shoot upon unarmed students. His outsider status in no way left him untainted by the inequality and authoritarianism that increasingly vocal critics attributed to the PRI.

Echeverría's solution was to neutralize social mobilization by throwing all the state's resources into social redistribution and development. Campaigning under the slogan "development with income distribution," he sought to restore the political hegemony of his party by turning the prevailing development model on its head. Accordingly, the PRI embraced Keynesianism in its strongest expression and began a decade of highly expansionist fiscal policies. As Newell and Rubio argue, "The consequence of this political shift was that financial decisions came to be made not by financiers, but by politicians" (1984: 141). While Mexican finance policy had long been used for political purposes, only with Echeverría did its politicization begin to undermine macroeconomic stability.

Although Echeverría began his term by continuing the conservative fiscal policies of his predecessors, by 1972 continued political mobilization and disappointing economic performance persuaded him to undertake a major policy reversal. The president turned to increased public spending to salvage the PRI's damaged legitimacy. The president's political strategy was to preserve the PRI's domination by responding to demands for political opening and equality by transforming the government's role in production and employment. As two Mexican political scientists argue: "Echeverría's main objective was to solve a political crisis: larger government participation and a reassertion of control of the economy were seen as the medium through which the crisis would be solved" (Bazdresch and Levy 1991: 252). Faced with the demands of a radical opposition movement, the new leader "used the budget to give them satisfaction, even at the cost of self-defeating indebtedness and instability in the longer run. The overwhelming issue has been the need to strengthen political legitimacy" (Ibarra 1988: 112).

As Echeverría maintained, economic policy existed only to promote social policy, which was the realm in which "governments born of revolution . . . evidence their legitimacy and effectiveness" (Suárez Gaona 1987: 149). In a remarkable illustration of the link between social order and policy choices, the president argued during his third state of the union address that "inflation is a lesser evil than political conflict" (Rubio 1990: 251).

The Echeverría administration concluded that under Stabilizing Development, the private sector had neglected investment in important economic areas, which stifled both development and social equity. "In place of the self-congratulatory rhetoric of his predecessor, Echeverría seemed most at ease when elaborating on the shortcomings of the revolution and attacking what he called the 'tragic complacency' of previous regimes" (Hellman 1983: 189). As a sympathetic chronicler notes, "The productive plant had grown and diversified, but the social conditions of the popular masses had not improved" (Dávila Aldás 1995: 126). In recognition of the failure of the model, the president advanced a new economic program for Mexico, which he called "Shared Development." As one of Echeverría's top economic advisors recalls, the main goals of the new model were "to increase the capacity of the economic system for absorbing manpower, to improve wealth distribution, and to sustain economic growth" (Solis 1981: 107).

Most agricultural and small industrial enterprises lacked access to credit, while the banks financed only the most profitable production and retail projects, goods, and services that were consumed primarily by higher income groups (Ejea et al. 1991: 31). In the face of the this so-called *huelga de capital* (investment strike) the government renounced its traditional goals of low inflation and budgetary discipline and boldly assumed the role as engine of growth. As one of the PRI's most prominent economic officials recalls, during the 1970s, "the economic policy of the Mexican government began to make a 180 degree turn away from the policies of stabilizing development" (Gurría Treviño 1994: 11).

### The Politics of Fiscal Expansion

The main issue confronted by any government contemplating a major budget increase is how the state will procure the needed capital. There are two basic ways to generate funds for public spending: income or debt. That is, the decision to spend more forces a government to choose between increased taxes or borrowing, or both. In the case of the Echeverría administration, a combination of political constraints and errors led the government to abandon any serious attempt at increasing revenue, leaving debt as the only vehicle for expansion.

### The Failure of Tax Reform

Significantly, the Echeverría administration explicitly recognized the dangers of relying on foreign capital and asserted the need to respond with fiscal measures. Just months after the *sexenio* began, Finance Minister Hugo Margain warned—with disturbing prescience—that excessive foreign debt would lead to national bankruptcy and social disorder. In presenting their tax reform proposal, Finance Ministry officials sounded more like sociologists than economists: "If we want to avoid violence and anarchy by legal and peaceful means, there is no other way than carrying out a broad fiscal reform that will . . . increases public revenue [and] promote the redistribution of wealth" (quoted in Solís 1981: 73). At the beginning of his *sexenio*, the president acknowledged the need to end dependence on external capital: "It seems, then, necessary to finance public spending primarily through the tax system" (*Mercado de Valores* 1970: 779).

At the end of 1970, as a first attempt to address the need for both increased revenues and a more equitable distribution of income, Echeverría proposed a 10 percent tax on luxury items. The proposal was immediately attacked by the heads of all the major business associations, who argued that it was inflationary, encouraged the sale of contraband, and would actually hurt the middle and working classes. When Congress approved the bill in December, the private sector attacked not the substance of tax increase, but rather the contents of the list of "luxury" items subject to the higher rate. More significantly, it complained that it had not been invited to consult with the government, as had been the practice in the past. After intense negotiations with industrial and commercial leaders, the government passed the fiscal reform with a highly abbreviated list that significantly reduced the level of public revenue originally proposed (Green 1981: 83–85). The level of taxation barely increased at all, from 1.5 percent to 1.69 percent of GDP (Elizondo 1994: 166–167).

An even more ambitious tax reform plan was attempted in 1972. The government sought to close numerous loopholes, increase the highest personal income tax by over 20 percent, enlarge the tax base, and raise taxes on financial income. The plan, in short, was designed not only to increase total revenue, but also to redistribute wealth progressively. One of the most developmentalist aspects of the reform was the proposal to tax dividends on nontraded equity shares as regular income, while offering a much lower rate on traded shares; the measure would thus function as a strong incentive for closed, family-owned firms to go public.

Leopoldo Solís, head of central bank research and a key member of Echeverría's economic team, offers an insightful insider's view of the policy process, explaining how both internal dissension and private sector opposition ultimately derailed an essentially sound reform. From the outset, the business organizations unified against the proposal, attacking it once again as inflationary. At negotiations conducted at the home of Finance Secretary Margain, business leaders of the two main industrial associations, Concamin and Canacintra; the national chambers of commerce; the major independent business association, Coparmex; and the bankers' association "were very critical and presented a common front against [the tax bill]" (Solís 1981: 75–76).

However, while business certainly objected to the economic implications of the tax bill, what apparently fueled the intensity and unity of their opposition was the unilateral manner in which the government had undertaken the measure. As then Finance Subsecretary Carlos Tello recalls: "The protest was not directed particularly at the fiscal reforms, but concentrated on the fact that prior consultations were not conducted." Coparmex director Roberto Guajardo Suárez complained directly to the press: "In past years the country's highest authorities have followed the custom of informing the national business associations of legal initiatives, directly or indirectly, that can affect Mexico's economic life . . . they have brought us together to tell us of measures practically decided" (Tello 1979: 45–46).

But consultation was not the private sector's only concern. While state reformers saw their proposal as supporting the long-term interests of capital—by stimulating economic growth without fueling inflation—big business saw the tax plan as a slippery slope leading to the erosion of property rights (Elizondo 1994). Particularly in light of Echeverría's use of revolutionary rhetoric, business interests feared that the seemingly arbitrary manner in which the government sought to expropriate their wealth was a harbinger of far more radical policies of redistribution and "social justice."

As a consequence of business protest, officials within the government began to doubt the wisdom of implementing the fiscal changes. In a December 1972 cabinet meeting, "those still opposing the reform warned that they still feared a flight of capital. . . . The [finance] officials argued that the tax reform would damage financial stability, growth and that it might provoke an attack on the peso" (Solís 1981: 75, 99). As a Mexican economic historian concludes, reform "was blocked by entrepreneurial forces in alliance with highly placed financial officials opposed to the state's increasing participation in the economy and market" (Dávila Aldás 1995: 130). Echeverría himself was never fully committed to the tax proposal. Because of limitations in the state's financial bureaucracy and the private sector's incentive to hide income, he doubted his administration's ability to collect the tax in the first place (Elizondo 1994: 169).

Potentially small gains in revenue made an open confrontation with the country's richest constituents a politically dubious undertaking. The president clearly had the authority to push the tax bill through a rubber-stamp

Congress. However, given the readily available alternative of foreign borrowing, he chose the path of least resistance and allowed the proposal to fade from his political agenda. Solís concludes: "Because of this [business] opposition, or some other issues unknown to me, the reform did not take effect" (Solís 1981: 76).

In spite of the government's withdrawal of the reform initiative, however, the political damage had been done. On one hand, the administration was still eager to increase its legitimacy through populist policies and rhetoric. If it lost to business in the fiscal arena, it would pose a challenge elsewhere. On the other hand, business was hardly convinced of the state's trustworthiness even after it backed down from the tax hike and continued to view the Echeverría administration as a significant threat to property rights (Elizondo 1994).

### Spending, Devaluation, and the Rupture with Business

If Echeverría lost in taxes, he won in spending. Although the private sector was particularly disturbed by inflation, growing budget deficits, and foreign debt, the president went on a public sector shopping spree of unprecedented scale. Echeverría's fiscal excess illustrates the inconsistency of the Mexican state's policy-making autonomy. On one hand, the structural power of capital over investment decisions appears to have given Mexican business veto power over tax increases. On the other hand, despite the disapproval of every major business association, the Echeverría administration successfully pursued inflationary and destabilizing deficit spending.

In the effort to put a break on price increases during the first two years of the *sexenio*, the president turned to price controls, which became a source of further business irritation with the government (Newell and Rubio 1984: 126). In 1973, Echeverría responded to increasing inflation by approving an across-the-board salary increase of 18 percent. Over the next two years, he would raise wages three more times, doubling nominal pay by 1975 (Solís 1981: 80). By the end of the *sexenio*, inflation surged at over three times its 1970 rate, public spending had more than doubled in real terms, rising by almost half as a proportion of national income, while the public deficit had more than tripled as a percentage of GDP (see Figure 2.1). New government borrowing had multiplied eleven times from 1970 to 1976, from $443 million to $5.1 billion.

The main targets of spending largesse were public employment and public investment, particularly in urban areas. Government job spending doubled during Echeverría's *sexenio*; state owned enterprises increased capital spending at an annual rate of almost 30 percent. Social security coverage was increased by a third, covering ten million more workers, while the National Workers Housing Fund created 100,000 units of af-

**Figure 2.1**
**New Public Borrowing\* (1970–1981)**

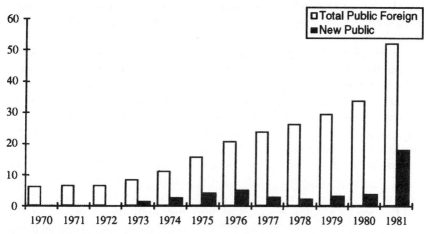

*Note:* \*billions of dollars

*Source:* Banco de México, *Indicadores Económicos* (cited in Zedillo 1986).

fordable housing. The education budget increased fivefold. By 1976, the number of technical institutes had increased from 281 to 1,301 (Hellman 1983: 191).[4]

As the current account deficit, budget deficit, and inflation mounted, confidence in the government's ability to maintain the exchange rate diminished. In 1975, the administration undertook a timid stabilization effort by tightening monetary policy. However, with foreign capital still plentiful and cheap, there was little political incentive to actually reduce public spending. Having alienated the private sector and middle class, a budget cut would now only serve to anger the working class and popular sectors whose support the PRI had sought to recapture in the first place (Bazdresch and Levy 1991: 246).

The persistence of uncontrolled expansion eventually turned the erosion of confidence into panic. Mexico's financial and industrial leaders were not just refusing to invest; they were taking massive amounts of liquid assets out of the country and battering the peso in the process. By the end of Echeverría's term, massive government borrowing was barely keeping pace with capital flight. The government abandoned its futile defense of the peso in September 1976. The exchange rate that had remained unchanged for over two decades was fell by 60 percent, a *sexenio*-ending shock to which Mexico would soon grow accustomed.

The government's blatant disregard for macroeconomic discipline angered and frightened the business community. At the same time, Echeverría's uncompromising antibusiness rhetoric represented a sharp break from the PRI's long-standing partnership with Mexican capital. In his last years in office, the president regularly engaged in fierce polemics to demonize what he characterized as a traitorous and cowardly private sector. During his 1974 state of the union address, Echeverría digressed momentarily from his prepared speech to express his outrage over capital flight, denouncing those who had recently bought large quantities of dollars in anticipation of devaluation. "The little rich Mexicans who buy dollars . . . are despised by their own sons, because they are not strengthening the fatherland" (quoted in Solís 1981).

In response, the private sector closed ranks, cooperated, and organized. Attacking the government as antagonistic, authoritarian, and sympathetic to Marxism, in May 1975, all of the country's major industrial, commercial, and financial associations joined under a new umbrella organization, the Coordinating Enterprise Council (CCE), which would now represent an autonomous and united front against what was perceived as the government's populist excesses (Story 1986: 90–91).

### Explaining Defeat and Victory

What explains the government's tax defeat and deficit-spending victory? The global economic environment clearly contributed to the new development model. Indeed, Mexico was hardly alone among developing nations in increasing the role of the state. By the early 1970s, a battered U.S. economy and a global trend toward sluggish expansion suggested the limitations of an export growth strategy. At the same time, the availability of low-interest petro-dollars during the 1970s facilitated foreign borrowing. Indeed, the inflation-adjusted interest rate between 1973 and 1976 was actually negative (Zedillo 1986: 968).

However, international opportunity cannot explain the timing or degree of Mexican expansion. Echeverría turned to international capital markets over two years before they were flooded by petro-dollars. Furthermore, the presence of affordable credit and oil revenues does not adequately explain how the state could generate a deficit of over 16 percent of GDP by 1982. Mexico's stimulus program went far beyond even the most enthusiastic Keynesian prescriptions of growth.

Much of the explanation for Echeverría's policy choices lay in the political visibility of taxation and borrowing. A tax hike is a *fiscal* policy; it is easy for the average citizen to see, and its effect are readily understood. Moreover, to the extent that progressive taxation targets the wealthier classes, it entails immediate and significant extraction of economic resources from a focused group. In contrast, the expansion of the public deficit is a *finance* policy. Even though the state must eventually repay that debt, the question of where that revenue comes from—increased growth, higher tax rates, or reduced services—tends to remain off the political agenda.

## LÓPEZ PORTILLO: ADJUSTMENT DEFERRED

When López Portillo took office in December 1976, the Mexican economy was in a state of disorder. High inflation, increased debt, and a growing budget deficit tied the president's hands from the beginning. However, the discovery of Mexico's virtually limitless oil reserves and the surge in oil prices provided the new president with the resources to continue the populist spending policies of his predecessor. At the same time, global stagnation made the resumption of deficit spending seem a reasonable proposition. As the United States and most of Europe settled into a long economic funk, continued domestic growth became problematic.

In 1970, the ruling party had been in danger of losing the legitimacy of its political control because of opposition to authoritarian rule. Six years later, for the first time since the Revolution, its economic competence was being fundamentally questioned. After the 1976 devaluation and the virtual state of war with the private sector, López Portillo found his options limited. Any attempt to further the excesses of his predecessor would only trigger more capital flight and intensify the "capital strike" of big business. It appeared as if the limits of populism had been reached. In short, because of insurmountable (but temporary) structural constraints, finance policy was largely taken off the political agenda at the outset of López Portillo's term. The PRI had to put Mexico's financial house back in order.

Accordingly, López Portillo started out with considerable discipline. During his first year, under the shadow of an International Monetary Fund (IMF) stand-by loan agreement, a standard austerity package was implemented: The central bank restricted the money supply; public investment declined in real terms; and wage growth was restricted to well below the inflation rate. After just one year, the new president had reduced the budget deficit from 9.9 percent to 6.7 percent of GDP (Buffie 1990: 430). In addition, a more flexible exchange rate made Mexican exports more competitive and reduced opportunities for speculation.

Inheriting the economic dislocations caused by Echeverría's overspending clearly forced movement toward fiscal discipline and might well have led to six years of moderate austerity. Indeed, the first two years of the term appear a model of responsibility and restraint in comparison with the last half of Echeverría's *sexenio*. Although public spending growth resumed in 1978, it was a measured response to a somewhat disappointing 3.4 percent economic growth in the previous year. The results were promising: GDP rebounded to a robust 8.3 percent, even as inflation fell. For at least a couple of years, it seemed as if Mexico had found a sustainable Keynesian solution to the stagnation of Stabilizing Development and the traditional import substitution model.

### The Petroleum Boom

Unfortunately for Mexico, international economic turmoil and domestic opportunities intervened. On the global front, by the late 1970s, most of world's industrialized powers were gripped by recession. The United States, Mexico's major trading partner, had discovered "stagflation." As employment and demand plummeted, not only did American imports fall, but protectionist demands were suddenly receiving a hearing in Washington. The few countries continuing to grow, particularly Japan and the Asian "tigers," were highly competitive and notoriously insulated economies, hardly representing an opportunity for Mexico to expand exports. In short, Mexican policy makers saw little reason to believe that international trade would fuel national growth in the 1980s.

At the same time that global constraints made domestic expansion desirable, the availability of valuable natural resources made such a program feasible. López Portillo took office just as Mexico's vast petroleum reserves were being discovered. Furthermore, not only was the amount of petroleum under Mexican soil found to be almost three times previous estimates, but the second "oil shock" of 1979 doubled the foreign exchange value of each barrel. When oil soared to over $30 per barrel in 1980, the value of Mexican petroleum reserves reached almost fourteen times the country's annual gross national product.

The discovery of such wealth would prove bitterly ironic. By dramatically increasing the state's direct control over economic resources, oil allowed political leaders to renew and accelerate the expansionary project begun by Echeverría. The new economic opportunity allowed the ruling party to defer the difficult economic decisions that might have jeopardized its hard-won image as both engine of growth and provider of social justice. The caretaker of Mexican financial policy would no longer be the despised IMF. In short, oil returned financial policy to the political arena.

Just as Echeverría had pursued tax reform to reduce Mexico's dependence on foreign credit, López Portillo extolled the "financial self-determination" that oil would make possible. Rather than bow down before multilateral lenders and forego improvements in the living standard of millions, oil revenue would make simultaneously possible the economic goals that would ensure PRI's undisputed domination: growth and social redistribution. Building upon the patriarchal mission of the state with which Lázaro Cárdenas solidified the ruling party's control in the 1930s, López Portillo's strategy reflected a political culture that . . . sees the government as a provider. And oil, in this culture, removed any reasons why the government should not provide. The outburst in public spending was not the outcome of a single individual intoxicated by terms of trade shock: it was also produced by a set of institutions that simultaneously placed great expectations on what the government should provide and few restraints on the nature of its intervention in the economy. (Bazdresch and Levy 1991: 247)

Finally, if the rapid expansion of public deficit and external debt had concerned anyone in the administration, such worries were ended with the "second" oil shock late in 1979. With prices doubling yet again on an export commodity seemingly without limit, the president pushed public spending to unprecedented heights. Between 1978 and 1981, public investment doubled in real terms, mostly in energy production (Gurría Treviño 1994: 12). To finance the exploding budget deficit, the López Portillo administration relied increasingly on foreign loans.

The money was used to pursue developmental, social, and political objectives. Moreover, the windfall from petroleum production seemed to make all these compatible. For example, the president quickly offered an olive branch to the private sector by extending state resources to producers. Replacing "Shared Development" with the more sober "Alliance for Production," López Portillo sought to repair much of the damage done under Echeverría. Under the new model, the government offered business fiscal incentives, investment in infrastructure, and cheap inputs (such as energy), in exchange for a commitment to invest in production and expand exports. At the same time, the new program was designed to shore up the government's central sources of social support. As one development scholar explained,

The "lubricant" relied upon to make the Alliance acceptable to investors and workers alike is oil wealth, which allows the government to subsidize industrial imports and grant credits for production, while offering increased social benefits to workers in the form of higher public investments in education, health, housing, and job training. Mexico's government evidently rests its hopes on a consensus model of development: it believes that sacrifices can be kept minimal thanks to the nation's abundant resources. (Goulet 1983: 78–79)

Aside from tremendous investments in oil, electricity, and infrastructure projects, as well as increased jobs and benefits for labor, the government also focused its attention upon problems of social inequality, particularly outside of urban areas, which had exposed the PRI to criticism in the 1960s. For example, López Portillo significantly expanded the Program for Integrated Rural Development (PIDER), a program initiated by Echeverría in 1973. While direct benefits of PIDER included access to education health care, one of the most important objectives of rural development was to replace the corrupt and exploitative system of agricultural production that prevailed in the countryside with the resources of a benign central state. The new president sought

to break the hold of intermediaries over the peasantry. New storage and marketing facilities, sources of credit and the rest were meant to liberalize the subsistence producer from the obligation to borrow on usurious terms, or depend on a variety of local middlemen and caciques who buy and transport the harvest, and siphon off any marginal profit the peasant might anticipate. (Hellman 1983: 193)

In addition, the Mexican Nutrition System (SAM) was established in the 1980s to make the country self-sufficient in cereals productions. Subsidized credit for agricultural inputs and the use of state-owned food warehouses served as the main instruments not only to reduce hunger among Mexico's poor, but also to increase the party's popularity in the countryside as well as its control over peasant organizations (Goulet 1983: 79–91).

Increased social justice notwithstanding, the price of the government's fiscal largesse was the alienation of the business community. Although the new president abstained from the militant antibusiness rhetoric of his predecessor, his administration's populist policy making contributed to the continued rightward shift of business and the independent politicization of the private sector against government encroachment (Gibson 1992). In particular, efforts to achieve economic redistribution, uncontrolled deficits, and inflation continued to alarm the newly organized and active business interests. (See Figure 2.2.) In 1979 the president proposed and achieved a modest tax increase on capital, while lowering the burden on labor (Story 1986: 60–69). While the fiscal reform did not come close to closing the enormous budget gap resulting from repeated spending increases, it did put further strain on business-government relations.

Despite macroeconomic alarms sounding in all directions, the state made no move toward adjustment. Notwithstanding López Portillo's conciliatory rhetoric and his Alliance for Production, big business was powerless to reverse or even slow the government's spending behavior.[5] As Mexico entered the new decade, the availability and high price of oil, in addition to the exigencies of the upcoming presidential election, precluded efforts to achieve financial discipline. "Although the [1980] budget approved by Congress called for an unchanged nominal fiscal deficit, in practice no serious attempt was made to achieve fiscal restraint. Just as Echeverría had done earlier, López Portillo overrode the Congressional budget by routinely authorizing *ampliaciones presupuestales* (out-of-budget expenditures)" (Buffie 1990: 442). Deficits continued to spiral out of control, while inflation edged ever higher.

**Figure 2.2**
**Consolidated Budget Deficit as Percent of GDP (1971–1982)**

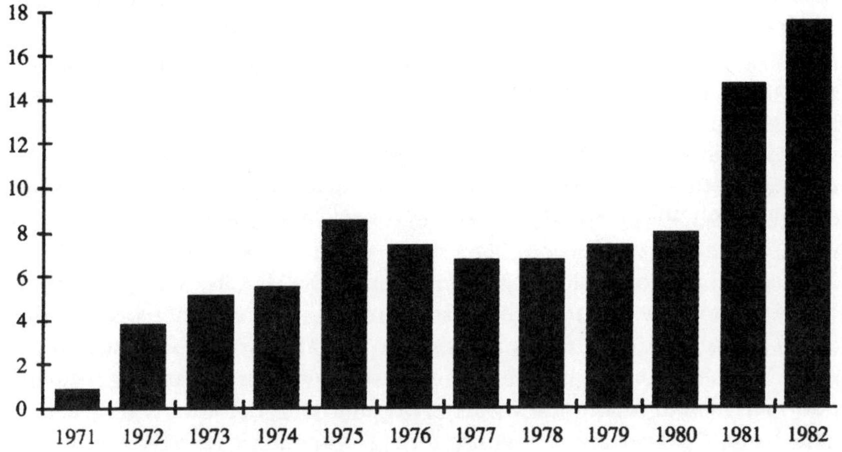

*Source:* Banco de México, *Indicadores Económicos.*

### Capital Flight and the Bank Nationalization

On September 1, 1982, frustrated by the banks' refusal to invest in production and infuriated by their removal of the nation's capital, the outgoing president lambasted Mexico's financial community as "traitors to the fatherland" and announced the end of the private banking system to a cheering Congress. In his final state of the union address, López Portillo triumphantly promised Mexico: "They won't plunder us again."

Scholars who justify the government's action argue that capital flight gave the state no choice but to expropriate the institutions draining the nation of wealth. Those who criticize the nationalization maintain that the populist policies of López Portillo undermined economic stability to such a degree that capitalists had no choice but to send their money abroad. The present study is not an adequate forum to resolve this debate. However, it will be useful to briefly describe the pressures leading up to the state's decision, the political impact of which would reshape the economic orientation of all future administrations.

After the 1976 devaluation, the government anchored the peso to the dollar in order to re-establish monetary stability, depreciating the peso by only fraction every day. However, because Mexico's inflation rate was far higher than that of the United States, the peso gradually became overvalued and increased the current account deficit. In an environment of pervasive uncertainty, anyone with liquid assets looked for a safe haven for their money, which in practice meant looking overseas. Despite the daily transfer of the nation's wealth to the north and relentless pressure on foreign exchange reserves, the government refrained from either floating or weakening the currency through 1981. "Devaluation and stabilization were seen as equivalent to a surrender to its enemies, as these measures implied a substantial revision of the government's growth strategy" (Bazdresch and Levy 1991: 251).

As inflation continued to spin out of control, expectations of devaluation became self-fulfilling. As both domestic and foreign speculators shorted the Mexican peso, everyone took refuge in dollars. While most simply tried to buy any greenbacks they could get their hands on, the rich transferred billions abroad, intensifying the massive capital flight already well in progress. It is difficult to speculate what would have happened, or for how long, had the high price of oil been maintained. But just as factors beyond the control of the Mexican president had created the opportunity for further expansion, so irresistible economic forces eventually destroyed the entire project.

By the end of López Portillo's term, the international economic environment that had made borrowing easy and inexpensive was transformed and rendered Mexico unable to service its foreign obligations. In 1981, the price of oil plummeted. Shortly thereafter, under pressure from massive financing of U.S. deficits, the variable interest rates to which Mexican foreign debt was tied began to soar. The result was far less foreign exchange available to make significantly higher interest payments.

Not surprisingly, most wealthy Mexicans were unwilling to risk their capital in what the state viewed as national priority sectors. In an atmosphere of shattered economic confidence, the president became increasingly frustrated by his inability to make private financial institutions channel credit to productive investment. In late 1982, a government-appointed director of Mexico's largest bank complained: "For the last five years [Banamex] did not create one job. It bought up shares in existing companies. It created wealth for bankers. The profit margins were as wide as the street out there" (*Euromoney*, October 1982: 50). In his historical treatment of the pre-nationalization financial period, Javier Márquez remarked that by the late 1970s the private bankers "didn't have much confidence, and perhaps not much interest either, that the multiple bank enter the field of new investment. Rather there persisted among them the thesis that investments (long term resources and risk capital) are not the function of those who obtain liquid resources from the public" (1987: 204).

In a now-infamous speech made in late 1981, López Portillo promised to defend the peso "like a dog." In his memoirs, the president blames the traitorous *saco-dolares* who drained the government of its currency reserves and kept their money abroad. In a histrionic account of his refusal to devalue, he characterized the struggle to maintain currency stability as that of "Prometheus against the vulture; against the greed of a class that ate the innards of the country, even though it hurt itself in the long run. The speculators! The question for me was to find a way out. To protect the peso, ourselves" (López Portillo 1988: 1227–228). Notwithstanding his patriotism, on February 18, 1982, with government coffers virtually emptied of foreign exchange reserves, López Portillo abruptly floated the currency, leading to an immediate devaluation of 57 percent.

The government was desperate to maintain a semblance of control, but its denial of crisis conditions merely intensified the frantic removal of financial assets from the country. Indeed, whereas the purpose of foreign loans had originally been to finance the governmental budget deficit, in the final years of the López Portillo *sexenio*, it had been used to finance capital flight (Zedillo 1987: 178). A Federal Reserve Bank study reported that Mexican investment and hard currency deposits in the state of Texas had increased by a factor of three between 1975 and 1981, to almost $25 billion. The U.S. border was just the tip of the iceberg. "According to conservative estimates, $14 billion was deposited in Eurobanks, $12 billion in foreign currency accounts in Mexico, and at least another $25 billion in real estate purchases in the United States" (Hellman 1983: 222).

For most of 1982, the Mexican economy was hit with a spike in inflation and a serious international credit crunch. With dollars scarce and foreign obligations high, the administration adopted a dual exchange rate system in early August. However, as this measure only increased the public's (accurate) fears of impending permanent exchange controls, capital flight reached a fever pitch (Gil Díaz 1984: 353).

On August 13, 1982, the government temporarily closed all foreign exchange operations. More importantly, on that day the government seized and converted all dollar-denominated bank accounts, worth an estimated $12 billion.[6] In the effort to stem further foreign exchange losses abroad, the government ordered the banks to pay account holders only in pesos. Because devaluation had already taken about a third of the value of the national currency, the result was that Mexican citizens—mostly from the middle class—collectively donated about $4 billion of their savings to the government (Elizondo 1992: 192). Of course, it was not enough; Mexico was left without sufficient foreign exchange to meet even short-term international obligations, triggering the Mexican debt crisis.

The decision to take control of the banks was facilitated by the fact that by late 1982, the financial community had few resources or weapons with which to sanction the government. Indeed, the foundation of the bankers' influence had always rested with their ability to withhold investment and remove wealth. "The immediate economic cost of nationalizing the banks was lower at this moment [September 1982] than before, because property holders had weakened the basis of their structural power, namely, the menace of capital flight. As capital had already been transferred abroad, they were in a weaker position" (Elizondo 1992: 185).

In an environment of widespread panic, those with liquid assets sought to convert them into dollars and other foreign assets. The banks' primary function during this period was to serve as a vehicle of capital flight. In his diary entry for August 31, the day before the announcement of expropriation, the president wrote:

Mexico has been pillaged. . . . At least $14 billion in Mexican accounts in the USA, $30 billion in real estate, of which $9 billion has already been paid in down payments and interest. . . . It's incredible, all the foreign investment in our history comes to $11 billion, $8 billion from the US. Mexican investment abroad is five times higher. How shameful! How disgusting! I'm going to take action, no matter what the consequences. (López Portillo 1988: 1232)

Immediate nationalization of the banks was made possible by the virtually unlimited powers available to the Mexican president. Indeed, under the provisions of the Law of Expropriation, López Portillo did not even have to consult with Congress or his cabinet.

## FINANCING A BIGGER STATE

Although foreign borrowing represented a major part of the capital that the Echeverría and López Portillo administrations used for deficit spending, both presidents also utilized domestic finance regulation to increase and protect the supply of capital available to the public sector, as well as to compensate the business community for the effects of a credit crunch. These policies ranged from typical measures of government intervention and extraction, to liberalizing innovations and institutionalization required to create and deepen key financial markets. The remainder of this chapter describes how the populist presidents of the 1970s tailored diverse financial policies to respond to address political exigencies.

### Banking Regulation

The growth of Mexico's financial system under Stabilizing Development had been slow but steady. In particular, the proportion of income that private citizens kept in the banking system had grown from an anemic 9.9 percent in 1954 to over 31 percent by the beginning of Echeverría's term. The increase in intermediation, in turn, meant a greater base of capital from which the private sector could borrow. During this period, although the government strictly controlled interest rates that banks could charge their clients, financial authorities were careful to maintain a healthy, positive real interest rate. Interest rate controls helped the government prevent usury on the part of price-setting banks, as well as contain credit expansion that might send prices skyward.

However, as Echeverría turned his focus upon rapid growth and turned a blind eye to inflation, he began to use banking regulation as a way to ensure a stable supply of capital rather than a stable macroeconomic environment. While he intensified government intervention in credit markets, he also initiated the earliest attempts at banking deregulation in postrevolutionary Mexico. Rather than an ideological contradiction, this policy change illustrates the state's objectives of procuring capital for both a high level of public spending and continued private sector investment.

*Financial Repression*

Two of the most important policies available to Echeverría in the search for capital were government restrictions in financial markets: interest rate controls and reserve requirements on private banks. While these regulations may seem to represent policy continuity—after all, both had been in place since the 1940s—in fact, they represented a sharp break with finance policies carried out under Stabilizing Development. This is because rather than serving as an anchor of macroeconomic stability, state intervention in the market for bank capital now served as a tool of credit expansion for the state.

In the realm of interest rate controls, for the first time since the Revolution, Mexican financial authorities in the early 1970s allowed both loan and deposit interest rates to dip below the rate of inflation. In 1974, a sharp spike in inflation made an interest rate increase necessary. The government responded by creating the weighted average deposit rate (CPP) to set rates more flexibly. Although loan rate controls were eventually eliminated completely, deposit rates continued to be controlled (Coorey 1992: 38). Indeed, as inflation began to climb, interest rates became negative between 1973 and 1977. In effect, the government used the national banking system as a vehicle for providing itself with cheap credit. As a consequence, putting money in a bank quickly became a money-losing proposition. Domestic savings plummeted, leading to a severe reduction in deposits. As financial intermediation fell, the amount of capital available for private investment fell accordingly (see Figure 2.3).

Past administrations would have made rapid adjustments in order to increase domestic savings and halt the process of financial disintermediation. However, since Echeverría's model for economic growth was based on public spending and the expansion of credit, his administration allowed the banking system to fall into a state of disrepair. In effect, Shared Development made traditional financial intermediation an unviable activity. In response, both the bankers and their clients took their business elsewhere and increasingly abroad.

Interest rate controls were not the only way through which the Mexican government intervened in the financial system to make possible the increased spending levels required to carry out PRI's political strategy. Even

**Figure 2.3**
**Financial Intermediation and Real Interest Rate (1971–1981)**

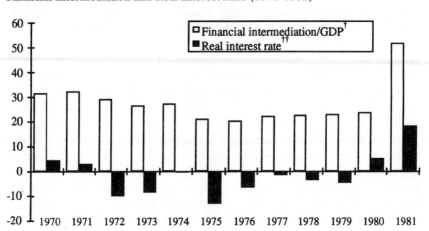

*Notes:* †Savings and checking accounts as a percentage of national income.

††Average nominal return of most representative financial instruments minus annual inflation rate.

*Sources:* *Estadisticas Históricas de Moneda y Banca,* Banco de México, cited in Gil Díaz (1984); Banco de México, Dirección de Investigación Económica (cited in Zedillo 1987).

as interest rates plummeted, the state also raised existing reserve requirements to ensure an adequate supply of financial assets for the public sector.

While the ratio was modestly increased during the first three years of Echeverría's term, by 1973 inflation and the ballooning deficit led the government to capture an increasing share of banking assets. Used both to "sterilize" credit resources and to help the government meet its spending obligation, the following year the central bank raised reserve requirements on deposit banks once again and implemented new requirements for mortgage banks. By the end of 1974, the shortage of foreign exchange had become acute, and the banks were forced to channel virtually all of their dollar-denominated assets to the central bank (Tello 1979: 128–130).

*Self-Serving Deregulation*

Ironically, it was precisely the problem of capital scarcity that led Echeverría to implement not only draconian restrictions, but also to undertake the liberalization of important elements of commercial banking. Even as the populist administration siphoned off private banking assets, it simultaneously pursued the deregulation of international capital movements in an effort to neutralize the effects of capital flight and create new sources of domestic savings. In August 1973, deposit banks were authorized to receive deposits from Mexican nationals living abroad. The following year, dollar restrictions were lifted for other financial institutions. In March 1976, the government responded to constant speculation against the peso, rampant rumors of devaluation, and the increasing flight of capital by authorizing private financial institutions to accept up to 10 percent of their liabilities in dollars from Mexican residents.

Although the measure achieved the desired effect of providing the capital-starved banks with deposits, deregulation within a heavily controlled economy posed new dangers. Indeed, the "disguised internationalization of Mexican finances" increased economic vulnerability. Since restrictions made it difficult for domestic banks to attract sufficient local capital, they were forced to rely increasingly on dollar-denominated accounts (Quijano 1983: 348).

Mexico's promotion of these deposits amounted to a financial fiction that never achieved full credibility. Savers deposited their dubious currency in national banks, and like water into wine, the pesos were pronounced dollars. The only way to make this transubstantiation possible was for the government to assume the dollar obligation. A Universidad Nacional Autónoma de México (UNAM) economist explains how capitalizing banks with foreign currency only increased Mexico's foreign obligations: "Upon completing this kind of deposit, usually in national currency, achieving its magical conversion into dollars simply through an accounting operation, the Banco de México, guardian of our international reserves . . . was obliged to contract external debt in order to increase artificially our reserves" (Ruiz Durán 1989: 249–250).

The effort to stimulate dollar deposits was too little and too late. The macroeconomic imbalance was so acute that the fraction of assets held in dollars could hardly stem the tide of capital flight. Indeed, the 10 percent limit was reached quickly and investors pressured for an expansion of the dollar ceiling. As Carlos Tello put it: "Either the dollarization limit was going to be raised or money was going to be taken out and invested abroad. The dollarization of the banking system implied, in fact, covering the exchange rate risk for investors" (Tello 1979: 139). In other words, by liberalizing capital movements, the government found its ability to loosen the exchange rate seriously compromised. The same policies designed to ensure an adequate inflow of foreign capital effectively chained monetary authorities to an unsustainable overvaluation of the peso.

Because public financing depended so heavily on bank reserve requirements, and because the level of bank reserves depended directly on domestic savings, the dollarization of Mexican financial assets can be seen as the most expedient way to provide the government with sufficient levels of capital to continue its high spending political project. The liberalization of capital, therefore, had nothing to do with an ideological change of heart. On the contrary, the state internationalized bank deposits in order to expand the broader policy of increasing its own access to credit. In sum, financial repression and capital deregulation were consistent with the PRI's ultimate goal of gaining access to capital for politically motivated public spending increases.

### Creating Economies of Scale

From the postwar period until the early 1970s, Mexico had promoted a highly specialized, fragmented banking system. Reflecting to a large degree the U.S. banking model, institutional differentiation was promoted to stimulate competition and reduce banking collusion. In practice, the state had not seriously impeded a long-term trend toward concentration of several different banking areas into the hands of a small number of major firms.[7] However, even Mexico's poorly enforced system of financial specialization had effectively prevented the concentration of all major financial services.

As Mexican financial authorities worked out their strategy for coping with the economic environment of the 1970s, the antitrust vision underlying existing banking legislation gave way to the need for size. As a ranking financial administrator explained: "The small size of many banks and financial institutions and their excessive specialization . . . precluded the supply of adequate and efficient financial services to the economy," adding that "steps were taken toward the establishment of full service or integrated banks. The government actively promoted mergers and consolidations" (Ibarra 1988: 114–115).

As a result of the PRI's strategy to preserve its legitimacy through spending, in addition to the belief among the main economic policy makers that a global credit crunch was imminent, the guiding principle behind Mexican bank policy since the early 1970s became the facilitation of international capital access and the strengthening of domestic financial institutions. Near the end of Echeverría's term, the governor of the Banco de México articulated the government's concern with the growing competition for international funds—ironically just as Organization of Petroleum Exporting Countries (OPEC) petro dollars began flooding global capital markets with excess liquidity. Noting with alarm that "some traditionally capital exporting countries like England, France, Italy and others . . . have now become solicitors of [financial] resources," the governor argued that "to attract and retain the international resources that Mexico and Latin America require in the circumstances which will prevail in the following years, I believe it is absolutely necessary to strengthen and enlarge even more our banking and financial institutions" (Fernández Hurtado 1975: 23).

In 1974, the Echeverría administration passed the Law of Credit Institutions, which began the evolution of what were to become "multiple banks." Although *de facto* concentration already prevailed, the government accelerated the trend by facilitating mergers among banking, insurance, brokerage, and trust companies (Gruben et al. 1993). Whereas in the postrevolutionary period Mexico's commitment to bank specialization was characterized by benign neglect, by the mid-1970s the government had decided to openly reverse its long-standing promotion of financial service decentralization.

In Echeverría's last year, the state stepped up the pace of concentration by implementing the 1976 Multiple Bank Law, in which commercial banks were officially permitted to combine services previously provided only by specialized financial service companies. At the same time, the government offered significant tax breaks and other incentives for firms to merge. Between 1975 and 1982, bank fusions were increased dramatically, as the number of banking institutions fell from 243 to 60. Of these, over half were "multiple" banks.

The multiple bank was not only seen as a vehicle to provide access to foreign capital. Equally importantly, it also represented a response to Mexico's perceived financial vulnerability. According to an official financial history, "The multiple bank can achieve, almost by definition, a diversification and portfolio composition far superior to that of the specialized bank, with consequent greater profitability and less risk. . . . As it has been said: 'diversification is still the best protection for a bank in an uncertain world'" (Márquez 1987: 78).

Because his expansion project depended largely on private banking funds, López Portillo offered no resistance to the financial initiatives of his predecessor. The larger the growth of bank assets, the larger the base of forced reserves from which to draw. As a UNAM economist recalls, in the late 1970s, "what was good for the banks was good for the government."[8] Given the growing gap between the state's financing needs and available resources, the government also sought to facilitate bank access to foreign capital. On the first day of 1979, in an effort to attract frightened capital back to Mexico, the López Portillo administration broadened the financial internationalization initiated by Echeverría. Through reforms made to the General Credit Law, it legalized the establishment of foreign bank branches within Mexico, whose operations were confined exclusively to credit operations with Mexican nationals living outside of the country (*Diario Oficial* December 27, 1978: 10).

### Capital Markets

Although the administrations of Echeverría and López Portillo are best remembered for their fiscal excesses and subsequent dependence on both external and internal financial savings, they were also instrumental in the modernization and development of what were to become crucial financial markets in Mexico. These populist presidents did not simply deregulate Mexican capital markets; they virtually created them from scratch. Indeed, without their initiatives in the regulation and issuing of equities and corporate and public debt, there would not have been much of a financial system to liberalize.

The paradox is resolved by two aspects of the market-creating project: First, rather than reduce its role in economic activity, the state gave itself new regulatory powers and established new institutions in its quest to develop financial markets. Second, far from an ideological contradiction, these new markets represented the state's effort to provide the capital necessary for the viability of the expansionary economic program, a key to the preservation of the PRI's legitimacy.

### Stock Market Development

By the end of the Echeverría administration, public spending was absorbing so much bank capital that even big businesses were effectively being squeezed out of capital markets. Yet large corporations were the primary engines of Mexican growth and modernization. Thus the government's expropriation of bank capital had the unintended effect of undermining both the political support of business and weakening economic growth, the primary objective of state spending in the first place.

Unfortunately, private enterprise had few alternatives to traditional bank financing. In spite of fiscal incentives for equity investment—both capital gains and dividends were tax exempt—the Mexican stock market in the mid-1970s was undeveloped. Few investors even knew about the tax breaks. Potential interest in equities was quashed by the small, illiquid, and unevenly regulated market. Leading business journals featured articles explaining the most rudimentary aspects of equities; even among investors the issuing of shares, liquidity, and the primary and secondary market were poorly understood concepts.

The Mexican stock market had been a nonfactor in providing new capital to business. A major reason for its poor development was a long-standing tax policy that allowed massive deductions for interest payments on debt, a regulation that more than negated the tax break on capital gains and dividends. Firms that borrowed money were able to retain virtually all of their profits, a major disincentive to go public. Indeed, the purpose of holding stocks was not to trade or receive dividends. Rather, business owners used their shares as collateral to obtain loans from banks, which they could then deduct from their tax bill. "It can be said that the stock market was used to finance stockholders, not corporations, and that it dealt mainly with debts, not with equities" (Hakim-Simon 1988: 22).

In 1975, near the end of one of Mexico's most populist administrations, President Echeverría approved the Securities Market Law. Of little consequence at the time, the legislation would become the "fundamental pillar" of the money market, such as commercial paper and corporate bonds, as well equity capitalization (Ortíz 1994: 26). It signaled the government's first serious attempt to stimulate investment activity through financial channels other than traditional loans. Such an effort required nothing less than the state's creation and maintenance of a new market for financial instruments.

In the context of a corporate credit squeeze caused in large part by public sector borrowing, the government sought to ensure that major private sector firms had sufficient access to investment capital. As the National Securities Commission reported the year after the law's implementation, the government's objectives included "providing small and medium savers with alternative opportunities to save and invest, [which] will permit . . . industrial and commercial enterprises to have a greater diversification of financial resources, and with it, less dependence on bank credit" (Ejea et al. 1991). The agency's president, Gustavo Petricioli, viewed the new financial instruments "as a source of long-term, peso-denominated financing for the public and private sector" (*Expansión*, January 18, 1979: 45–46).

To carry out these goals, the law created a new public institution, the National Securities Commission (CNV), which authorized and regulated the securities market, gathered financial statistics on securities and brokers, and arbitrated disputes. In addition, the stock market was streamlined and made into an autonomous institution. The three regional stock markets (in Mexico City, Guadalajara, and Monterrey) were merged to form the *Bolsa Mexicana de Valores*. In order to institutionalize the securities trade and enable the CNV to monitor its activities, the government authorized brokers as the only legal securities traders and mandated that all securities transactions undertaken by banks be conducted through those agents. Finally in 1975, the finance ministry imposed a 4.2 percent reserve requirement on banking assets to be channeled directly to the purchase of stocks and another 2.1 percent requirement to develop brokerage firms (Cardero and Quijano 1983: 233).

The results of the Echeverría's innovations were felt almost immediately. The new Mexican stock marketed experienced an unprecedented boom. The capitalization of the *bolsa* grew by over half in 1977, over 130 percent in 1978, and doubled in value once again in the first half of 1979—before beginning its steady downward spiral into 1982.

However, as would be the case in later surges, governmental action contributed to the *bolsa*'s rise more than corporate performance. While the 1978–1979 boom was accompanied by economic expansion, as we have seen, that growth was based more on fiscal expansion than increasing productivity or exports. In addition, one of the main reasons for the sudden attractiveness of equities was the negative interest rate prevalent among traditional financial instruments. Because the government controlled interest rates that banks could pay on deposits, savers began looking for alternatives.

But government stimulation was not the only factor leading to the boom. The financial strategy of Mexico's banking-industrial conglomerates contributed to the wave of euphoria. The concentration of brokerage firms and their tight linkages to banks made price manipulation by brokers and their corporate clients easy and commonplace. The tremendous growth in capitalization was not accompanied by significant growth in primary stock issues. From 1978 to 1981, just ten brokerages controlled two-thirds of all transactions, while the largest, owned by Banamex (Banco Nacional de México), controlled over one-fifth. In 1978, over 80 percent of transaction volume was on the secondary market, reaching almost 90 percent the following year (Ejea et al. 1991: 55).

Two Mexican economists explain the emerging corporate strategy. Firms sold off large shares of overvalued stock (but not enough to lose control over management), obtaining a large cash infusion. They then invested that capital in interest-earning financial instruments overseas. In order to "make up" for this lost capital, the firm borrowed a like sum of money from its affiliated bank at a preferential interest rate or from an international bank at a relatively low market rate. Aside from the interest earned in its speculative investment, the company received an additional benefit provided by state regulation: Interest payments made on loans were tax deductible. (Cardero and Quijano 1983: 237–238) In this way, Mexico's largest corporations utilized the stock market to leverage lucrative financial investments and maximize the benefits of fiscal incentives rather than as a vehicle for direct capitalization.

The boom was short-lived. The crash came in 1979, as high inflation, high debt, and global opportunities made the stock market relatively unattractive and risky. Whereas 50,000 brokerage accounts existed at the peak of the 1979 boom, by the middle of 1982, only 5,000 investors were playing the market. International financial opportunities rapidly surpassed those available in the Mexican *bolsa*. In the United States, the end of President Jimmy Carter's term coincided with a global pummeling of the dollar, a devaluation that triggered significant increases in the interest rate in order to continue attracting foreign capital. It was also during this year of widespread financial insecurity that the value of gold reached historic levels, at times commanding over $800 per ounce. Faced with such competition, even Mexico's lively stock market ceased raising eyebrows. Risk-averse investors fled to the security of American treasury bills, while gambling speculators boarded the golden roller coaster in search of extraordinary profits.

The 1979 crash relegated the stock market to financial oblivion for over three years. The vast majority of novices experienced enormous losses when the market sank. Those embittered investors would no longer risk their savings in equities. As the *Wall Street Journal* reported in the early 1980s, with fewer investors around, the market was characterized by illiquidity, price volatility, and a low degree of brokerage professionalism (July 6, 1982: 29).

In addition to the government's own contradictory policies, the availability of plentiful and relatively cheap foreign capital prevented the stock market from becoming a genuine source of investment capital for Mexican firms. International bankers made the same dubious risks with the private sector that they did with the federal government. The same recycled petro-dollars that fed Mexico's ballooning budget deficit also fueled the dramatic expansion of its largest private firms. With foreign creditors more than willing to lend, Mexican entrepreneurs had little incentive to risk control of their firms by issuing shares to the public.

### The Money Market

One of the most momentous changes in the Mexican financial system occurred in 1978, with the creation of the country's first publicly sold debt instrument, short-term treasury bills. These public securities, called *Cetes*, would soon become the foundation of a modern, liberalized money market. Initially, however, they were created to respond to economic distortions caused by Echeverría's and López Portillo's irresponsible fiscal policies.

Until the late 1970s, banks were the only players in capital and money markets, which were extremely underdeveloped. They raised capital by issuing *bonos financieros*, long-term securities, to individuals and firms. Although *bonos* were technically securities, they actually served as a kind of interest-paying checking account, since the banks promised to buy them back at the prevailing interest rate back at any time without penalty (Hakim-Simon 1988: 21).

One of the results of the 1976 devaluation was an increase in inflation and the pervasive (and correct) belief that holding currency was unwise. The result was a massive withdrawal of private savings from bank accounts. As we have seen, however, because the government relied so heavily on bank reserves to finance itself, these withdrawals were tantamount to a reduction of resources available for state use. At the same time, government deficits mounted under President López Portillo, who began to accelerate his predecessor's spending levels in 1978. Thus, Mexico increased its reliance on foreign loans and let its fiscal imbalance spin out of control, even as its access to domestic savings was drying up.

Mexican treasury bills entered the financial system over the pointed objections of the banks. Already subject to high reserve requirements and obligatory credit allocation to parastatal enterprises, the banking sector became alarmed at the prospect of direct competition with the state for scarce domestic savings. At the 1978 convention of the Mexican Bankers Association, President Eraña García voiced his colleagues' preoccupation over the government's new capacity to absorb capital otherwise destined for deposits and suggested that the banks might find the resources needed to finance private investment limited. (White 1992: 89) However, the PRI did not seek to undermine the relatively positive business-government relations that still prevailed in the late 1970s.

The *Cete* was invented in large measure as a response to the government's need to finance its budget deficit. The treasury bill greatly enhanced the government's access to capital (Hakim-Simon 1988: 24). Although interest rates were initially controlled by the central bank, the new instrument provided unprecedented liquidity in the debt market and made more domestic savings available for public sector use.

At the same time, *Cetes* also helped the state improve macroeconomic management. Before *Cetes*, the central bank's only instrument for controlling the money supply or capturing savings was reserve requirements. While this regulation had sufficed during the period of fiscal conservatism, during the deficits of the 1970s, the capital siphoned off from reserve requirements was pumped back into the economy. Moreover, any decline in deposits would translate directly into a decline in reserves. According to David Ibarra, López Portillo's finance minister and one of the engineers of the new instrument, "Its purpose was also to stabilize internal savings and provide the state with capacity to perform open market operations."[9]

In addition to a new debt instrument, the state also modernized the institutional infrastructure for securities transactions. In 1978, the same year the *Cete* was unveiled, it created the Institute for Securities Deposits (Indeval). Acting as a custodian of debt instruments, Indeval made possible the "accounting transfer" of securities. The new clearinghouse eliminated the need for the physical storage and movement of actual paper and dramatically reduced the transaction costs associated with capital market activity in Mexico (*Sistema* 1990: 45; AMCB 1991). It was also designed to act as a break on highly speculative trading; by registering all transactions and eliminating anonymity, it could more easily monitor irregularities (*Proceso*, June 20, 1987: 18).

Ironically, the government's promotion of the public debt market contributed to the fall of the stock market. *Cetes* quickly became a principle force behind the sensational gains on the *bolsa* and represented a profitable and safe alternative to stock holdings. The widespread availability of a high yield domestic instrument provided an attractive option even for investors lacking the capital or connections to invest abroad. As the *Wall Street Journal* suggested on the eve of the debt crisis, the government began to crowd out the very equity markets it had earlier sought to develop; the introduction of *Cetes* now represented an important opportunity cost: "Interest rates on Mexican Treasury bills are 52.46%. If investors can get that kind of return on government securities, why should they buy stocks, which are riskier?" (July 6, 1982: 29).

## CONCLUSION

The administrations of Luis Echeverría and José López Portillo represented a turning point in both the political and economic stability of Mexico. In order to appease left-wing groups mobilizing in opposition to the ruling party's domination, lack of political accountability, and social inequality, Echeverría increased the level of government intervention in the economy and openly attacked private sector interests. In the following administration, López Portillo continued the populist agenda, using Mexico's newly discovered oil wealth to secure financing of deficits required to increase the state's role in production and employment.

The populist politics of these leaders and economic turmoil tore apart what had been a successful alliance between the private sector and the state. Although Echeverría attempted to heal some of the wounds of big business by deregulating and internationalizing part of the financial system, his undisciplined expansion ultimately provoked economic instability and the mobilized opposition of the private sector.

Facing less vitriolic opposition and armed with oil wealth, López Portillo followed a "please all" strategy, attempting to repair the alliance with the private sector at the same time that he continued highly popular social and development policies. In the attempt to increase the state's capacity to finance itself, he undertook important measures in creating capital markets. However, changes in global markets ultimately made his fiscal excesses unsustainable and plunged Mexico into a lengthy economic crisis.

## NOTES

1. For a discussion of the relationship between banking and large industrial interests in the 1940s and 1950s, see Mosk (1950: ch. 2). For more detailed analyses of financial-industrial cross-ownership and credit allocation practices, see Jacobs (1981); Jacobs and Nuñez (1982); and Camp (1989: ch. 8).

2. Stevens (1974) chronicles the major episodes in which the Mexican government has relied on force to quell movements of social opposition. In the broad literature on Mexican co-optation, see especially Collier and Collier (1991: 236–250, 407–420, 574–608), Meyer and Sherman (1987), and Hansen (1971).

3. For a detailed chronicle of the event see Poniatowska (1971).

4. These remarkable increases contrast sharply to social welfare spending, which, after three years of moderate increases, was slashed to barely one-half its 1970 level by the end of the term. Indeed, in terms of income distribution, Mexico's poorest were hardly better off at the end of Echeverría's *sexenio*. Reflecting on the failure to maintain spending levels and subsidies that mostly benefited those with limited incomes, one economist muses, "It is difficult to understand Echeverría's reputation as a 'populist' . . . [a term which] apparently derives from [his] rhetoric and his lenient approach to public finance issues. An examination of the fiscal records reveals that Echeverría was a statist, not a populist; his main priority was to increase the role of government in the economy" (Buffie 1990: 421).

5. For a sympathetic study of the events leading up to the nationalization and written by the central banker who carried it out, see Tello (1984). A similar perspective is offered by Aguilar et al. (1983) and Colmenares et al. (1982). White (1992) and Cockcroft (1983) offer neo-Marxist, class-based analyses. Story (1986: ch. 7) gives a useful summary of the economic pressures Mexico created for itself leading up the nationalization, while Brannon (1986) provides an analysis of its economic effects.

6. Such accounts were one of Echeverría's financial innovations. See following section.

7. Mexican banking practice often undermined existing legislation, which officially prohibited the combination of financial services and linkages between banks and industry. Even the Mexican Banking Commission acknowledged that financial holding companies had existed in Mexico well before they were legal (CNB 1992: 22).

8. Interview with Ramón Pieza, April 22, 1994, Mexico City.

9. Interview with David Ibarra, August 13, 1996, Mexico City.

# 3

---

# Crisis from the Right (1983-1988): The Rise of Brokerages, the Decline of Banks, and the Search for State Solvency

When the administration of President Miguel de la Madrid began in December of 1982, it confronted both political and economic challenges. Politically, a mobilized business community fought against the Institutional Revolutionary Party's (PRI) excessive power. The party sought to recover the support of the private sector, which demanded an end to the PRI's lock on power. The "radical faction" of big business called for limits on executive authority and for the development of a viable party system. The private sector's social legitimacy, influence over public opinion, and independent resources made it impossible for the PRI to use traditional means of co-optation. Business demands for political opening were based more on protecting private property than on furthering democratic ideals. Yet business leaders expressed opposition to reckless economic policies by attacking the ruling party's mandate to govern.

Economically, de la Madrid was constrained by economic and political forces beyond his control. Before he even took office, most international lending was cut off. The government was virtually insolvent. While inflation ran wild, the collapse of the peso had sent a large fraction of the nation's wealth abroad and plunged Mexico's major industrial firms into an international debt crisis of their own.

De la Madrid responded to these challenges by liberalizing the economy. However, the move toward the market was complicated by the continuation of government intervention in financial institutions. Furthermore, even those finance policies that were consistent with liberalization had perverse economic effects, providing rent-seeking opportunities and destabilizing the economy. The government-implemented policies appeared ideologically contradictory yet were politically coherent. Even as bank capital was expropriated, the securities sector was liberalized. Both policies increased the public sector's access to capital, while the latter also helped rejuvenate big business.

## BUSINESS OPPOSITION

De la Madrid's most serious political weakness was the open hostility of the business community toward the government and its demands for genuine party competition. Two populist administrations had generated not only capital flight, but also growing support for the market-oriented National Action Party (PAN), which until the 1980s had been a negligible force in Mexican politics.

As a result, the ruling party was dedicated to re-establishing its partnership with the private sector. De la Madrid's primary goals were to overcome both the political crisis of confidence and the economic crisis of stability. While frequently utilizing the revolutionary rhetoric of social justice, the president quietly built the foundation for a new, symbiotic relationship between the state and capital.

### The Private Sector Strikes Back

Throughout the 1980s, Mexico's business class dedicated all of its energies toward reigning in the state's policy-making authority, demanding an end to what it saw as arbitrary interventionism and securing concessions for the private sector (Loaeza 1992a). During the final moments of the López Portillo administration, the private sector watched Mexico's creditworthiness disappear, the value of its currency cut in half, and its financial institutions expropriated. Opposition was orchestrated by a group of powerful Monterrey industrialists, "who perceived the bank nationalization as the final blow to a decades-old accommodation between business and government" (Maxfield 1989: 221).

Although the private sector's hostility was intense, the relatively probusiness de la Madrid administration initially underestimated the political danger. In December 1982, the president's first month in office, the PRI deepened the wrath of the private sector by implementing constitutional changes designed to specify the economic rights and responsibilities of government and business. Changes to Article 25 formalized and protected the private sector's role in economic activity, while giving the state "rectorship" over economic policy and defining the "social sector." Article 27 was amended to specify "strategic areas" over which the government would exercise control.

By codifying property rights for business and acknowledging the social objectives embraced by populists and labor leaders, the administration was simply trying to kill two birds with one stone. Although the language used to address the demands of the popular sector was little more than legal window dressing, the legislation rubbed salt into business wounds at the worst possible moment: "In an effort to please the left, and in particular the left-wing members of the PRI, who had apparently strengthened their position due to the popularity of the nationalization, the reforms were in such a populist rhetoric that they had the unexpected effect of severely damaging the credibility of Miguel de la Madrid" (Elizondo 1992: 229).

The bitter response of business took the government by surprise particularly because the legislation did virtually nothing to change the status quo. As Luis Rubio recalls, "Even though the constitutional amendments simply formalized what had been the practice for many years, the private sector's interpretation was that it had been displaced." (1990: 254). The ruling party had provoked business opposition simply by creating legislation "to raise planning, state tutelage of the economy, and the notion of a 'social sector' to constitutional status" (Bailey 1986: 125).

In a 1986 speech, Luis Pazos, a conservative intellectual, articulated the fear and frustration of the Mexican business community. Not only did de la Madrid fail to nullify the bank nationalization, but he also "elevated state planning to the constitutional level by [changes to] Article 25 . . . a paragraph copied almost literally from the Cuban constitution. In this paragraph, almost unlimited powers are given to the government to interfere in all spheres of private economic activity" (1986: 75). The president of Confederación Patronal de la Republica Mexicana (Coparmex) went so far as to suggest that recognizing a "social sector" was part of a Communist plot to divide society and promote class conflict. Even moderate businessmen who belonged to officially linked economic chambers worried that the reforms gave the state too much policy-making discretion (Elizondo 1992: 233, 237).

Given the market-oriented character of de la Madrid and his top cabinet officials, the right may have been posturing. Indeed, the legislative changes, while codifying the nature of government authority in the economy, actually improved private property rights. The reform of Article 25, in particular, actually institutionalized the rights of entrepreneurs and put them on an equal footing with those of the state, a perennial demand among Mexican business leaders. However, the concession meant little because the private sector "sought formal (or at least informal) guarantees that civil society would play virtually no role in the determination of national policy. . . . Traumatized as it was by the bank nationalization, the business elite badly misinterpreted the posture assumed by the administration for its first three years" (Cypher 1990: 178).

Making matters worse for the government was its own inept response to business criticism early in the *sexenio*. In January 1983, the Mexican Chamber of Commercial Enterprises organized a forum in Toluca with independent business associations to denounce the nationalization and exchange controls imposed by López Portillo. The PRI responded by taking out advertisements in the major newspapers, which declared that the chambers "are not political institutions nor adequate channels for the expression of ideological positions," and even hinted that their behavior might be sanctioned (Story 1987: 263). Far from being intimidated, the private sector redoubled its criticism of government authoritarianism.

Business demands to end the PRI's hegemony represented an even greater political threat to the PRI than radical mobilization had in the previous decade. While the Mexican Left had called for a more open political system in the 1970s, its influence over the ruling party, though significant, was mostly symbolic. Indeed, despite the militancy of their rhetoric, most social progressives understood that the PRI's self-proclaimed mandate to promote the social goals of the Revolution was their main source of political leverage. They wanted to reform the ruling party, not to destroy it.

In contrast, when corporate leaders became champions of democracy in the 1980s, their mission was put an end to the PRI's centralized control over the policy-making process.[1] In order to increase its own political leverage, the radical faction from the north "demanded a redefinition of the system of representation in the political structure" (Luna, Tirado, and Valdés 1987: 29). As John Bailey observed halfway through de la Madrid's term, "to restore business confidence, it is necessary to limit presidential power. This should be done through constitutional reforms, bolstered with real decentralization, greater citizen participation, and vigorous opposition parties competing in honest elections" (1986: 133–134). To most PRI leaders, such a solution amounted to political suicide.

Equally importantly, unlike the radical intellectuals before them, the leaders of Mexico's private sector organizations controlled the resources to back up their threat. The PRI was particularly concerned with the giant industrial conglomerates of Monterrey. The associations that represented these firms, particularly Coparmex and the Consejo Coordinador Empresarial (CCE), were independent, highly organized, and well funded. They had the clout to get serious press coverage. Unlike other social organizations in Mexico's corporatist political system, the groups representing Mexico's largest industries did not depend on the ruling party for financing, membership, or recognition; "the bulk of the Mexican private sector and its political associations remain outside the confines of the Party" (Story 1987: 262).

Finally, the PRI was alarmed at the growing linkages between the private sector and PAN, the main opposition party. Electoral victories in the northern border states suggested that the long-time right-wing nemesis was beginning to emerge as a viable political institution, and business influence, money, and organization was a major reason for the party's increasing success. Although PAN was far from presenting a national electoral threat in the 1980s, its future was looking increasingly bright. Business organization demands for greater party competition boded ill for the PRI, given that their leaders had in mind an actual, existing alternative rather than an abstract call for more robust democracy.

Confronting organized opposition and economic chaos, the new president possessed few resources with which to assert a bold, new agenda. Unlike the two previous administrations, the de la Madrid *sexenio* was characterized by a highly defensive political posture. The Mexican state focused its energies on regaining international investment and reversing capital flight. This required painful economic adjustment. As Lorenzo Meyer observed in 1983, the government "finds itself with few economic options. Its primary and almost exclusive concern has been to control the social contradictions accentuated by the crisis and to implement the required austerity program, while attempting always to keep the political system intact" (1983: 119–120).

As a result of the economic crisis and the new assertiveness of the private sector, the PRI no longer focused on the approval of mass constituencies or even the principal social organizations. Rather, it now struggled primarily to appease the country's most powerful entrepreneurs and restore financial stability. As de la Madrid recalled, his principle goals were to "win back the confidence of the private sector and to bring back capital."[2] By the end of 1982, "unable to procure significant resources to maintain its expansionary policies, [the Mexican government] could no longer challenge domestic or international capital, but had to seek the approval of these sectors in order to remain financially viable" (Centeno 1994: 69). In short, the PRI's political future would now be tied to both the state's economic survival and reconciliation with the business sector.

### Concessions in Policy and Politics

In his efforts to reverse capital flight, de la Madrid made numerous concessions to big business. The 1983–1988 National Development Plan, unveiled at the beginning of the *sexenio*, was an undisguised attempt at reconciliation with the private sector as well as the international financial community. Its fundamental goals were to rationalize prices, regain fiscal stability, and remove the state from key areas of production and commerce.

In order to demonstrate its commitment to economic discipline and to qualify for an International Monetary Fund (IMF) stand-by loan, in 1983 the administration unveiled the Immediate Program of Economic Reordering (PIRE). Through severe austerity measures, policy makers proposed to reduce the deficit from over 16 percent of GDP in 1982 to 8.5 percent in 1983, 5.5 percent in 1984, and 3.5 percent by 1985 (Campos 1993: 163). Whereas spending on education, health, and social welfare accounted for 24 percent of the national budget in 1980s, by the end of de la Madrid's term these programs absorbed less than 10 percent of total spending

(Guillén Romo 1990: 87). The development plan and the PIRE were designed "to show, on one hand, the coincidence of interests between the public and private sector, and on the other, the willingness of government to eschew activities that could be identified with previous administrations" (Casar 1992: 296).

In addition, the de la Madrid administration began to liberalize trade. Unilateral tariff cuts in 1985 signaled the beginning of the end of Mexico's import-substitution strategy, as domestic businesses suddenly found themselves exposed to international competition. Despite occasional rhetoric about forcing Mexican business to modernize, the initial purpose of the trade opening was clearly to put a brake on inflation, which was among the private sector's greatest concerns. "The determination with which the de la Madrid government pursued anti-inflationary policies can be seen as the heart of a strategy to restore the alliance with the private sector and a basic consensus with the middle class" (Loaeza 1992b: 65–66).

To demonstrate its commitment to discipline, the de la Madrid administration adopted a monetarist approach to deficit financing. The 1985 Organic Banking Law included a provision that specifically prohibited the central bank from covering public deficits by printing money. By deliberately tying its own hands, the state sent an important signal to the private sector that government borrowing decisions would be strictly regulated by the market. As we will see, the monetarist rule would lead to the explosion of government securities issues and the transformation of Mexico's public debt.

In August 1986, Mexico deepened its commitment to free trade by joining the General Agreement on Tariffs and Trade (GATT). The action was more symbolic than economic, since Mexico was granted significant concessions and long phase-in periods. However, membership in the free trade organization cultivated Mexico's emerging status as a modern, disciplined economy. Significantly, Mexico did not undertake trade liberalization in order to join GATT; indeed, it had already met or surpassed policy requirements to become a member in unilateral measures taken earlier. Rather than an acceleration of reform, the accession to the GATT represented "a signal by the Mexican policy makers . . . to enhance the credibility of the program with both domestic investors and foreign financial institutions" (Ten Kate 1992: 666).

In addition to actual policy reforms, de la Madrid made explicit efforts to indicate to the business community that both the ideology and excesses of his predecessors were over. One of the new president's first decisions was to dismiss Carlos Tello, central bank director and architect of the nationalization. De la Madrid affirmed that by appointing the staunchly orthodox Miguel Mancera to head the Banco de México, he meant to "send a very important signal to the private sector."[3]

In spite of the president's efforts at conciliation, the private sector would not easily forgive Mexico's political leadership for its past sins. A decade of alienation could not be undone in a moment. Business leaders demonstrated "uncertainty regarding the policies that the de la Madrid administration would implement to normalize relations with the private sector ... [and doubted] how consistent the public sector would be in applying the medicine of structural adjustment" (Valdés Ugalde 1994: 220–221). In short, economic discipline alone was insufficient to win back the private sector.

Once again, however, the PRI utilized the financial system to confront the breakdown of its traditional social alliance. Just as the party had used public spending increases in the previous decade to buy off the Left—fiscal policies that led to the creation of the securities sector—it now engineered a series of financial policies designed to channel massive economic benefits to those business interests most adamantly opposed to its domination. At the same time, to survive massive debt and deficits without access to foreign capital, the government had to ensure its own solvency as well as that of Mexico's most important firms.

The president promoted and developed new financial institutions through which Mexican big business could recapitalize the national economy and make a lot of money in the process. Unable to generate sufficient capital from domestic savings in traditional institutions, the PRI turned to the liberalization of the securities markets in order to procure the capital required to keep the state solvent and reinvigorate Mexico's largest firms. Combined with a generous corporate debt restructuring program, these policies helped the ruling party regain its credibility among Mexico's economic elite.

## THE ADVENT OF SECURITIES

A major part of the government's solution to the problems of private sector mistrust and capital flight was the development of the brokerage industry. Although they had existed in Mexico since the late nineteenth century, the *casas de bolsa*, or brokerage houses, remained an extremely small part of financial activity in Mexico. As we saw in the previous chapter, a speculative frenzy in the late 1970s ended with a crash, leaving the brokerage sector moribund. To the de la Madrid administration, the *casa de bolsa* represented much more than a financial services firm facing tough times; it was the channel through which Mexico would be recapitalized.

### Reprivatizing the Securities Sector

In January 1985, the passage of the Organic Banking Law authorized the government to sell off 100 percent of non-bank financial institutions, the most important of which were the *casas*. In the spirit of private sector reconciliation, the ex-bankers were given the first opportunity to buy these shares and could even use their indemnification bonds in lieu of cash. The privatization culminated a long process of bargaining initiated by industrialist and brokerage owner Agustín Legorreta and negotiated by stock exchange president Manuel Somoza. The brokerage industry—composed mainly of ex-bankers—had argued that in the absence of bank re-privatization, the least the state could do to restore confidence in the private sector was to leave the *bolsa* to those whose property had been confiscated (*Proceso*, July 20, 1987: 21).

The sale of the brokerages was initially not seen as an event of major economic importance either in government or private sector circles. One reason was that only those brokerage houses that were subsidiaries of commercial banks became state property. Many of the largest firms had always been independent. As finance economist Jonathan Heath remarked, "In 1984 the brokerages were just little fish. Nobody in government really cared what happened to them."[4]

While the reprivatization was consistent with expanding the securities market, its primary purpose was to help re-establish confidence in the business community. Since reprivatization of the banks was not a viable political option in the mid-1980s, returning the brokerage houses to private hands was the government's most noncontroversial way of reassuring Mexican capital that it intended to protect private property and reduce its control over the financial system (White 1992: 135). According to the government, the return of the brokerages to private ownership was "the most important development of the year, from a confidence standpoint" (*Economía Mexicana* 1984: 94).

The brokerage reprivatization increased the ex-bank owners' share of the lucrative corporate financing business. Not only did they earn commissions on the trading of securities, they also acted as investment banks in the actual underwriting of new issues. Given the unavailability of traditional bank loans for the private sector, their contribution to business finance during the 1980s was impressive: the issuing of private securities tripled between 1982 and 1987 (Manchaca Trejo 1989: 11). Commercial paper, in particular, underwent an unprecedented expansion. In 1985, placements of commercial paper in the *bolsa* grew by almost 80 percent, while placements outside the stock exchange soared by 3,000 percent. "The underlying cause behind this was the increasing shortage of bank credit, which forced businesses to look elsewhere for working capital" (*Economía Mexicana* 1985: 101). In the following year, as a direct result of the persistent credit crunch, the placement of both registered and unregistered commercial paper grew by around 150 percent (*El Financiero*, August 6, 1987: 32; *Economía Mexicana* 1986: 75).

### Liberalizing the Money Market

In its very first days, the de la Madrid administration turned to the market in order to increase the state's access to private savings. Just a month after the nationalization of the banks, in October 1982, the government authorized the free auction of *Cetes* (Mexican treasury bills) for the first time. The marketization of Mexican internal debt led to the rapid development of a secondary market for government securities and to the birth of the modern Mexican money market, a crucial development for both financing the public sector and controlling money supply in a liberalized economic environment.

The liberalization of treasury bill yields did not lead to an immediate increase in internal debt. Rather, financial authorities adopted free auctions in order to provide them with the flexibility to borrow domestically. As long as the stable recovery continued, major new debt was not needed. For the first two years of the *sexenio*, gradual progress toward stability and deficit control allowed the central bank to moderate increases in the issue of treasury bills. However, adjustment and austerity led to a severe recession by the end of 1984. Tax receipts fell below anticipated levels and inflation began to heat up.

New financial regulations included in the 1985 banking law also liberalized institutional participation in the money market. Perhaps most importantly, the government authorized the establishment of *sociedades de inversión de renta fija* (fixed income mutual funds). These funds offered checking accounts and other services. While they had to hold at least 30 percent of their funds in government paper, they could also invest in any financial instrument other than stocks (e.g. commercial paper, bonds). Although technically they were allowed to invest only in domestic securities, in practice they represented one of Mexico's earliest efforts to compete for international capital—or at least to reduce capital flight. As an Instituto Tecnológico Autónomo de México (ITAM) economist explained, "Even though these funds do not invest in international money markets, they can be considered part of them, since the opportunity cost for a Mexican investor buying [domestic money market shares] includes not having bought shares in the foreign money market" (Mansell 1992: 152).

The result of persistent deficits, the self-imposed marketization of borrowing, and the liberalization of the money market was an explosion in the issue of treasury bills. The state "opted for the issuance of *Cetes* instead of relying on monetary expansion to finance the fiscal deficit" (Castaneda 1988: 33). Because monetizing the deficit was now prohibited, the government's only financing option was the market. To cover the shortfall in 1985, the government began what would become an unprecedented expansion in the issue and trading of public securities.

In 1985, the central bank increased the sale of *Cetes* on the open market by 200 percent. The government's promotion of securities led to a boom in capital markets that was based almost entirely on fixed rent securities (Márquez 1987: 74). In fact, over 92.5 percent of all transactions in 1985 were in the money market, while stocks accounted for just 7.5 percent. The following year, the money market absorbed 91 percent of *bolsa* activity, leaving 9 percent for equities. In other words, while some large Mexican firms were recovering their value, most of the *bolsa* boom was driven by the growth in government securities.

For the remainder of the decade, during which Mexico remained virtually barred from further international borrowing, the internal money market increasingly replaced bank loans as the country's primary debt instrument. In fact, as Figure 3.1 indicates, Mexico's dependence on foreign capital fell from well over half the budget deficit in the early 1980s to just one-fifth during the first year of the debt crisis and less than one-tenth by the middle of the decade.

An unintended and unwanted consequence of the state's increased reliance on the market to cover its internal debt was the significantly higher interest rate the government had to pay for the privilege of borrowing. The high yields investors demanded on *Cetes* both fueled inflation and soaked up scarce government revenue. In September 1985, with internal debt servicing absorbing an ever higher share of discretionary spending (see Figure 3.2), the state authorized the commercial banks to participate in *Cetes* auctions directly, on behalf of third-party investors.

Unfortunately, the goal of driving down the cost of financing through increased competition with the brokerages failed to produce interest rate reductions. The disappointing results were due to the banks' limited ability to increase the client base willing and able to participate in public debt auctions. Desperate for interest rate relief, the state threw the brakes on liberalization in October, terminating the free auction of Cetes and appointing an official committee to fix rates at a lower level. The immediate reaction was inevitable: vocal protest from the brokerage houses, whose most lucra-

**Figure 3.1**
**Internal and External Financing of Public Deficit (1980–1986)**

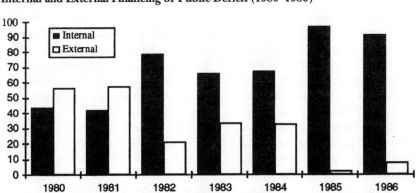

*Source:* Banco de México, *Indicadores Económicos.*

**Figure 3.2**
**Federal Internal Debt (1980–1988)***

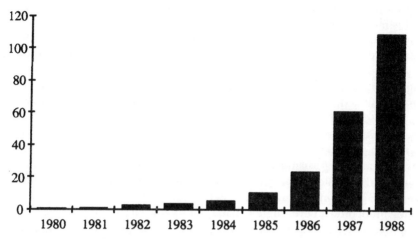

*Note:* *billions of new pesos

*Source:* Banco de México, *Indicadores Económicos.*

tive source of income had been interrupted, as well as a substantial reduction of *Cetes* purchases (*Economía Mexicana* 1985: 101).

With treasury bill sales flat and falling, by 1986 the government was forced to continue free auctions. During the year, in which the state relied even more heavily on securities to cover the deficit, the placement of Cetes soared by an astonishing 272 percent. In addition to the burden of foreign debt payments, internal debt servicing increased by 28 percent from September 1985 to September 1986. Total payments on the public debt increased from less than 10 percent of government spending in 1980 to over 63 percent in 1988 (Guillén Romo 1990: 87). Financing the deficit on the free market "turned out to be almost as big a problem for the de la Madrid administration as the foreign debt was previously" (*Economía Mexicana* 1986: 51).

In the second quarter of 1986, the government again attempted to reduce its ballooning interest payments by taking treasury bills off the market and setting weekly *Cetes* rates by committee. As before, "this tactic was openly rejected by the brokerage houses, which began to move their money into other instruments with better yields." (*Economía Mexicana* 1986: 74) By the middle of July, as its main private source of financing dried up, the government once again acquiesced and returned to the free auction system. By 1987, the yield on *Cetes* had increased by almost 40 percent in real terms, and the quantity of *Cetes* held outside of the banking sector more than doubled (Casteneda 1988: 33).

Nonbank banks, which included those brokerages that had been sold back to the private sector, were best positioned to assume the leadership in financing the government. Only those with sufficiently large quantities of capital to invest in the securities market enjoyed the high returns available outside of the traditional banking system. The existing concentration of income, opportunities for profits at the brokerages, and a highly regressive system of taxation led to a massive transfer of wealth from the middle class and poor to the privileged. According to Luis Acevedo, "The efficiency of the brokerages houses was significantly greater than that of the nationalized banking system, and led to the concentration of income and distortion in savings" (*El Financiero*, May 7, 1990: 4). As a result of the expansion and high interest of securities issues at the end of the de la Madrid *sexenio*, "the transfer of resources from the treasury to its internal creditors during 1988 and 1989 was of an extraordinary magnitude, 49 trillion pesos and 49.4 trillion pesos respectively in interest payments" (Sosa 1990: 77).

Was Mexico's conversion to internal debt motivated by the technocratic goal of disciplining and stabilizing the financial system? Government officials insisted that the development and deepening of financial markets was essential to long-term growth and viewed internal debt as economic progress. As the financial manager of Banco de México concluded, "*Cetes* stimulated the money market, developed independent financing of the public deficit, and contributed to the modernization and effectiveness of monetary activities" (Palencia Gomez 1992: 34).

In contrast, two economists considered money market development irresponsible and counterproductive: "The government, searching for funds, fell into the perverse spiral of internal debt because it had to obtain increasing credit with very short maturity in order to pay off previous debts" (Ejea and Leriche 1991: 51). Another economist explains the government's failure to achieve its "explicit objective" of reducing debt and inflation as the result of fulfilling its "implicit objective [of creating] a space for speculative profitability" for big business. Indeed, by 1988, the private sector received more income from interest payments on *Cetes* than it paid out in taxes (Guillén Romo 1990: 89).

As Bolsa Mexicana de Valores (BMV) president Manuel Somoza stated in 1987, "Of course we have counted on the support of the administration. Paradoxically, the bank nationalization pushed us stockbrokers ahead. It opened up a space that we intend to fill in a very big way. A space that . . . consisted in financing the federal government through the placement of Cetes" (*Proceso*, October 5, 1987: 11–12). In sum, while the government explained its decision to fund the deficit on the market as a purely technical response to structural constraints, the evidence also suggests that the political priority of creating profitable investment opportunities for the private sector contributed to the adoption of public debt policy that undermined stability.

### Corporate Recovery and Stock Market Boom

In the latter part of the decade, the Mexican stock market underwent a spectacular surge in valuation. In 1986, the inflation-adjusted stock price index grew by a phenomenal 220 percent. Stock prices began to rise to levels that did not correspond to even the most fantastic predictions for economic growth and profitability. In 1986, the shares prices of beer brewing giant Moctezuma jumped almost 1,800 percent, beverage company Grupo Continental multiplied tenfold, while petrochemical manufacturer Cydsa grew almost sevenfold (*Economía Mexicana* 1986: 71). For the first nine months of 1987, glassmaker Vitro saw its share price multiply seven times, while shares of Cemex grew eight times (*Economist*, October 3, 1987: 87). The *Wall Street Journal* proclaimed in June 1987, "The Mexican stock market has outperformed every other market in the world this year" (June 29, 1987: 32). Euphoria characterized a financial environment in which even novice investors earned huge and seemingly effortless profits.

The stock market's profitability led to tremendous growth in the client base for equities. In 1982, only 66,000 market accounts were registered with the *bolsa*. By the beginning of 1987, that number had tripled to 200,000, and before the year's end it had reached 400,000. While barely 600 professionals made their living through the *bolsa* in 1982, on the eve of the *crac* (crash), the number stood at over 10,000 (*Economist*, October 3, 1987: 87). Success fed upon itself, as the media spread the news of easy wealth to thousands of middle-class Mexicans.

The spread of mutual funds provided a convenient vehicle through which *novatos de inversión* (investment rookies) could park their money. In 1986, fixed yield funds offered an average gain of 126 percent, while stock funds reached 156 percent (*Economía Mexicana* 1986: 71). Anyone with capital to spare (or borrow) looked to the *bolsa*. Newcomers who did not know T-bills from stocks left the technical question of risk to glib brokers assuring easy money. As a financial executive from Monterrey remarked, "The word has gotten out about the profits to be made, and everyone wants a piece of the action. Now you're seeing housewives and middle-class professionals who would never have thought of the *Bolsa*" (*New York Times*, January 13, 1987: 32).

But something was odd about this "miracle." The boom took place during economic stagnation, poor expectations for future growth, and instability. "The world's stock markets could hardly have a more unlikely star" (*The Economist*, October 3, 1987: 87). More disturbingly, virtually all the *bolsa*'s gains came from increasing values of existing shares, not from an expansion of the market. With the revealing exception of financial firms, growth was not based on new equity. Less than fifty firms actively traded on the *bolsa*. Between 1982 and 1987, existing companies issued hardly any new shares, while no new companies came to the *bolsa* (*New York Times,* January 13, 1987: 32). Throughout the 1980s, the stock market raised less than $1 billion dollars in primary and secondary issues (Heyman 1991: 31). From 1985 to 1987, the *bolsa* financed less than one percent of total risk capital. (Dávila Flores 1990: 133). Even the typically sanguine president of the Comisión Nacional de Valores (CNV) conceded, "What the capital market needs now are greater primary issues . . . it's the same companies that come out everyday [that have so much] money that have come into the market" (*Proceso,* April 13, 1987: 13).

### Government Incentives

Why did the value of stocks grow so much while macroeconomic conditions were unfavorable and new issues limited? Why did nonfinancial firms—the main component of economic output and employment—receive such a small share of new equity capital? Economic stagnation and instability made productive investment more uncertain. But much of the reason for this growth can be found in the kind of incentives the government offered in its promotion of equity markets. Financial reforms made it safer and more lucrative to trade stocks on the secondary market, while a government bail-out of foreign-indebted corporations resurrected the *bolsa*'s major players.

*Regulation, Intervention, and Stimulation*

De la Madrid's first response to Mexico's sagging stock market was to improve transparency in trading. The crash of 1979 had burned thousands of investors. One of the most important shortcomings in the stock market was the lack of protection for small investors. The major brokers and their largest clients not only took advantage of privileged information, but also often cooperated with each other to manipulate prices.

In 1983, the state addressed the problem of market manipulation by officially regulating the use of "insider" information and collusion on listed stocks and assigned the Mexican Securities Commission the task of monitoring illegal activity and levying sanctions against violators. Two years later, a special "contingency fund" was created to protect investors from fraud and other illegal actions on the part of brokerages (Hakim-Simon 1988: 25).

In addition to improving transparency, the state also helped stabilize and stimulate the stock market by participating directly in trading activities. It did so primarily through the public development bank Nacional Financiera (Nafin), which routinely bought up shares whose price was slipping. Although the law protected the anonymity of all investors, making the precise level of Nafin's *bolsa* transactions impossible to quantify, the bank's role in maintaining price levels was widely recognized. According to the business editor of *El Economista*, "Everyone knows about the *mano negra* (hidden hand) of Nafin. We don't know how much, when or for which companies, but we all know that it keeps the stock market stable by buying and selling whenever there's a significant fluctuation."[5] Indeed, the very knowledge that such a powerful agent was monitoring price stability helped calm investor jitters and prevented price dips from turning into panics.

The government also undertook the privatization of the *bolsa*'s regulatory infrastructure. In December 1986, it sold off much of the administration and monitoring of the stock exchange by surrendering control of the securities clearinghouse (Indeval) to the brokerages. Originally created as a monitoring institution to control artificial booms in the fledgling market, Indeval soon became a source of irritation to the new brokers, who accused the state of hampering the development of the market. "Since the government knows through Indeval who buys and who sell shares in the *bolsa* . . . there won't be 'confidence' to invest. By privatizing Indeval, the 'law of investor secrecy' will be passed into the hands of the brokerages" (*Proceso*, December 15, 1986: 10). Six months later, with its sale of Somex, the state's own brokerage house and one of the largest, the government ended its direct involvement in the management of the securities.

The state's exit left a regulatory gap, which was not filled by the National Securities Commission (CNV). The *bolsa* operated "with little supervision from the Government. Although [the CNV] is legally responsible for overseeing the stock market, it is widely regarded as lacking enough power to police the market and seems uninterested in exercising what power it has." Mexican brokers and investors agreed that "the Mexican market is virtually unregulated" compared with the United States Securities and Exchange Commission (*New York Times*, October 13, 1987: 32).

Finally, the state stimulated the stock market through fiscal incentives. Since the 1950s, firms had been allowed to deduct the total amount of their interest payments, a loophole that created heavy incentives to incur debt. A 1986 tax code change that eliminated the deduction was implemented to promote equity financing (Castaneda 1988: 14). In the short term, however, the measure simply contributed to the erosion of the commercial banks' share of corporate finance and failed to stimulate new equity financing.

The reason was a tax incentive on speculation. The finance ministry kept the capital gains tax exempt, which created strong incentives to play the stock market for price fluctuations rather than consistent corporate performance. The *bolsa* was already Mexico's most lucrative investment; tax-free profits on the sale of stocks made it even more irresistible. Traders who engaged in "strategic buying" in order to nudge an inexperienced and euphoric market into raising prices could now make an untaxed fortune. Far from providing incentives for real productive investment—the issue of primary shares—this tax break stimulated speculative purchases of existing shares on the secondary market and encouraged price manipulation (Lissakers and Zamora 1989: 14).

The tax exemption on capital gains had such perverse effects on financing that it was criticized even by the political right. In October 1987, PAN Diputado (Congressional Representative) Humberto Ramirez argued that the circumstances that originally justified the tax break—the need to develop a negligible stock market—no longer prevailed. He submitted a bill in Congress to impose a 21 percent tax, calling the exemption "most damaging to equity and justice" (*Proceso*, October 5, 1987: 11). The measure was poorly understood by most legislators and quickly buried by the PRI majority. Even the Frente Democrático National (FDN), which had far more ideological reason that the PAN to oppose exemption, declined to make it a political issue.

### Exchange Rate and Foreign Debt Relief

Exchange rate policy during the first four years of de la Madrid's term was engineered to prevent the peso from gaining value. Policy makers pursued two goals by weakening the national currency. First, the exchange rate helped Mexico's major corporations recover through export expansion. Second, it reduced the opportunities for speculation and the possibility of sudden, sharp fluctuations in the peso's value.

At the beginning of 1983, the state adopted a dual exchange rate system. While a "managed" float prevailed for most routine currency transactions, a "preferred" or "controlled" rate was extended for imports, exports, and certain foreign debt obligations. In practice, the two rates were kept relatively close to each other. In September, a crawling peg was adopted, applying a moderate break on the rate of devaluation. In the first quarter of 1986, with inflation approaching 100 percent, oil prices plummeting and foreign exchange scarce, the government found itself subsidizing the controlled rate. Realizing the futility of defending the peso without massive reserves and strong foreign income, the government was forced to devalue substantially the controlled rate, in effect unifying the two rates and ending dual system.

In the context of initial tariff reductions in 1985, followed by Mexico's 1986 entry into the GATT, the floating peso promoted international competitiveness and helped foreign sales grow. According to the central bank, "From 1983 to 1987, the main objectives of the exchange rate policy were to cope with the balance of payments difficulties caused by the fiscal imbalance, the strong deterioration of the terms of trade, and the insufficiency of external financing, as well as to maintain the margins of competitiveness for domestic producers in the face of trade liberalization" (Banco de México 1993: 94). As the central bank director affirmed, "The policy of peso devaluation has provided a generous incentive for manufactured exports, and therefore constitutes a generator of foreign exchange"

(*Proceso*, June 15, 1987: 24). Between 1982 and 1987, Mexican firms tripled the value of their industrial exports. While the weakened currency clearly contributed to the increase in inflation for 1986, it was also largely responsible for the surge in industrial exports and a dramatically improved balance of payments position.

The government plausibly justified the float on technical grounds as the most effective way to revitalize Mexico's leading industrial enterprises and prevent destabilizing currency fluctuations. Critics who argued that an undervalued peso sapped buying power and undermined price stability viewed the policy as politically inspired. "In a country with a profound currency crisis, the government opted to maintain a floating exchange rate policy, despite its negative impact on the economic plans proposed by the President, and which put at risk the entire scheme of financial restructuring. However, the re-establishment of confidence and the reelaboration of the social pact with the finance sector were issues of the highest priority, and oriented government actions" (Ruiz Durán 1989: 262).

A far more direct effort of the government to re-establish the confidence of the private sector elite was recovering corporate solvency. The devaluations of 1982 devastated the private sector, above all the large conglomerates that had enjoyed access to cheap and plentiful foreign capital. In December 1981, a dollar bought 26 pesos; two years later it bought 144 pesos. The result was a massive increase in the real debt burden upon firms that had borrowed abroad. The weakened peso made dollar-denominated interest payments unbearable and threatened to send a number of Mexico's most important sources of employment, output and technology—not coincidentally the country's most influential business leaders—into bankruptcy. To revive both the vitality and political support of the country's largest industrial firms, the Mexican government provided exchange rate protection for companies that had incurred large foreign obligations and provided them with dollars to negotiate advantageous restructuring arrangements with creditors.

In May 1983, under the direction of future president Ernesto Zedillo, the de la Madrid administration launched the Trust Fund for the Coverage of Exchange Rate Risk (Ficorca). Although the operation of the fund was enormously complex,[6] the logic behind the program was simple: Private companies serviced their foreign debt by making peso payments at the Banco de México, while the central bank committed itself to making dollar payments directly to creditors as foreign exchange became available.

Under the most common payment system, the indebted firm loaned dollars to Ficorca, which then directly assumed repayment to the creditor beginning in the fifth year of an eight-year contract. Ficorca, in turn, replaced the lost dollars with an eight-year peso loan, upon which the company began making monthly payments immediately. However, since the peso loan principal was tied directly to the exchange rate existing *at the moment* of contract, any slide in the peso's value would be absorbed by the government, rather than the original debtor. In effect, the Mexican government sold dollars to the companies at a protected rate. A Bankers Trust analyst explains: "Ficorca permitted firms to pay only a portion of the installment due and capitalize the remainder. Thus, the firm's peso debt grew in nominal terms while theoretically declining in present value terms. The formula gave firms a needed cash flow boost" (Riner 1989: 22).

Perhaps the most important contribution of the exchange rate program was to enable Mexico's indebted firms to aggressively negotiate the terms on which they would repay much of their foreign debt. Because so much corporate debt was short term, and neither government nor business was prepared to pay it in the early 1980s, it became necessary for the foreign banks to restructure most private sector obligations. Because Ficorca ensured that borrowers would be able to repay at least part of their obligations, it provided both Mexican firms and their creditors with an incentive to restructure loans by themselves (Orme 1989: 24). The extra cash flow, combined with later debt discounts, "gave cash-rich firms an opportunity to reduce their liabilities. . . . Companies canceled their Ficorca contracts, received the rescue value . . . in cash, complemented it with funds from their treasuries and repurchased their debts at prices ranging from 55 to 90 cents on the dollar" (Riner 1989:22). Eventually 65 percent of foreign private debt was restructured through the program (Gutiérrez 1992: 859).

For many of Mexico's largest companies, a weak peso helped increase foreign sales but also increased real foreign debt. As long as Ficorca protected the largest firms from surges in foreign-denominated debt obligations, they benefited from the floating exchange rate. For this reason, it has been argued that Ficorca was essentially a political program to repair relations with a business class that had been battered by the López Portillo devaluations (Loaeza 1992b).

The de la Madrid administration earned not only the gratitude of big business, but also respect for the efficacious manner in which the PRI's technical talent implemented the complicated and ambitious program. For example, steel and tourism giant Grupo Sidek was virtually saved from insolvency by the state when it became unable to service its $32 million foreign debt. According to Sidek executive Martinez Guitron, "Ficorca was the most valuable help the business has had from the government. It made the difference between growing and disappearing" (Conger 1995).

### The October *Crac*

Although *bolsa* gains temporarily helped reverse capital flight, the boom was unsustainable. Rather than contribute to an increase in productive investment, liberalization and stimulation of the stock market stimulated speculation, insider manipulation, and ultimately provoked a crash that is still remembered in Mexico simply as *el crac de 87.*

The stock market boom provided corporate financiers a fast and easy way to realize fabulous gains through investor ignorance, price manipulation, and insider trading. The profit euphoria of 1987 created a vast Ponzi scheme[7] within the *bolsa.* "The stock market may have been anticipating a rosier future, but it appeared to have simply risen on the assumption that a 'greater fool' would come forth at each higher level of prices." In the final stage of the bull market, "stock prices had no relation whatsoever with the economic fundamentals; all brokers and financial analysts became technicians willing to extrapolate rising prices and anxious to enlarge their portfolio of clients" (Castaneda 1988: 95, 98).

The head of Multibanco Banco Comericial Mexicana (Comermex) characterized Mexico as a "casino society" in which the obsession with short-term, fantastic profits had completely overtaken the concerns about productivity and growth (*Proceso,* June 15, 1987: 25). New clients were typically ignorant of brokerage operations and lacked an understanding of price fluctuations: "Amid such ignorance, they trust the promoter, the agent of the selected brokerage. The agent tells his client that the *bolsa* should be understood as a deal among gentlemen, that one's word is what counts. . . . If [an investment] fails, he has a thousand explanations to justify it." (*Proceso,* May 18, 1987: 9).

Stock market authorities vigorously denied the presence of insider trading or price manipulation. The market was now well diversified, composed of institutional and corporate investors, brokerages, the Mexican development banks, and foreign investors. Just weeks before the crash, *bolsa* general director Mario Segura declared, "These are large, long-term, institutional investments. The rest, the non-institutional investors, are few. . . . [W]e have a more professional market, managed by more people, with greater knowledge. . . . I believe that no mutual fund, no brokerage house, nor any other investor can manipulate the market" (*Proceso,* October 5, 1987: 13).

The evidence, however, indicated otherwise. Because large firms controlled so much stock and because close personal and economic linkages between the owners of brokerages houses and large firms were the norm, the stock market was subject to frequent and extensive manipulation. The practice of "orchestrated buys" on the trading flow was widespread (*Proceso,* May 18, 1987: 8–9). With economic growth low and expected to stay that way, it made little sense to invest in expansion, modernization, or training.

In the midst of the country's consumer doldrums, large corporations had to determine what to do with their capital: "The stock market turned out to be one of the best areas for businesses to invest working capital" (*Economía Mexicana* 1986:69). A 1987 study by three economists at the Autonomous University of Azcapotzalco affirmed that the high interest rates required for the government's tight monetary policy both prolonged Mexico's recession and, more importantly, led large firms to adopt a strategy relying on gains from the securities market. Reduced productive investment with tremendous portfolio investment led to a phenomenon dubbed "rich businessmen with poor businesses" (Quintana et al. 1987).

The companies were not disappointed. Firms listed on the BMV demonstrated a twenty-three-fold increase in profits in 1987, with earnings rising over sixteen times faster than sales. This performance was due to replacing working capital with investment in financial instruments, particularly in 1987 when the securities market offered the most fantastic yields (Castaneda 1988: ch. 6).

International opportunities, however, eventually altered the strategy of the financial officers that had been pouring corporate capital into the stock market. Responding to an initiative from foreign banks to offer steep discounts on existing foreign debt in exchange for immediate cash payments, Mexico's largest companies jumped at the chance to reduce their external liabilities. In a massive debt restructuring, Mexican industrial and commercial conglomerates wrote off billions of dollars in foreign debt through a series of negotiations with their U.S. and European creditors. During 1987 and 1988, just four firms—Alfa, Cydsa, Visa, and Vitro—restructured over $5 billion of foreign debt on very favorable terms. By 1989, Mexican private sector medium- and long-term foreign debt stood as low as $3 billion, down from well over $20 billion during the mid-1980s (Orme 1989: 20).

In order to take advantage of this opportunity, indebted firms had to get hold of cash quickly. The resources were available. Corporate treasuries were overflowing with stocks, bonds, and public securities. By "getting out" in time, Mexico's multinational corporate sector made itself well situated to enter the free trading 1990s. However, by selling off massive quantities of paper, they not only procured the cash needed to dramatically improve their overall financial position, but also contributed to the crash.

On October 5, 1987, then Budget and Planning Minister Carlos Salinas was officially named by the PRI to become de la Madrid's successor at Los Pinos. The news that the staunchly neoliberal market reformer would soon be Mexico's leader quickly drove the *bolsa* to an all-time high, amid a wave of euphoria so intense that trading was interrupted. Two weeks later, on October 19, Mexico's investors woke up to *lunes negra* (Black Monday). The market plummeted by 16.5 percent, and continued its free fall over the next month. In mid-November, rumors of a massive intervention by Nafin to bolster share prices were dismissed when officials conceded the rescue effort would not be attempted.[8] On November 16, after a month of unrelenting sliding prices, the market fell over 18 percent. By the next day, the price index had dipped to under 105,000, a loss of almost three-quarters of its peak value (*Financial Times*, November 18, 1987: 1–16).

## THE POLITICS OF NATIONALIZED BANKING

In formulating banking policy, President de la Madrid attempted to address two contradictory goals. On one hand, the banks had been expropriated in the name of social and productive investment. The PRI's main pillar of support, labor, had eagerly supported the nationalization, and millions agreed with López Portillo's justification for seizing control of the country's financial institutions: The state would invest in Mexico much more than the owners had and recognize social obligations ignored by the private bankers. Moreover, many actors within the government, particularly the party faithful that filled leadership positions within the bank, sought to restore capacity of the financial system to pursue development goals.

On the other hand, as we have seen, the state sought to regain its lost credibility among both the Mexican business class and the international financial community. Recovering that confidence depended on restoring the protection of private property, as well as implementing a stable economic program. During the 1980s, these were not necessarily compatible goals. In the end, economic restraint prevailed, limiting not only the banks' role in social spending, but also keeping them in government hands throughout the decade.

### The Triumph of Discipline

Ex-bankers wanted their property back. Populists wanted increased social spending and public investment. Neither had their demands satisfied. In July 1983, the state passed the Law Pertaining to the Public Service of Banking and Credit, which offered the banks' owners and fifty thousand shareholders up to 34 percent ownership in the banking sector. The new instrument of bank ownership was a bond called Bank Ownership Certificates (CAPs). Their yield was set by the market, and they were highly liquid.

The leftist opposition characterized these measures as excessive concessions to the very *sacadolares* whose financial betrayal had provoked the crisis in the first place. Many argued that the government compensated the bankers quite lavishly (Brannon 1986: 35–37, Hamilton 1986: 171–172). After all, just months after the nationalization, the new administration had not only paid the ex-bankers for the property confiscated by the state, but also offered them partial ownership. Numerous scholars interpreted the rapid series of banking concessions as evidence of the irresistible political power of capital.[9] The day after re-privatization was announced, a *La Jornada* headline declared: "In Practice, the Bank Nationalization Lasted Only Three Months."

However, the concessions were actually quite limited and were far less than the bankers had demanded following the expropriation of their property.

For example, although the 34 percent offer of ownership was widely criticized as overly generous, it also preserved the state's control over the banks.
"The private sector maintained that if the government was not willing to con-
cede at least 75 percent of the bank shares . . . the sale made no sense economically or politically. That is, 34 percent doesn't guarantee control." In
fact, José María Basagoiti, president of Coparmex, Mexico's critical and independent business organization, pushed the ex-bankers to boycott the new
shares, arguing that to buy them "would signify the betrayal of the private
sector" (*Proceso*, November 10, 1986: 31).

Despite outrage over the government's offer, it is difficult to assess how
high the payment really was. The book value of the banks at the moment of
nationalization was about 47 billion pesos, but the government adjusted this
figure to 70 billion pesos. However, because the banking system was in such
chaos by late 1982, the stock value was unusually depressed. Owners demanded 150 billion pesos, over three times book value (Tello 1984:
162–167). The amount of cash the state paid out to take control of the
country's financial sector was just a fraction of what it would receive in selling it back. "When compared to the price the banks were sold nearly ten
years [after the nationalization], the government made a spectacular deal"
(Elizondo 1992: 253).

If the government gave the bankers a windfall, it was in the timing of the
creation of private bank shares. Although the bankers' indemnification was
approved in 1983, the actual shares were not sold back to the bankers until
February 1987, almost four years later. On one hand, the delay of the sale
gave the government breathing room. The cash-strapped treasury hardly
had billions to spare in the crisis-ridden years following de la Madrid's taking office. On the other hand, by the time the CAPs were released onto the
open market, not only had the state nursed the banks back to health, but
the stock market was booming in general. The value of the new bond multiplied on the secondary market within just a few days, generating tremendous profits for the owners who had exercised their right to buy back their
property.

Even more divisive than ownership issues during the nationalization period were bank policies dictating how the state would use the financial assets
of the institutions it had expropriated. The debate over economic priorities
was framed as financial austerity versus developmental spending and was
personified in the conflict between two top economic administrators: Banco
de México director Carlos Tello, champion of populism and architect of the
nationalization, and Finance Minister Jesús Silva Herzog, Mexico's voice of
economic discipline. Silva Herzog demanded that the banks not be used as
cash cows for social or development objectives and sought just compensa-
tion for the ex-bankers. Tello wanted the state's new financial institutions to
prime the pump of economic expansion that had been neglected under
private ownership (Maxfield 1990: 148–149).

The ability to channel public deposits directly into development banks for allocation to priority sectors constituted the main instrument of development policy (Quijano 1983: 364–365). The constitutional reform that de la Madrid sent to Congress—the legislation that so enraged the business community—precisely delineated the parameters of government participation in the national economy. "The administration began in seeming support of the principles that had produced the bank nationalization: state rectorship of the economy . . . and ratification of the primacy of the federal executive in economic matters by outlining strategic areas of exclusive state responsibility" (Valdés Ugalde 1994: 223).

Notwithstanding the president's social rhetoric, however, the nationalization was not used to continue the state's role in economic development. Although the nationalization clearly demonstrated the power of the Mexican government and its ability to challenge the interests of even the country's most influential economic actors, state ownership would not, as López Portillo had promised, lead to a radical renovation of credit policy.

The economic discipline championed by Silva Herzog won the day. Indeed, as mentioned earlier, de la Madrid quickly relieved Tello and replaced him with a monetary conservative. The end of international credit made the nationalized banks a primary resource for public sector financing. Banking policy during the de la Madrid administration consisted mainly in helping the state cover its massive deficits.

The *sexenio* became a six-year ordeal of fiscal austerity and recession. While financing for private investment did increase somewhat over the rock bottom levels of 1982, the state used far more banking resources to cover fiscal deficits and pay debt interest than for new social or productive spending. According to Mexico's main foreign debt negotiator, servicing debt interest was key to recovering economic stability. Moreover, "the public deficit had to be financed through bank reserve requirements and the creation of internal debt" (Gurría Treviño 1994: 15). While the authorities rhetorically accepted the banks as an engine of growth, "they run it as an effective instrument to contract the economy. . . . Dragged down by the monetary policy, [the commercial banks] have turned into nothing more than a cash register for the government" (*Proceso,* January 20, 1986: 12).

### The Banking Sector Declines

As a result of burdensome regulations, uncompetitiveness, and the rapid rise of brokerages, the resources and profitability of traditional banks began drying up. Prior to the nationalization, the banking industry had faced no significant competition. Since the Multiple Bank Law allowed them to control brokerage firms under a holding company structure, they could attract capital at all levels of intermediation. Following nationalization, this monopoly on financial services came to an end.

Regulation strictly limited banking activity. Half of all deposits had to be kept in reserve at the central bank and were used primarily to finance the growing fiscal deficit. In addition, between 5 and 6 percent of credit had to be allocated to selected sectors (ABM 1991). During the first two years of nationalization, even before competition from private brokerage firms, the private sector bank lending stagnated. Corporate financing was almost completely squeezed out by public sector borrowing. Total assets and the number of bank accounts actually declined slightly.

Persistent budget problems kept the banks on a tight leash. In spite of somewhat promising results of austerity in the early 1980s, the 1985 earthquake and the subsequent collapse of oil prices exacerbated the already severe credit crunch in 1986. The government further slashed public spending on both services and parastatals but could not overcome the budget shortfall. As a result of the crisis, which also led to a 7 percent shortfall in tax receipts, the government increased yet again the reserve requirements of the banks under its control: In the first half of 1986, banks had to keep 92 percent of their assets in government paper, while a relaxation of the requirement in the second half still absorbed almost three-quarters of bank capital (Castaneda 1988: 93).

In addition to severe restrictions on the financing of social and developmental projects, interest rate ceilings, strict deposit requirements, and costly financial services severely undermined the banks' ability to attract deposits. Perhaps the greatest handicap the banks endured was their inability to offer competitive interest rates to prospective savers. Following the nationalization, the only market-oriented savings instrument available through the banks was the "banker's acceptance."[10] However, because the banks were being used almost exclusively to fund the deficit, it made little sense to offer savers higher interest for capital that would be used to purchase government securities anyway.

As a Federal Reserve Bank economist explains, "The artificially wide spread between the interest rate on *Cetes* and the interest rate on bank deposits reduced the attractiveness of bank deposits, making it difficult for the banks to raise funds, which, in turn, weakened their ability to extend loans. Rather than depositing their savings in banks, individuals and firms found it preferable to lend directly to the government" (Moore 1993: 32). By selling its securities either directly to large corporations or to individuals through the brokerage industry, the government paid savers only the *Cetes* rate. Accordingly, the quantity of authorized acceptances was strictly limited by the Banco de México, and the banks had to observe a 100 percent reserve requirement for all acceptances beyond that ceiling (Coorey 1992: 38).

By the middle of the decade, the restricted credit access confronting industry, in addition to the government's inability to cover its deficits with banking resources, led financial authorities to initiate a program of deregulation. This approach was embodied in the January 1985 Organic Banking Law. The new legislation represented a rather timid effort at regulatory reform designed to give banks increased freedom in capital allocation. Previously, banks had to keep almost half of their assets in the form of deposits at the central bank. The new law, reflecting the state's shift toward monetarism, mandated that only 10 percent could be held by the central bank and only for the purposes of regulating the money supply.

However, the banks still had to keep 40 percent of their assets in government bonds in order to help the state cover its deficits and fund its development banks (Castaneda 1988: 33–34). In 1986, as the government attempted to reflate the economy after two years of austerity, the state redoubled its efforts to channel banking capital to public spending, soaking up even more of the scarce credit resources available for private sector investment (*El Financiero*, August 6, 1987: 32; Cypher 1990: 175).

When the brokerage industry burst upon the financial system in 1985, banks lost ground rapidly.[11] As Carlos Salinas's chief-of-staff, José Córdoba Montoya, wrote: "The bank nationalization and economic instability induced a rapid growth of the Mexican securities market, much greater than one would have expected given the per capita income of the country" (Córdoba Montoya 1991: 40).

Regulation made it impossible for the banks to compete. "The concentration of banks' financial resources in government hands and the impossibility of obtaining financing for private enterprises was one of the great impulses to brokerage houses" (Pineda 1991: 12). As the Mexican Banking Commission explains, "Financial intermediation of the banks contracted in favor of that stimulated by brokerage firms, given that banking instruments were subject to rigid time requirements and maximum interest rates fixed by the Banco de México" (CNB 1992: 25). Not only did 1985 deposits fall 40 percent below predictions, but the central bank froze the commercial banks' private sector portfolios at October 1985 levels. "This last measure was interpreted by many analysts as an increase to 100 percent the [reserve requirement] for the last three months of the year" (*Economía Mexicana* 1985: 85).

Compounding the effects of brokerage competition was the deregulation and direct stimulation of the stock market. Whereas in the early 1980s traders had complained that fixed high yields on *Cetes* were weakening the growth of the stock market, by the middle of the decade the tables had been turned decidedly against public sector financing. The government had created an equity monster that was gobbling up scarce capital needed above all to cover public spending.

Individuals reduced cash and demand deposits to the minimum real balances required for transactions purposes. While the government was attempting to increase the internal savings ratio for the purpose of financing the fiscal deficit, the equity market was booming. . . . The untaxed capital gains realized in the stock market undoubtedly served to reduce the savings ratio, thus countering the influence of the higher interest rate on Cetes and time deposits. (Castaneda 1988: 94)

Regulation and brokerage competition severely eroded the position of Mexico's traditional intermediaries. From 1982 to 1988, commercial bank absorption of capital as a proportion of GDP dropped from almost 20 percent to less than 13 percent. While in 1980 commercial banks' share of capital within the financial system stood at 96 percent, by 1987 it had fallen to just 72 percent; over the course of the decade, brokerage firms increased their capture of savings from 12 percent to 44 percent (*El Financiero*, May 8, 1990: May 22, 1990: 5).

By strangling the banks and promoting stock market speculation, the government succeeded in crowding itself out of the very credit markets it sought to exploit for its own purposes. Yet it was too late to reverse the liberalizing process. Any step backwards would have destroyed the precious investor confidence the state had worked for a half decade to restore and surely would have provoked a massive new wave of capital flight.

### State Bankers

The disjuncture between the promises of bank nationalization and its actual implementation would lead to some disagreement among PRI leaders. Ironically, the old guard *políticos* of the PRI who sought a more active developmental role for the bank pressured the *técnicos* to lift the most burdensome regulations on financial intermediaries. Unable to match a liberalized brokerage sector, the directors of the nationalized banking system pursued deregulation for their financial institutions.

Many had a political stake in the role that the banks could play in channeling credit to popular economic projects, from small business to parastatals. The public image of a group of state-appointed, party-affiliated administrators depended, in large part, on the bank's ability to fulfill the popular social and productive goals promised after nationalization: to channel public credit to the private sector and production priorities. Indeed, the primary goal of many of the public sector bankers was increasing market share, not efficiency.[12]

In order to increase income, the banks implemented a number of policies aimed at boosting profit, not productivity. At the end of 1985, the Mexican Bankers Association (ABM), now composed entirely of state-appointed managers, informed its account-holders that it would significantly increase the monthly checking account fee and would charge 250 pesos per written check. The measure proved to be a fiasco. The result of the decree stunned the state bankers, who were clearly out of touch with public opinion. Public outrage was swift and intense. Thousands of accounts were canceled and transferred to other savings instruments, particularly mutual funds. Worse still, a prominent group of businessmen publicly threatened to cancel collectively their checking accounts. In disgrace, the finance ministry stepped in to announce the indefinite postponement of the measure (*Proceso*, January 20, 1986, pp. 12–15).

While this episode was abruptly ended by public indignation, other legal changes made the banks far more profitable. Rather than increase fees, in 1986 the government allowed banks to impose stiff financial penalties. In addition, the finance ministry later "liberalized" charges for all sorts of basic financial services, such as checking accounts, money orders, and so on. Public response was far more limited because these later measures were not sudden, uniform increases and were therefore more difficult to detect and organize against. Although aggregates of these fees and fines were not publicly reported, they quickly came to represent an important source of bank income.[13]

In short, the banks' uncompetitiveness vis-à-vis the new brokers eroded the financial base from which the state funded itself, leading directly to the implementation of regulations undermining intermediation and efficiency. Not only was the result a further decline in the banking sector's ability to attract capital, it also deepened the public's suspicion and scorn for the financial institutions that were supposedly being run by the government to satisfy pressing social needs during hard times.

The state bankers did not take their demise lying down. Beginning in the summer of 1986, they embarked on a program of propaganda and behind-the-scenes political confrontation. In July, the ABM began a publicity campaign to shore up its falling rate of deposit, as well as its sagging image. Under the slogan "It's a good time to invest in Mexico," the bankers' association and Nafin, the largest development bank, paid advertisement costs of over half a billion pesos to bring back business. The commercials consisted primarily of "testimony" on the part of regular businessmen, whose affirmation of the banks' convenience and efficiency was supposed to generate credibility.

However, marketing research suggested that while the businessmen were received quite favorably among viewers, the government destroyed the credibility of the message: The results revealed "a climate of extreme irritation toward the government and a tremendous deterioration of its image." Common responses included: "They're always hiding something," The government "automatically makes me mistrustful," and "Anything the government says, the opposite is true." Respondents ridiculed the ABM as a "complete disgrace" and believed it was trying to bolster its image "by hiding behind the private sector." (*Proceso*, October 20, 1986: 12–15).

But the government bankers were not through. In June 1987, at the National Banking Convention in Guadalajara, the besieged bureaucrats who ran the state's cash registers staged a rebellion against the authorities in the central bank and the finance ministry. Reacting against their role as both laughingstock and villain on Mexico's colorful political stage, the members of the ABM challenged virtually every major aspect of the state's economic policy: monetarism, restrictions on banking operations and the use of bank funds to cover the deficit, and the promotion of stock market speculation.

ABM president Fernando Solana openly attacked the freezing of bank credit for the private sector, which he argued reduced productive investment and prolonged recession. Conceding that the brokerages had risen because of financial repression against the banks, he dismissed their role in real economic development. With less than 3 percent of the number of branches and a highly speculative orientation, they would never replace commercial banks as the principal means of business finance (*Proceso*, June 15, 1987: 22–23).

Outgoing ABM president Ernesto Fernández attacked the central bank's monopolization of banking resources through reserve requirements, which made a mockery of the purpose of nationalization—to provide capital to social and productive sectors neglected by the private bankers prior to 1982. He finished by calling for the creation of a joint commission of central bank, finance, and ABM officials to undertake changes allowing the banks to fulfill their central responsibilities, "with a character of unquestionable public service" toward the end of industrial development.

According to reports by those in attendance, the ABM accusations "provoked clear disgust in the director of the Banco de México, the Finance Minister and the President himself." After the bankers' assault had ended, central bank director Miguel Mancera staunchly defended monetarism as the only thing standing in the way of hyperinflation and accused the bankers of incompetence for not taking advantage of existing noninflationary measures of financing. Shortly thereafter, Deputy Finance Minister Francisco Suárez Dávila argued that the supposedly excessive control over the banks was necessary to prevent them from damaging the economy through credit expansion. Solana reportedly responded, "The bank can count on one resource that the authorities have not demonstrated: actual contact and the ability to see reality" (*Proceso*, June 15, 1987: 24–25).

Despite the state's face-saving performance at the banking convention, Mexico's policy-making leaders were clearly shaken. Above all, they worried about the impact of the conflict on the private sector. Any strategy that provoked mistrust and uncertainty in the market was the wrong strategy. Immediately following the meeting, Deputy Finance Minister Pedro Aspe gave orders to study the issues brought forward by the ABM.

Ironically, the response of the nationalized banking sector was to pressure for deregulation, particularly the end of reserve requirements. The goal was not to make the intermediaries more efficient or eliminate market distortions, but rather to liberate capital needed for expansion and socially oriented investment. Thus the austerity-minded neoliberal economists who occupied the government's highest financial offices found themselves in the awkward position of defending government restrictions on bank capital and confronting pleas for deregulation on the part of old guard PRI politicians who wanted the state to regain at least part of its role in directly promoting development.

## CONCLUSION: THE LEGACY OF INSTABILITY

By the end of the *sexenio*, de la Madrid had succeeded in recovering the ruling party's alliance with big business. In May 1987, the reconciliation was symbolically confirmed when the CCE elected as its president Agustín Legorreta, former head of Banamex. Previously an outspoken opponent of the nationalization, Legorreta now gave his seal of approval to the government's market orientation. His election as head of the country's powerful and independent private sector association was an "indicative sign that the former bankers had forgiven the regime for its past mistakes of expropriating the banks" (Elizondo 1992: 291). Moreover, because the bankers had largely reasserted their role in the economy through the brokerage sector, their influence in the nation's largest industrial and commercial enterprises remained paramount and helped the ruling party forge a common front of political support for its liberalization project.

In spite of the achievement of recovering business support, de la Madrid left office with the economy in shambles. Heroic adjustment efforts and years of painful austerity were unable to tame inflation. Nature and global commodity markets conspired to push the country's economic instability to new heights. In the two years following the inauguration, Mexico seemed to be muddling through the crisis with relative stability and even appeared poised to stage a moderate recovery. However, while luck cannot be predicted as a factor in economic performance or policy-making decisions, it cannot be discounted.

The 1985 earthquake in Mexico City caused damage equal to two percent of GDP, while the 1986 price of oil dropped by over half. Even as foreign exchange earnings plummeted, further public spending for recovery was unavoidable. Under these highly inflationary circumstances, stabilization under even a mildly reflating program became a quixotic effort. Pressures over which Mexico had no control brought the economy to its nadir. Fiscal discipline and the goal of bringing back Mexican capital appeared doomed. The legacy of that failure would fundamentally change the way the next administration approached macroeconomic discipline.

In 1987, de la Madrid responded by devaluing the peso one more time. Public criticism was virulent and certainly contributed the PRI's dismal showing in the 1988 election. However, just as the president had hoped, capital responded favorably: "While the policies were wildly unpopular, they convinced some investors that the government was willing to put economic health ahead of its own image" (*Wall Street Journal,* June 29, 1987: 32).

By the end of the *sexenio*, high inflation and macroeconomic instability had proven unstoppable. Austerity and trade liberalization had proven ineffective. In response, the ruling party orchestrated the first of what would become a long series of social "pacts" between business and labor, helping to keep both price and wage increases in check. To make the social accord work, the de la Madrid administration undertook direct price and wage controls and, equally importantly, used the exchange rate to apply an artificial break to inflation.

As a result of their inability to control the price spiral, financial authorities lost their faith in the beneficial effects of the peso's devaluation, which they now saw as a direct cause of inflation. With prices rising at well over 100 percent annually in the mid 1980s, then Budget and Planning Minister Carlos Salinas pronounced the fight against inflation as "the number one priority in economic strategy" and, in July 1987, unveiled a proposal for a heterodox stabilization plan that not only sought to cut spending, control prices, and open trade still further, but also replace the currency float with a fixed peg. (*Proceso*, July 27, 1987: 9).

Embedded formally in the Pact for Economic Solidarity (PSE), the peg represented the response to a political consensus among business and labor groups that prices had to be controlled. "Since 1988, exchange rate policy concentrated on supporting anti-inflationary effects and on providing certainty with respect to the evolution of the peso" (Banco de México 1993: 94–95). Exchange rate policy would now be directed primarily toward manipulating price level expectations. "The task of government through the late 1980s was to make agents believe that its policy was credible. By using a nominal anchor . . . the government pre-committed itself to . . . decreasing the expectations of inflation" (Baker 1993: 33–34).

As intended, the fixed exchange rate resulted in a steady, gradual appreciation of the peso. However, as we will see in the following chapter, the dynamic of currency overvaluation took on a political life of its own, even well after inflation had been reduced to one of the lowest rates in Latin America. While government intervention successfully pulled the Mexican economy out of chaos in the 1980s, it would be largely responsible for the next crisis.

**NOTES**

1. Interestingly, the bankers largely refrained from open criticism. They saw good relations with the government as the best strategy for recovering what they had lost in the nationalization. As finance minister Jesus Silva Herzog reportedly told the ex-bankers, "If you misbehave, I will not compensate you" (Elizondo 1992:194–196).

2. Author interview with Míguel de la Madrid, August 2, 1996, Mexico City.

3. Author interview with Miguel de la Madrid, August 2, 1996, Mexico City.

4. Author interview with Jonathan Heath, July 29, 1996, Mexico City.

5. Author interview with Jesus Rangel, August 30, 1994, Mexico City.

6. See Gutiérrez (1992).

7. A Ponzi Scheme is a fraudulent investment strategy—commonly called a "pyramid game" in the United States—which attracts naive investors in search of easy and spectacular gains. A group of investors pays a sum of capital into a pool, which is paid out to a smaller group of investors who contributed a like sum at a prior "round." When a sufficiently large number of investors later pays into the pool, they provide high returns for the intermediate group, and await the next, still larger group after them to realize a profit. The scheme always ends in a bust, because it is based entirely on a growing supply of hopeful investors who supply profits and keep the game popular.

8. Immediately following the crash, the brokerage houses and Nafin entered negotiations in which the development bank and private traders would buy massive amounts of stock to provide liquidity. Although the failure of the talks was initially blamed on differences over levels of public and private contribution, insiders acknowledged that Nafin simply lacked the capital to reverse the damage (see Lissakers and Zamora 1989: 12).

9. See Maxfield (1990), Cockcroft (1983), Tello (1984), and White (1992).

10. The term refers to the bank's acceptance of corporate deposits at an interest rate based on the prevailing Cetes yield and its obligation to repay with interest upon demand.

11. For an analysis of capitalization trends in the banking and nonbank financial sectors, see Ruiz Durán (1989). For general discussions of the trend, see Rodríguez San Martín (1990) and Barnes García (1989).

12. Author interview with Jonathan Heath, July 29, 1996, Mexico City.

13. Author interview with UNAM economist Ramón Pieza, April 22, 1995, Mexico City.

# 4

## Electoral Crisis (1989–1994): Recasting the Social Bases of the PRI

In 1983, social historian Lorenzo Meyer speculated that Mexico's economic crisis might force policy changes that could endanger the social alliance of the Institutional Revolutionary Party (PRI). "If those elements of populism which still remain in Mexico's political system, that is, its minimal redistributive elements, were effectively eliminated, the political elite would then have to seek other bases for their legitimacy or be prepared to rely more openly on force" (Meyer 1983: 122). Even though the PRI possessed the political resources to implement and endure the neoliberal transition in the short term, the breakdown of its traditional corporatist alliance forced the party to recast its social bases of support.

The central argument of this chapter is that, notwithstanding its fiscal discipline, the PRI did not cease politically motivated redistribution in the 1990s. What is often ignored in both political and economic analyses of the Salinas administration is that targeted pay-offs to social groups continued to be an integral part of the ruling party's strategy for survival. The evidence suggests that President Carlos Salinas, the successor to de la Madrid, relied on finance policy to allocate tangible goods to capitalists, the middle class, and impoverished Mexicans who were defecting from the PRI.

Largely because it sought ways to materially compensate such diverse social constituencies, the Salinas administration seems the most schizophrenic of those examined in this study. On one hand, it deregulated and reprivatized the banks and liberalized and internationalized capital markets. On the other hand, it protected the banks from both foreign and domestic competition and artificially propped up the value of the currency through exchange rate intervention.

While the fact that Salinas did not implement liberalization in every aspect of the financial system simultaneously is, in itself, not surprising, the nature of this uneven policy pattern requires explanation. At the ideological level, we need to explain why certain areas of the financial sector were deliberately exempted from market discipline, especially given the nearly religious adoption of neoliberal reform in other economic areas. An even more perplexing question arises in terms of economic logic, because bank and exchange rate policy directly undermined the stated goals of growth and financial stability. To understand these contradictions, we must turn to the political challenges confronting the PRI at the end of the 1980s.

## THE POLITICAL CONTEXT

By the 1988 elections, public disgust with six years of painful adjustments, stagnation, and instability had taken their toll. According to official figures, which many believe overstate the level of PRI support, the ruling party lost over 20 points between the 1982 and 1988 elections. The damage done by declining living standards during the debt crisis enabled the opposition to gain a significant share of voters for the first time. The PRI's rejection of nationalist economic policies and its conversion to market reform had gradually eroded support from its traditional allies in labor, the peasantry, and small business. In order to survive, the party sought to strengthen its relations with those groups that stood to gain from the new economic strategy and to find ways to re-establish partnerships with dissatisfied groups.

### Economic Mission

Because the PRI's electoral vulnerability was based primarily on a record of economic failure, Salinas had to achieve recovery and growth. His strategy was to move beyond adjustment and to radically accelerate the market transition. Largely because of the unusual degree of autonomy enjoyed by the Mexican president, Salinas's technocrats were not only able to deepen the liberalizing reforms initiated under de la Madrid, but to undertake the very transformation of Mexico's development model. Salinas is best remembered for successfully taming inflation, turning budget deficits into surpluses, selling off public enterprises, and lowering trade barriers. While these measures were directed primarily toward preserving macroeconomic stability and "modernizing" the economy, the new model also predicated growth on inflows of foreign capital and integration with the United States.

On one hand, international economic constraints were far less restrictive than during the previous administration. Indeed, the increasing availability of foreign capital seemed to validate the government's new, internationalized growth model. By the end of the decade, Mexico began to recover its economic credibility among foreign governments and investors. The International Monetary Fund (IMF) gave its blessing to Mexico's fiscal discipline, and the country's macroeconomic performance suggested a rapid return to stability. Equally important, historically low interest rates in the major economies made emerging markets irresistible to profit-hungry investors. In short, the global boycott of capital quickly turned into an avalanche.

On the other hand, while Mexican policy makers may have gained flexibility in the international realm, their room for maneuver in the domestic arena remained quite limited. The orthodox model served as a major policy-making constraint. The commitment to fiscal discipline and low inflation precluded deficit spending strategies to stimulate growth. Similarly, the government's renewed alliance with business and international investors—not to mention the goal of passing the North American Free Trade Agreement (NAFTA)—was predicated upon the continuation of sober fiscal management. Not even the most enthusiastic emerging markets fund managers could be expected to risk their clients' retirement savings in a country whose financial assets could be eroded by inflation or devaluation. As Keynesian options became unavailable, public sector spending could no longer be used to finance growth. Not only was macroeconomic stimulus ruled out as an expansion strategy, but social policies and programs could no longer be funded by borrowing.

### Civic Opposition and Contested Elections

By the end of the 1980s, the PRI faced its first genuine electoral challenge. In the 1988 presidential election, amid widespread vote-counting irregularities, Carlos Salinas officially narrowly defeated leftist Frente Democrático Nacional (FDN) rival Cuauhtémoc Cárdenas. Popular outrage over voting fraud and the mobilization of well-organized opposition parties exposed the ruling party to potentially devastating opposition for the first time.

The new Salinas administration confronted unprecedented popular protest from labor, professional and academic institutions (*New York Times*, July 17, 1988: A1). The PRI received particularly harsh treatment from the domestic press (e.g., *Proceso*, July 11, 1988: 6–17; July 25, 1988: 6–19). At the same time, while television news continued to be controlled by PRI allies, print journalism emerged as a tenacious critic of the government. By the beginning of the Salinas administration, Mexican investigative journalism and editorial assertiveness was subjecting the PRI to unprecedented levels of criticism. Weekly news magazines such as *Proceso* treated their readers to a steady supply of shocking exposés and governmental scandal.

The PRI was fighting for its political life. "The electoral fraud, ever present throughout post-revolutionary history, inflicted for the first time a distinct dimension of illegitimacy to an incoming government; an unequivocal sign that legitimacy through performance had deteriorated seriously, if not collapsed completely" (Crespo 1992: 31). Public outrage, repeated denunciations from both opposition parties, and increased international exposure put the PRI leadership on notice that future electoral victories—at least at the national level—would have to be legitimate. As a Mexican political scientist concluded shortly after Salinas's victory, "Persisting discrepancies between the population's declared preferences and electoral outcomes imply that the PRI's [imposed] victories will carry high costs for the legitimacy of the political system" (Guillén López 1989: 250).

The neoliberal policies implemented by the PRI under Carlos Salinas had damaged the party's traditional corporatist alliance. Market reforms were undermining patronage relations between the state and its long-time social allies, particularly labor and agriculture.[1] The economic pain of transition also made unintegrated groups available for recruitment by rival parties.

The party leadership openly acknowledged the need to create new alliances and partnerships in order to ensure political survival. Six weeks after taking office, President Salinas commented on the new challenges he confronted.

In previous decades, the PRI could count on campesinos who had received land from agrarian reform, and unionized workers who were the product of import-substituting industrialization. Now the country is experiencing a formidable process of transformation. We must seek new bases of support for the Party. We must build alliances with new groups, some of which are unorganized now. (Cornelius et al. 1989: 27–28)

In sum, Salinas confronted the most daunting political and economic challenge of his party's existence. To ensure the PRI's future viability, his administration had six short years not just to recover macroeconomic stability, but also to achieve tangible and visible results for diverse and divided interests. The following section identifies the most important of these groups, and describes the source of their influence over the PRI's political future.

### Middle Class and Small Entrepreneurs

The economic crisis of the 1980s had sent much of the Mexican middle class to the opposition. Diffuse, unorganized, and relatively small, this social sector nevertheless represented one of the PRI's top political priorities during the 1990s. Those with higher incomes and education levels not only wielded considerable voting strength, but also represented the most important political reference group for the rest of Mexican society (Loaeza and Stern 1990). Reflecting upon the social cost of economic crisis during the 1980s, Meyer warned that the "systematic containment of consumption in the middle classes cannot continue" (1983: 121–122).

Although the National Action Party (PAN) did not take significantly more of the 1988 vote than in the previous election, its gains among Mexico's more urban, educated, professional voters suggested a disturbing trend for the PRI.[2] An analysis of polling data from 1989 showed that "the most exaggerated relationship is between college-educated voters and preference for the PAN" (Camp 1993: 81). Alonso Lujambio, former director of the social science department at Instituto Tecnológico Autónomo de México (ITAM) and electoral counselor at Mexico's Federal Election Institute, stated: "Prior to the 1988 election empirical evidence on voter income and preference is scarce. However, it seems apparent that the economic crisis that erupted in 1982 and its effect on social mobility caused the middle class, which had enormous expectations of permanent improvement, to become frustrated, and they assumed an increasingly critical position against the post-revolutionary regime."[3]

Moreover, the PRI was losing support among the country's millions of small businessmen. Throughout the crisis-ridden 1980s, it was unable to "overcome the tensions with the private sector and diminish their growing support for the PAN." By the end of the decade, the ruling party was "fearing the further rise" of National Action (Morris 1995: 72). Between 1983 and 1987, entrepreneur support for the PRI fell from 51 percent to 32 percent, with the PAN picking up virtually all defectors (Basañez 1990: 225–229).

### The Poor and the Informal Economy

An even greater and more immediate electoral challenge was the leftist appeal among Mexico's poor (Guillén López 1989: 256–258). Lacking any kind of "officialist" representative institution, Mexico's growing legions of unemployed and impoverished citizens threatened the party's claim to revolutionary legitimacy. Living in sprawling slums on the outskirts of the capital, and in tens of thousands of rural municipalities around the country, Mexico's poor survived largely through the informal economy, virtually forgotten by the local PRI machines.

Public spending cuts eliminated what little had gone to the poor. Austerity and unemployment left millions to fend for themselves. The sidewalks and major avenues of the capital became markets to a booming informal economy. Peddlers wearing rags sold newspapers, used pornography, and candies in the middle of traffic, while school-age boys washed car windshields and performed circus acts during red lights in the hopes of collecting a few pesos from sympathetic motorists. Outside of the major cities, where the consumer market was much smaller, opportunities were even more limited, and social services were abysmal: Running water and electricity were luxuries, while access to education and medical care was often nonexistent.

Campaigning aggressively in urban slums, poor rural communities, and impoverished blue-collar neighborhoods, FDN leaders accused the PRI of abandoning the social principles of the Revolution. Their old-style populism was a bold and successful challenge to the legitimacy of the ruling party. The degree of support Cuauthémoc Cárdenas received in 1988 among the popular sectors previously loyal to the PRI suggested that the strategy was paying off (Bruhn 1996: 155).

How serious were the opposition's gains? Reflecting on the "pincer effect" of urban, educated votes to the PAN and rural, poor votes to the FDN, two election analysts concluded: "It would be difficult to exaggerate the relevance of this change . . . the consolidation of these tendencies would undoubtedly be devastating for PRI hegemony, because they form the bases for an electoral defeat, unless the party reconstitutes its electoral profile (Molinar and Weldon 1990: 252)." According to political scientist Roderic Camp, "Long term development trends . . . tend to favor the opposition, not the government's party. . . . Although none of the opposition parties yet has the strength to best the PRI nationally . . . the time will come when one of them, or some new opposition party, will effectively contest for primacy among the electorate" (1993: 156–157).

### Big Business

Finally, Salinas was committed to preserving the partnership with powerful business interests. The central pillar of PRI social and financial support and backbone of the neoliberal agenda, the multinational finance-industrial elite was the only group capable of fulfilling the developmental objectives of economic integration. Large manufacturers, distributors, and bankers presided over the country's most dynamic growth sectors. They were also the primary source of investment capital and foreign exchange, the life-blood of Salinas's market reforms. By designing financial policy to channel rents to big business, the PRI sought to deepen its alliance with the private sector actors who supported the new "outward-oriented" economic strategy.

In addition to their economic role in development, the influence of these firms lay in their control of the major business associations. The Coordinating Enterprise Council (CCE) was created in 1975 to mobilize against populist economic policies; the Coordinator of Foreign Trade Enterprise (COECE) consisted of 114 business sector representatives that consulted with each other and the government during the negotiation of NAFTA provisions; the elite Council of Mexican Businessmen (CMHN) was composed exclusively of the country's wealthiest and most powerful capitalists from industry, finance, and commerce. The leadership of the Association of Mexican Bankers (ABM) included what would soon be the new owners of the reprivatized banks.

Big business support was not only important to the PRI because of its control over private sector organizations, but also because economic liberalization threatened to erode the traditional base of support among small producers, typically represented within Cámara Nacional de la Industria de la Transformación (Canacintra). Trade opening had savaged thousands of

Mexico's backward industrialists. Because of the PRI's control over Canacintra's organizational resources and its ability to prevent independent
organizations from stealing Canacintra membership, Salinas was able to
prevent the small producers from effectively articulating their opposition to
neoliberal policies (Shadlen 1997). However, the ruling party needed more
than grudging silence from business to bolster its economic agenda and
looked to the financial-industrial conglomerates to provide that voice.

## RIDING THE MARKET OUT OF CHAOS

The PRI responded to the need for change with a bold economic reform
project based on stabilization and international capital. Neoliberal reforms
would stabilize prices and the currency, invite mountains of foreign capital,
and make the economy internationally competitive. Stability would be the
foundation of the ruling party's political viability. The new executive not
only vowed to deepen the deregulatory reforms initiated by his predecessor,
but to pull the Mexican economy up into the ranks of the developed countries by limiting the role of the government and promoting the forces of
market discipline.

The recovery of macroeconomic stability during the first half of the
Salinas administration was so impressive that it made Mexico a virtual show-
case of successful market reform for the rest of the developing world to fol-
low. The mainstays of liberalization were the privatization of parastatals,
further budget reductions, elimination of controls on foreign investment,
and economic integration (tariff reductions and NAFTA). In addition,
Mexico successfully renegotiated the payment of its foreign debt, with the
Brady Plan significantly reducing the country's interest obligations. By the
early 1990s, economic indicators for inflation, budget, and debt-to-GDP ratio demonstrated a remarkable return to stability.

The most impressive accomplishment of the Salinas administration was
bringing inflation under control in just a few years. The de la Madrid government, inheriting the debt crisis and facing a virtual stoppage of international credit, regularly saw inflation rates top 100 percent, reaching a
frightening 159 percent in 1987. It was during this year that the first of a series of social "pacts" was approved, uniting business, labor, and government
in a common effort to control price increases. In addition, the central bank
began to run a very tight money regime, constraining available credit and
monetary aggregates. During his tenure as budget minister under de la
Madrid, Salinas had made inflation control his number one priority. As
president, his attention to this goal remained undiminished; the inflation
rate was cut by over half in the first year of the *sexenio* and to below 10 percent by 1993.

A major factor in the struggle against inflation was the taming of public
finances. The Mexican budget had become undisciplined since the populist

days of the Echeverría administration and spun out of control during the petroleum boom of the López Portillo *sexenio*; the public deficit reached an astonishing 14 percent of GDP in 1987. Just three years later, Salinas had virtually closed the gap. By 1992, massive budget cuts and the sale of unprofitable public enterprises turned the budget deficit into a slight budget surplus. See Figure 4.1.

The availability of foreign exchange also contributed to economic stability and confidence. Beginning in the late 1980s, the central bank assiduously built up its international reserves. As a result of the net inflow of capital, the government more than tripled its reserves between 1988 and 1993.

One of the most impressive and oft-cited achievements of the Salinas administration was the relative reduction in Mexico's debt burden. Through debt restructuring under the Brady Plan and the liquidation of principal using funds raised through the privatization of parastatal enterprises, the government was able to reduce Mexico's debt/GDP ratio by more than fivefold in just eight years. (See Table 4.1.) In 1988, over 44 percent of the total budget went to pay debt interest. Just three years later, the debt consumed only 20 percent of the budget. Over the same period, the share of GDP spent on debt servicing fell from 17.7 percent to 5.7 percent (Baker 1993: 24–26).

**Figure 4.1**
**Budget Deficit/Surplus as Percent of GDP (1984–1992)**

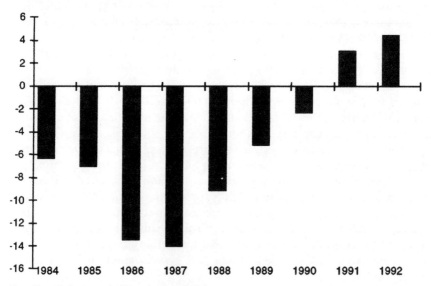

*Note:* Years below zero indicate budget deficit.

*Source:* Banco de México, *Indicadores Económicos.*

**Table 4.1**
**Net Public Debt as Percent of GDP (1984–1994)**

|          | 1984 | 1985 | 1986  | 1987  | 1988 | 1989 | 1990 | 1991 | 1992 | 1993 | 1994* |
|----------|------|------|-------|-------|------|------|------|------|------|------|-------|
| External | 43.6 | 56.5 | 88.7  | 87.2  | 48.3 | 41.3 | 29.4 | 20.4 | 16.3 | 13.3 | 16.6  |
| Internal | 22.4 | 21.3 | 28.4  | 27.5  | 20.0 | 19.5 | 19.5 | 15.9 | 8.4  | 8.5  | 4.9   |
| Total    | 65.9 | 77.8 | 117.0 | 114.7 | 68.3 | 60.8 | 48.9 | 36.3 | 24.7 | 21.8 | 21.5  |

Note: *January–June.

Source: Banco de México, *Indicadores Económicos.*

The question of why Mexico chose to liberalize when it did is not particularly puzzling. Proponents, the government, and even many critics concur that liberalization was the most viable economic response to the obvious failure of traditional inward-oriented economic policies, changes in global financial markets, and the pressing need for capital in the wake of the debt crisis. At the end of the de la Madrid *sexenio,* a Universidad Nacional Autónoma de México (UNAM) political scientist reflected the conventional wisdom: "The present conjuncture thus greatly favors laissez-faire policies. This coincides with the interests of the radical faction [of business] and also represents the predominant tendency in world capitalism" (Luna et al. 1987: 27).

By the early 1990s, many believed that the PRI's emphasis on maintaining and obtaining global capital had already paid off politically. Political scientist Miguel Angel Centeno argued:

By the middle of the Salinas *sexenio* prices were (relatively) stable, the economy was growing and no longer so dependent on oil revenues, and the political stability of the regime was no longer so fragile. This last point was perhaps the most impressive accomplishment. . . . The harsh living conditions [under de la Madrid] had produced the strongest challenge to the regime since 1968, but this had apparently been defused by 1992. The key to Mexican success seemed deceptively simple . . . economic efficiency before social justice, international support before national sovereignty. (1994: 20)

The economic transformation undertaken by the Salinas administration was by no means a unique phenomenon. Clearly, the growing forces of capital mobility and the pervasive failure of inward-oriented economic policies had caused countries in Latin America, Africa, Asia, and even Europe to turn to market reforms. "*Salinastroika* was part of a global revolution of the market. In the developing world, states reduced public subsidies, competed for links with the developed economies and investment capital from multinationals" (Centeno 1994: 21).

It is not surprising that the government was able to implement such fundamental changes in the nation's economic model. While many governments
have experienced great difficulty in politically managing the move from insulated to liberalized economies, those characterized by a high degree of "state
autonomy" have weathered the transition far more easily. Mexico stands out
among the world's developing countries for its institutional domination of
popular social sectors and control over political resources. The puzzle is not,
then, why the state undertook financial liberalization, nor how it was able to
do so. Rather, the main question of this chapter is why the government implemented policies that undermined markets, growth, and stability. Notwithstanding the accomplishments of Salinas's economic "revolution," a large part
of the president's policy agenda also consisted of measures that undermined
and distorted financial markets. These contradictory reform efforts appear
even more inexplicable when viewed in the context of other liberalization efforts—trade, in particular, was opened much more quickly and extensively
than finance, despite tremendous costs to Mexican producers.

Officially, the PRI's *political* strategy consisted entirely of *economic* strategy,
which was based entirely on market orthodoxy and stabilization. World
leaders, international investors, and most economists agreed that the PRI
pursued genuine liberalization measures to rescue the economy from instability and, by extension, to improve its political standing. The present argument, however, is that it also implemented antimarket policies to address
electoral vulnerability.

The PRI needed an economic mechanism with which to appease middle
class and poor voters who now had real party alternatives, as well as to preserve the commitment of big business. Unable to pursue traditional populist
solutions, which typically called for fiscal stimulus, the government turned to
the financial sector to generate resources to satisfy large and socially disparate constituencies. The remainder of this chapter explains how the PRI
used banking and exchange rate policy to recover its political dominance.

## BANK REGULATION AND PRIVATIZATION

When the Salinas administration sold the banks back to the private sector
halfway through the *sexenio*, Mexican financial liberalization was pronounced complete. Given the extensive deregulation that preceded the
reprivatization, the painstaking and highly transparent procedures of the
sale, and the impressive jump in private sector lending following the sell-off,
it seemed clear to the international community that Mexico had fully embraced market reform and would soon reap the rewards of the efficient allocation of capital.

However, progress in Mexican banking liberalization was achieved at the
expense of competition. The maintenance of high barriers to entry would
ensure high profits for the privatized banks, provide the PRI with massive

amounts of extra capital to fund popular social programs, and seal the ruling party's alliance with finance-industrial capital. The price of this political victory would be excessive interest rate burdens on domestic borrowers and the weakening of financial stability.

### Deregulation

It is significant that bank deregulation was implemented before the reprivatization. By reducing or abolishing perennial restrictions, the government made Mexico's financial institutions more attractive to prospective buyers. As Sergio Sarmiento argued, "Paradoxically, now, with the new [deregulatory] measures, the state's banking institutions enjoy greater freedom than they had under private ownership" (*El Norte*, April 5, 1989). Indeed, the nationalization so feared by the private sector initiated a period of unprecedented freedom and growth of banking activities.

The starting point was the elimination of mechanisms of financial repression. Interest rate controls on deposits had prevented banks from competing with nonbank financial institutions and reduced traditional bank savings. The only market-rate savings instrument available during the de la Madrid administration was the "banker's acceptance," a corporate deposit whose quantity was strictly controlled. In September 1988, the Finance Ministry lifted all quantitative restrictions on bank acceptances, signaling "a *de facto* liberalization of interest rates" (Mansell 1994a: 118). By April 1990, 80 percent of all savings was kept in the new accounts. (*New York Times*, April 10, 1990: D10; *El Financiero*, May 8, 1990: 8).

Salinas aggressively liberalized other financial activities. In 1989, the reserve requirement was converted into a less burdensome "liquidity" requirement. Banks now only had to keep 30 percent of available capital at the Banco de México. As the government turned to the market for financing, "banks were released from the credit harness that had at times restricted their private sector lending to 10% or less of their funds" (*The Banker*, April 1990: 50). During Salinas's first year, bank credit to the private sector increased by 20 percent, while direct credit to the state fell by almost half (*El Norte*, March 13, 1990). At the same time, the new president moved to end the obligatory allocation of capital. By 1990, the entire selective credit system was abolished, and minimum reserve requirements were reduced to international levels (Aspe 1993: 80; Lustig 1992: 108).

### Concentration and Competition for Foreign Capital

As Salinas eliminated banking restrictions, he also accelerated the trend toward concentration. Fears of an international shortage of capital led the government to promote the size, rather than quantity of financial firms. The government's main objective was now to ensure that financial intermediaries could effectively compete in global markets. If foreign capital was going to fuel economic development, the banks would serve as the engine.

An official financial history acknowledges that "beginning with the nationalization, the financial authorities implemented a policy designed to diminish the number of institutions and promote the strengthening and expansion of those existing" (CNB 1992: 25). The number of Mexican banks dropped from 64 to just 18 by the time they were reprivatized. The three largest banks, Banamex, Bancomer, and Serfin controlled over 70 percent of total deposits.

In his second year as president, Salinas pushed bank concentration to its logical conclusion. The July 1990 Law for the Regulation of Financial Groups promoted consolidation and the fusion of financial activities, allowing *casas de bolsa* and commercial and investment banks to operate under the same roof. Banks could now invest directly in domestic or foreign firms, as well as invest in a broad range of financial instruments, from money and securities markets, to options and currency trading. Mexico had formally adopted a "universal banking" model." (Marray 1992: 148; Aspe 1993: 89).

The new law dramatically expanded opportunities for financial *grupos* (highly integrated financial-industrial conglomerates) to participate in global capital markets (Villegas and Ortega 1991: 94). As a securities lawyer observed, "The creation of non-bank [brokerage-linked] financial groups . . . is of transcendental importance to the financial system, in that it will permit the organization of economies of scale . . . to compete at the domestic and international level" (AMDB 1990: 24). As a ranking bank regulator remarked, "The formation of solid universal financial groups with greater competitive capacity will allow us to face future decisions more confidently" (Palencia Gomez 1992: 38). According to the Mexican Banking Commission, "The policy of stimulating the integration of multiple banks had as its purpose to give greater strength to credit institutions, avoiding vulnerability and underdevelopment which at times affected those of smaller size" (CNB 1992: 22).

The private sector concurred. Just months after the announcement of the reprivatization, the president of the Mexican Stock Brokers Association wrote: "We will only be able to respond to the challenge [of access to capital markets] with large integrated financial groups" (Madariaga Lomelí 1990: 60). Former ABM president Carlos Abedrop concurred: "It would be a grave error that because of the existing prejudices against oligopolies (a word which in Mexico has an almost satanic meaning) we do not promote the creation of large and powerful Mexican banks that have the capacity to participate in international financial markets" (*Proceso*, September 30, 1991: 19).

### Protection and the Politics of Reprivatization

On May 2, 1990, President Salinas announced: "Today it is time to modify the exclusive state property of the bank, because the circumstances that motivated the [nationalization] project have changed" (*La Jornada*, May 3,

1990: 1). He then charged the Congress to reverse the constitutional changes with which President López Portillo had nationalized the banks eight years earlier. Notwithstanding opposition from the Left, the initiative received the support of every PRI lawmaker.

The reprivatization of the Mexican banks was one of the largest and most complex sales of public assets in the history of the developing world. The government undertook painstaking steps to ensure adequate information and transparency in highly visible public auctions. Between June 1991 and July 1992, the government sold off eighteen banks. Financial holding companies and brokerage firms, which had made their fortunes in the 1980s from the profitability of public lending and the stock market boom, bought fourteen of the banks. Unlike industrial conglomerates laboring under high debt levels, the brokerages had enormous quantities of liquid capital available. For those lacking sufficient cash, their balance sheets ensured extensive borrowing capacity. Several new owners leveraged their purchases by borrowing abroad.[4]

The most notable feature of reprivatization was the very high price paid. While typical U.S. and European banks sell for about 2.2 times book value, Mexican banks were sold at a remarkable average of over 3.5 times book value, netting the government over $12 billion. The bidders were influenced by several factors that suggested robust financial performance.

First, as previously noted, deregulation and universal banking made Mexico's financial institutions more attractive to prospective buyers. Second, the government had returned the banks to life during the nationalization period. By the beginning of Salinas's term, the banks had regained solvency and by 1992 were profitable.[5] Finally, financial growth indicators augured well for banking. The banks were sold off from mid-1991 to mid-1992, a period of robust expansion. Moreover, both corporate and consumer demand for financial services was expected to explode in the 1990s; with less than 10 percent of the population holding bank accounts, Mexico was "underbanked by almost every measure" (*The Economist*, February 13, 1993: S16).

Nonetheless, these factors hardly guaranteed the banks' long-term profitability. Indeed, Mexican economic expansion was quite slow, while the country's low rate of savings limited capital for loans. While deregulation and recovery made financial assets relatively more attractive to investors, they were clearly not sufficient to generate the stratospheric bidding levels achieved during the reprivatization.

The extremely high prices largely reflected the bidders' anticipation of the rents that would be obtained under protectionism. The same Mexican negotiators who conceded trade and service concessions in NAFTA fought tenaciously with the United States to guarantee that Mexican banks would not be exposed to foreign competition. Chapter fourteen of NAFTA, which includes the terms for trade and investment in financial services, stipulated strict ceilings on foreign participation in Mexico's financial sector. No U.S. or Canadian bank was initially allowed to buy a Mexican bank until 1998, and even then, foreign acquisitions were to be limited to banks with less than 4 percent market share. Moreover, the combined total of all foreign banks could not exceed 8 percent of net capital until the year 2000.

According to a Federal Reserve report, the Mexican strategy allowed "U.S. banks to enter in the phase-in period only in a very limited part of the market" (Gruben et al. 1993). The "free trade" treaty thus ensured that foreign banks would not challenge the position of Mexico's domestic institutions for the foreseeable future: "NAFTA protects the financial sector for a very long time. With this the process of liberalization and globalization will not break the oligopoly power of Mexican commercial banks. It can be concluded that, regarding finance, NAFTA represents essentially a model of financial protection" (Gutiérrez Pérez and Perrotini 1994: 93).

While the Mexican government restricted foreign competition in the banking sector, it acknowledged the need to increase domestic competition.[6] However, notwithstanding the licensing of a handful of new banks between 1990 and 1994, banking regulation under Salinas imposed serious barriers to domestic entry. The minimum level of capitalization required to charter a new bank was set at 0.5 percent of combined capital and reserves of the entire banking system. By 1993, that figure represented almost $30 million (Musalem et al. 1993).[7] As three financial economists concluded, such a sum represents an "ante that would exclude a large proportion of would-be [foreign] entrants . . . capital minimums serve to impede entry and thus competition in the industry without necessarily serving the intended purpose of enhancing institution solvency" (McComb et al. 1994: 226).

Because of an obscure NAFTA provision that Mexican negotiators had demanded, the capitalization minimum went far beyond discouraging the formation of local banks. The treaty also stipulated that all foreign banks had to enter the Mexican market as chartered national subsidiaries, rather than branches. Permission to open foreign branch offices would have enabled hundreds of smaller U.S. banks, many located near the Mexican border, simply to invest in a modest building and staff to serve local credit needs. The requirement that all entrants had to procure such a massive amount of capital represented an insurmountable barrier to many American banks that were otherwise well-positioned to compete in Mexico's retail banking market (Vega Cánovas 1995; Mansell 1994b: 31).

Government protection of the banks was motivated by two political goals. The first was straightforward: to cement the PRI's partnership and alliance with Mexico's wealthiest and most powerful capitalists—precisely those who had bought the banks. The second was indirect: By using the windfall from the bank sale for social programs, the PRI sought to recover support from the poor. The chance to earn the gratitude of entrepreneurs as well as a cash windfall for public spending was a political opportunity too attractive to sacrifice in the name of ideology or increased competitiveness.

### Strengthening the Business Alliance

The negotiation of NAFTA's financial services provisions represented the fulfillment of a deal between the government and the new bankers. Without the assurance of protection rents, reprivatization would have given the Mexican financial-industrial elite less incentive to offer its allegiance to the ruling party, and bank bids would certainly have been much less enthusiastic. Significant foreign penetration would have meant both reduced market share and downward pressure on interest rates. Just as much of Mexican industry had responded to sudden foreign competition by failing to adjust, it was widely believed that much of the long-protected finance sector would be unable to defend its share of the domestic market.

The bankers demanded protection by applying a variation of the nationalist "infant industry" argument to the financial sector. Past bank protection had led to inefficiency, which would make Mexican banks vulnerable to foreign pressure should finance markets be opened quickly. They needed time to become internationally competitive and avoid the (unspecified) danger of foreign-controlled banking.

Over a year after the reprivatization, Javier Fernández, strategic director for Bancomer, stated: "We've barely come out of a system that was nationalized for ten years. It would be childish to think that the entire financial system can be transformed in only 18 months" (*Excélsior*, October 6, 1993). Shortly following the announcement of the bank reprivatization, the Mexican Bankers' Association stated that national control over banks could not be compromised (AMB 1991). During financial negotiations, Alfredo Harp Helú, ABM executive and co-owner of Banamex, argued that "we must defend our financial sovereignty and determine up to what point an opening is opportune" (*El Financiero*, November 21, 1991: 15). Antonio del Valle, director of Banco Internacional and head of the elite Mexican Council of Businessmen, observed with satisfaction that NAFTA's ceiling on foreign participation "allow the national banks to have a comparative advantage and be able to compete efficiently in the future" (*El Norte*, August 14, 1992). Similarly, an executive of Banacci, Mexico's largest financial group, maintained that a rapid financial opening offered Mexican banks "little to gain" and that policy "should consolidate the internal market, in order to become more [internationally] competitive" (*El Financiero*, February 13, 1992: 3).

After the legal provisions of NAFTA had finally been hammered out, journalists, bureaucrats, academics, and elected officials concurred that protection was the political price of the sale. Business columnist Arturo Hanono argued that the high prices paid were the consequence of "guaranteed protection for the privatized banks . . . keeping markets closed for some years allows the recuperation of investment" (*Expansión*, December 11, 1991). Another, Antonio Gershenson, observed that forcing the new banks to compete against foreign rivals "would be seen as violating an explicit or implicit compromise" (*La Jornada*, February 16, 1992). The director of industrial promotion at the trade ministry acknowledged that "protection was a precondition for selling the banks,"[8] while a Panista congressman remarked that "the condition of protection for the bank sale to go through was common knowledge."[9]

The government publicly attempted to justify protection and the resulting high interest rates as necessary for sustaining adequate capitalization levels.[10] However, when pressed to defend the bank protection on purely technical grounds, a high-ranking finance ministry official stated, "We wanted to keep the payment system in Mexican hands." As for the neoliberal argument that competition would result in a more efficient financial system and lower interest rates, he conceded that "the Mexican team was guided by more subjective criteria. The economic argument in favor of competition is valid."[11]

### Targeting the Poor

The PRI's second goal was to broaden its appeal among the poor. Like any government trying to improve its political stature, the fiscally orthodox Salinas administration needed money. Because protection enhanced the profit-making potential, and therefore the price of the banks, reprivatization provided the government with the extra cash it needed for targeted social programs. The most important of these was the National Program for Solidarity (Pronasol), the federal program that issued block grants for infrastructure and education directly to municipalities.

Solidarity was widely characterized by scholars, journalists, and opposition parties as a return to clientelist politics.[12] According to Centeno, Pronasol was "the core element of the Salinas administration's formula for maintaining control . . . it was a perfect example of classic PRI tactics, whereby opposition and discontent could be coopted through patronage" (1994: 65–66). Statistical analysis revealed that Pronasol funding was not targeted to maximize poverty alleviation, as maintained by the government, but rather to maximize the PRI's political gains (Molinar and Weldon 1994).[13]

The Salinas administration used the proceeds of Mexico's vast privatization program to fund Pronasol. Of more than 2,000 firms eventually sold off to the private sector, the sale of the eighteen banks alone generated over $12 billion. (The 1990 sale of Teléfonos de México, which also enjoyed many years of protection and extremely high profits, also netted the government almost $2 billion.) Technically, virtually all of the money gained through these sell-offs went into a "contingency fund" to pay off large parts of Mexico's public debt, which was bleeding the treasury of billions of dollars in interest payments. By significantly reducing its debt burden, the government increased its level of discretionary spending for more politically valuable activities. As a Mexican scholar explained, "Employing privatization in this way allowed Mexico to reap larger margins from public savings . . . and direct them toward welfare and growth" (González Turbicio 1994: 72).

The use of reprivatization revenue for Pronasol was not merely acknowledged by the government; it was a point of pride. "When Mr. Salinas visits communities to dedicate new Solidarity projects, he never fails to mention that the money came from the privatization program."[14] The president's brother Raúl Salinas, then coordinator of Pronasol's System of Evaluation, declared in 1992, "Part of what we get from the bank purchase, of course it will go to the programs of Solidarity" (*Wall Street Journal*, January 8, 1993: A7). A government press release describes how cash from reprivatization was used to enable the government to channel more resources to spending programs. "Most of the resources obtained from the bank sales have been applied to debt reduction, allowing the Government to reduce principal as well as interest payments, thus making more resources available to allocate them in social and productive investment" (*Mexico on the Record*, July 1992: 4). As Salinas declared: "The resources obtained from the ending of state banking will contribute to strengthen the stability of the country's economy, expand long-term development perspectives and attend to the most urgent needs of those who have the least" (*Proceso*, May 7, 1990: 9).

At the end of the Salinas *sexenio*, almost half of all public investment was channeled through Solidarity projects (Contreras and Bennett 1994: 282). By 1993, the government had spent $12 billion on Solidarity programs (Cornelius et al. 1994). It is certainly a coincidence that this figure approximates the sum of capital raised by the bank sale. Obviously, even if the banks had been sold without the promise of protection, their sale would have provided the government with a sizable chunk of cash. While Pronasol was not the only reason the government backed bank protection, the windfall received by the government from high bidding prices clearly strengthened the ruling party's efforts to expand politically crucial poverty-abatement programs.

### Bank Performance: A Costly Boom

The economic consequences of protecting the newly privatized banking sector were dismal. The financial "opening" was expected to increase the level and efficiency of investment and provide stability for the banking system. Yet as a result of the high interest rates made possible by protection, Mexico's new bankers were able to make extremely high profits, despite pervasive inefficiency in the financial sector (see Table 4.2).[15] Writing just before the bank sale, economist Javier Gavito, who would become president

**Table 4.2**
**Profitability of U.S. and Mexican Banks (1992)**

|                  | Banamex | Bancomer | Large U.S. Banks |
|------------------|---------|----------|------------------|
| Return on Assets | 2.3%    | 2.0%     | 0.9%             |
| Return on Equity | 32.8%   | 27.9%    | 13.4%            |

*Source:* Keefe, Bruyette and Woods, Inc., Salomon Brothers, Inc. (cited in Smith and Zellner 1993).

of the National Securities Commission under President Ernesto Zedillo, wrote that the concentration of banks during the nationalization period generated "an oligopolistic structure that has allowed extraordinary benefits" (Gavito 1991: 26).

Even before the peso crisis hit in December 1994, the rate of default threatened the stability of the banking sector. The eventual collapse of the nation's loan portfolio can be understood, in part, as the result of three factors: budget balancing, banking deregulation, and protection. The disappearance of the federal deficit in the early 1990s coincided with the liberalization and reprivatization of the banks. As the need for heavy reserve requirements evaporated, the state allowed the banks to lend more capital to the private sector.

The problem was that for almost a decade Mexican banks had not had to perform any kind of risk analysis.[16] When a bank's major activity consists of buying government securities, risk assessment becomes a moot point. However, by the early 1990s, the banks found themselves flush with capital; at the beginning, the new owners greatly increased private sector lending but failed to make commensurate improvements in risk assessment. "Unfortunately," as a Banco de México analyst remarked, "it was a good short term strategy but a bad strategy in the long term. Those banks could lend freely and charge good interest rates, but they had no experience in credit analysis."[17] As Table 4.3 demonstrates, Mexican banks underwent unrestrained increases in consumer lending.

By 1992, Mexico, the world's fifteenth largest economy, occupied sixth place in the world in credit card use (*El Financiero* May 22, 1992: 26). Revolving credit lines, which offered the tantalizing promise of easy money to millions of inexperienced consumers, were remarkably easy to obtain. In the early 1990s, customers applying for the basic credit card at either of the country's largest banks needed to show proof of a salary of about $335 per month (Geyer 1991: 4).

While credit card profits exploded, so did the growth of nonperforming loans. (*Expansion*, August 18, 1993: 349; *Los Angeles Times*, September 8,

**Table 4.3**
**Percent Growth of Consumer Credit (1989–1992)**

|                   | 1989 | 1990 | 1991 | 1992* |
|-------------------|------|------|------|-------|
| Credit Cards      | 109  | 116  | 71   | 65    |
| Consumer Durables | 125  | 124  | 181  | 196   |
| Home Loans        | 341  | 147  | 268  | 171   |
| TOTAL             | 125  | 119  | 97   | 96    |

*Note:* *August 1991–August 1992.

*Source:* Banco de México (cited in Mansell 1993).

1993: D4). While the latter is typically factored into risk analyses, the eye of default far surpassed rates of expansion of consumer credit. Table 4.4 demonstrates the alarming increase in the rate of default in the Mexican banking system.[18]

Although the collapse of the banking sector eventually became a debacle for the PRI, during Salinas's presidency the political fallout from protection was minimal. The main reason was that the groups most harmed by the policy were either politically marginal or could not readily perceive the distributional consequences. In addition, middle-class consumers, after ten years of austerity, were delighted with the easy credit offered by the new bankers. During Salinas's term, the most salient fact about privatized banks for millions of Mexican consumers was the satisfaction of years of pent-up demand.

Small and medium business represented the only organized voice against protection. While most smaller entrepreneurs remained squeezed out of the credit markets, even those qualifying had to pay interest spreads far higher than their counterparts in countries they now had to compete against in open markets.[19] Two years after the reprivatization, two ITAM economists found that compared with a sample of industrialized countries, "the Mexican banks demonstrate higher [interest] rates. . . . This might be additional evidence of the monopoly power and the lack of competition faced by Mexican banks" (Gavito and Trigueros 1994: 203).

A report by a CIDAC, an independent Mexican research institute, concluded that requirements for small business were made prohibitively strict: "The present instruments of financing are designed for large firms, limiting access for smaller ones: the requirements are excessive, credit is scarce and expensive, collateral is very high" (*El Financiero*, October 19, 1992: 40). ANIT, an independent association of small industrialists, complained that

Table 4.4
Non-Performing Loan Portfolio of Mexican Commercial Banks* (1988–1994)

| | 1988 | 1989 | 1990 | 1991 | 1992 | 1993 | 1994** |
|---|---|---|---|---|---|---|---|
| Manufacturing | 197 | 344 | 556 | 1,095 | 2,026 | 3,070 | 3,685 |
| Construction | 130 | 154 | 250 | 571 | 1,003 | 1,969 | 1,993 |
| Industry, Energy, Mining | 429 | 589 | 993 | 1,940 | 3,771 | 6,243 | 7,232 |
| Consumer Credit | 86 | 196 | 467 | 717 | 3,495 | 5,475 | 6,697 |
| Transport | 8 | 14 | 42 | 108 | 275 | 544 | 633 |
| Service Sector | 192 | 420 | 1,019 | 1,638 | 4,911 | 7,447 | 10,131 |
| TOTAL (combined industry and services) | 621 | 1,009 | 2,013 | 3,578 | 8,681 | 1,3690 | 17,364 |

*Notes:* *Millions of new pesos
       **Through May

*Source:* Banco de México, cited in Salinas de Gotari (1994: 119).


limited banking competition denied small firms the opportunity to recapitalize and increase competitiveness" (*El Financiero,* June 3, 1992: 14). Even the officially linked industry association Canacintra expressed its displeasure. Vice President José Antonio Murra remarked: "Sincerely, it's a scandal that the negotiation of financial services didn't consider that the second most important resource of an enterprise—after human capital—is money. We disagree with the lack of credit competition that we have" (*El Norte,* October 8, 1992).

However, while large in number, small business did not represent a significant political threat to the PRI. First, because the financial system had been so shallow for so long, utilized mostly by large corporate borrowers, by the end of Salinas's term less than a quarter of microenterprise had even applied for bank credit in formal markets (*El Financiero,* December 9, 1994: 30A). Indeed, although small business loans were scarce and costly, the privatized institutions were offering more credit than the nationalized banks had in the previous decade.

Second, and more importantly, small business simply did not have much political clout in the 1990s. Its representative association, Canacintra, had been powerless to halt the rapid pace of trade liberalization in the late 1980s. Because of the PRI's control over Canacintra's organizational resources and its ability to shield the association from independent organizations seeking to steal its membership, Salinas was able to prevent the small producers from effectively articulating their opposition to government policies that threatened the interests of its members (Davis 1992: 664–666; Shadlen 1997).

If interest groups did little to oppose bank protection, opposition parties did even less. On the left, the PRD might have been expected to demand economic relief for small producers and portray the financial sector as betraying ordinary Mexicans struggling to make ends meet. However, the party's economic nationalism and suspicion of U.S. domination made it difficult to support selling a major part of the financial sector to foreigners. PRD candidate Cárdeñas declined to openly support a greater opening to foreign banks (*El Financiero*, June 12, 1994: 45). On the right, the PAN also failed to make a campaign issue out of bank protection. Although PAN *diputado* David Vargas declared that his party would support a financial opening in principle, when asked why this perspective had not translated into an articulated political position, he explained: "To be frank with you, PAN has not done much research on this issue. We have many other important issues during this election, and this one has not received much attention among our candidates."[20]

## GLOBAL CAPITAL AND FIXED EXCHANGE RATES

The dramatic expansion of the securities sector and the central role of foreign capital under Salinas were made possible by Mexico's return to international investment credibility. While the internationalization of capital was consistent with the technocrats' new development model and liberal ideology, it also reinforced the political support not only of the wealthiest finance capitalists who bought the banks, but also the major industrial and commercial entrepreneurs who benefited from Mexico's triumphant return to the global market.

The dark side of this openness to capital, however, was the government's dangerous overvaluation of the exchange rate. The so-called 'crawling peg' was largely responsible for the speculative currency bubble that burst during the first weeks of the Zedillo administration. The peg flew in the face of the government's objectives of long-term macroeconomic stability and balanced trade. The policy reflects the PRI's effort to maintain the price stability that underlay labor's acceptance of liberalization and, more importantly, to subsidize consumption and borrowing for middle-class and corporate constituencies.

### Internationalization and the Exchange Rate Commitment

Whereas the de la Madrid *sexenio* was characterized by the ceaseless effort to repatriate Mexican capital back to within national borders, the Salinas years were distinguished by their aggressively global orientation. The linchpin of the economic transformation was international capital. By itself, argued its leaders, Mexico lacked the resources to modernize its backward and uncompetitive economy. As Mexico's leading business weekly observed near the end of Salinas's term, "The incapacity of the Mexican financial system to provide enterprises with necessary credit flows, the high cost of credit, and economic globalization, have led to a constant search overseas for alternative financing" (*Expansion*, February 3, 1993: 17). As President Salinas explained,

The evolution of the national economy is influenced more and more by the changing conditions of the international economic environment. We are determined to direct this external impact and not to receive it passively. That is why we diversified and deepened our linkages to countries and blocs which are the indisputable signs of the dynamic world transformation. (*Gobierno Mexicano*, April 1991: 30–31)

Mexican policy makers realized that foreign capital inflows could not be taken for granted. According to Salinas's chief-of-staff José Córdoba Montoya, "During the decade of the 90s, the capacity to compete for financial resources will define the opportunities to revitalize the productive apparatus [and] undertake structural changes" (Córdoba Montoya 1992: 61–62).

### The Bolsa Goes Global

In April 1990, the new Mexican Stock Exchange building opened on Paseo Reforma, a gleaming blue-glass skyscraper dominating the capital's crowded skyline and seeming to confirm Salinas's promise that Mexico was leaving behind its third-world status. The stock market was the vehicle through which the Mexican government would procure capital for development and strengthen its alliance with big business. By eliminating most restrictions on foreign participation in the Mexican stock market, and by stimulating Mexican equities trading abroad, the Salinas administration enabled the country's largest corporations to increase their value and gain access to unprecedented levels of financing.[21] The global orientation of the *bolsa* put billions of foreign dollars at the disposal of Mexico's leading companies.

The *Bolsa* has been, in practice, the backbone that sustains in large measure Salinas' economic policy. It plays a key role in three principal aspects of the neoliberal reforms of the *sexenio*: modernization and opening of the economy, attraction of foreign investment, and the strengthening and concentration of large capital. (Carlsen 1993: 108)

A number of factors contributed to the phenomenal growth in the value of the Mexican stock market during the Salinas years: an improved economic environment, reduced debt obligations, lower interest rates and higher oil prices all contributed to "an atmosphere of abundance and optimism that surrounds and probably injects resources into the current stock market boom" (Ejea and Leriche 1991: 52).

In addition, the government expanded opportunities for domestic firms to trade on the *bolsa*. In April 1992, the Comisión Nacional de Valores (CNV) eliminated the restriction upon brokerage houses to trade stocks on their own account. In effect, it let brokers "play the market" themselves, rather than playing exclusively for the commissions received from investor clients. According to a U.S. Treasury analyst, "This change is expected to increase the volume of shares traded and to provide liquidity for more issues" (Low 1992: 36).

Using its development bank, the government also continued to promote the stock market through direct purchasing and trading of shares. As the *bolsa* recovered from the 1987 crash, Nacional Financiera (Nafin) returned as one of the market's most influential players. As during the de la Madrid administration, official figures of Nafin's participation were not made public. Yet it was widely understood among traders that the bank played a pivotal role in stabilizing prices and ensuring liquidity. As an analyst from Banobras recalled: "It was amazing. There might be a slide in the price index for most of the day. But like magic, just before the trading closed, you'd see the index suddenly start to move up. Everyone knew what was going on."[22]

While the stock market became more attractive as a result of economic and regulatory improvement, as well as public sector intervention, what brought the avalanche of foreign capital were direct changes in rules that internationalized Mexican equity markets. The 1989 Act to Promote Domestic Investment and Regulate Foreign Investment expanded the level of foreign shareholding permitted in domestic companies. Firms that sought the active participation of foreign partners could now issue up to 49 percent of stock capital to foreigners through series "B" shares. In 1990, foreign participation was further stimulated when Nafin set up a trust fund through which foreigners could buy corporate shares previously restricted to Mexican nationals. In the same year, the CNV created series "C" stocks for banks and brokerages, shares made available to foreigners (without voting rights) for up to 30 percent of total ownership.

In just a few months, over eighty Mexican firms were listing stock through Nafin. A Washington-based investment banker beamed: "It opens up virtually the whole market" (*Wall Street Journal*, March 26, 1990: C12). By September 1990, after less than a year of operation, the Nafin fund had attracted over half a billion dollars from overseas (*Mercado de Valores*, October 1990).

At the same time that Mexico pursued foreign participation in its securities market, the U.S. government liberalized the rules by which foreign firms could be listed on American stock exchanges. In April 1990, so-called 'Rule 144' and 'Regulation S' reforms made by the American Securities and Exchange Commission (SEC) enabled Mexico's largest companies to issue American Depository Receipts (ADRs). By 1993, Teléfonos de México (Telmex) ADRs became the most actively traded foreign issue on the New York Stock Exchange, and Mexico boasted the second largest placement of ADRs in the world, trailing only England (*El Economista*, March 17, 1994: 17).

The results of liberalization and reform of equity markets were impressive. Between the end of 1987 and 1991, trading increased fivefold, while market capitalization reached $101 billion, a tenfold increase. During the same period, the price index of the *bolsa* multiplied twelve times; almost 120 percent in 1991 alone (*LatinFinance*, July 1992: 53). In 1993, the average yield in the Mexican stock market reached 48 percent, almost triple the interest offered on twenty-eight–day Certificado de la Tesorería (Cetes) (*Excelsior*, January 7, 1994).

Moreover, this growth was clearly driven by foreign investment. (See Figure 4.2.) By 1992, foreigners controlled over $28 billion worth of the Mexican stock market. Whereas foreign capitalization of the Mexican stock market stood at 11 percent in 1990, by 1993 it reached over 22 percent (Baker 1993: 31). However, this figure is misleading, as it covers all stocks listed on the Bolsa Mexicana de Valores (BMV), the vast majority of which were illiquid. When only traded stocks are considered, by the end of Salinas's term, foreign control probably approached half the market. In 1992, Mexico captured over 40 percent of all ADRs issued through Rule 144A, more than three times the amount of Taiwan, its nearest competitor (*LatinFinance*, May 1993: 41). According to BMV planning director Benardo González, "Foreigners control more than 50 percent of the float [trading]

**Figure 4.2**
**Foreign Investment into Mexican Stock Market (1989–1993)***

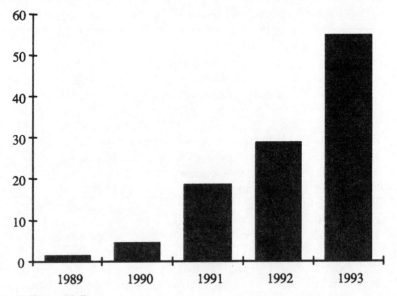

*Note:* *Billions of dollars

*Source:* CNV, *Annual Report.*

in the market," adding, "in many stocks, like Telmex and ICA, they have almost complete control" (*LatinFinance*, March 1993: 33).

Notwithstanding the fantastic statistics of growth in Mexican equity markets, very few enterprises listed on the BMV actually benefited by the expansion of foreign participation. Just as the banking industry was dominated by a few large firms, so did a handful of giant corporations receive the vast majority of capital invested in the BMV. By 1993, just five firms received 77 percent, and of this group, Telmex alone took over half (*El Financiero International* April 19, 1993).

### Trade Deficit and Foreign Capital

The Achilles heel of the Mexican model was the balance of payments gap, which was the result of trade opening and an increasingly overvalued currency. A modest trade surplus in 1987 had become a $14 billion deficit by 1991. In 1994, Mexico imported $30 billion more than it exported, a shortfall equal to 7 percent of GDP. In December 1987, the central bank had reserves equivalent to one full year of imports, compared to just over two months in 1994 (*El Financiero*, December 5, 1994: 4). Even if Mexico reduced the growth of imports by half between 1994 and 2000, while increasing its exports by half, the commercial deficit would still grow by 46 percent, requiring over $100 billion in fresh capital to cover the gap (*El Inversionista Mexicano*, August 29, 1994: 2).

Despite growing concern that the Mexican imbalance was unsustainable, financial authorities shrugged off criticism with two arguments. First, the deficit was evidence that the country was acquiring needed capital to modernize and increase competitiveness. In his final annual report, President Salinas explained: "Such a deficit proves the country is making use of foreign resources to expand the productive plant at a faster pace than it could if it depended solely on national financing" (Salinas de Gotari 1994).

Unfortunately, Mexico's export growth was inextricably linked to buying ever greater amounts of goods from abroad. Notwithstanding the government's claims, from 1987 to 1992 purchases of foreign capital goods remained stagnant as a proportion of the total import bill, while consumer imports more than doubled, reaching over half the amount of the trade deficit by 1994. More ominously, intermediate goods, typically premanufactured inputs used by Mexican exporters, continued to account for well over half of all imports. From 1989 to 1993, while Mexican non-*maquiladora* (foreign-owned manufacturing and assembly plants in Mexico) exports rose 31.9 percent, from $22.8 billion to $30 billion, an annual increase of 7.2 percent, non-*maquiladora* imports rose by an astonishing 109 percent, from $23.4 billion to $48.9 billion, an average of 20.2 percent per year (*El Inversionista Mexicano*, August 29, 1994).

Second, the government argued that because the Mexican economy was attracting more than enough capital to cover the trade gap, the country had regained international confidence (*Carpeta Mexico* 1993: 27). In other words, the reason the current account deficit had become so large was that the global investment community had enough faith in Mexico's new development model to fund the gap.

However, the data show that the vast majority of foreign capital was invested in Mexico for the unambiguous purpose of extracting financial rents, while a decreasing proportion went to direct investment. As Figure 4.3 shows, foreign investment was practically negligible in 1988 but reached well over $30 billion by 1993. Moreover, while direct foreign investment increased, mostly through Mexico's growing *maquiladora* industries, by 1992, it amounted to only 1.6 percent of Mexican GDP, less than one-third the level received by Chile and a number of Asian competitors (*LatinFinance,* July 1992:58).

To cover the gap, Mexico looked to foreign capital, "the oxygen of Salinas' economic strategy" (*The Banker,* April 1990: 49). In 1990, the Salinas administration changed regulations in the Mexican securities market to allow foreign investors to enter for the first time since before the Revolution. Moreover, because treasury bills and longer term bonds were auctioned on the open market, they offered extremely attractive yields, especially when compared to the historically low rates offered on American T-bills during the first years of the decade.

In order to cover Mexico's growing current account deficit, the central bank had to acquire massive amounts of dollars abroad. Because the main-

**Figure 4.3**
**Breakdown of Mexican Internal Debt (1987-1993)\***

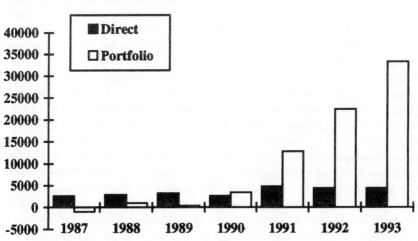

*Note:* \*Millions of dollars

*Source:* Banco de México, *The Mexican Economy:* 1997, 297.

tenance of Mexico's trade deficit was dependent on the steady and growing inflow of dollars from abroad, the state took measures to ensure investor confidence. During the first year of the Salinas administration, at the end of 1989, the Finance Ministry authorized the creation of several new public debt "hedging" instruments, whose main purpose was to sustain the flow of foreign capital by eliminating the risks of future macroeconomic adjustments. The *ajustabono* was a long-term instrument that paid interest after adjusting for inflation, while the *tesobono* guaranteed payment indexed to the exchange rate at time of purchase.[23]

The creation of the *tesobono* represented the government's pledge to investors that it would not let the value of the currency slide. The private sector correctly interpreted these capital market innovations "as a self-binding commitment to fulfill the intended discipline in public finances" (Aspe 1992: 325). The director of the central bank's economic research unit explained: "The use of the exchange rate as a nominal anchor implies that the government is committed to adjust all its policies so as to guarantee the stability of the exchange rate" (Carstens 1994: 75).

The foreign response to Mexican interest rates and the sophisticated array of instruments offered was astonishing. In fact, the vast majority of foreign capital invested in Mexico went into public debt instruments, particular Cetes and, toward the end of Salinas's term, hedging instruments. By September 1993, foreigners possessed 60 percent of short-term Cetes, which offered real rates twice as high as U.S. notes; 87 percent of *tesobonos*; and 57 percent of *ajustabonos* (*La Jornada*, October 13, 1993). Although the Salinas administration could boast that it had reduced Mexico's internal debt from 28 percent to 10 percent of GDP, well over half of this total—over $22 billion—was in the hands of foreign investors (*Alto Nivel*, November 1993: 4–5). According to the *bolsa*, foreign participation in the placement of government securities grew by 756 percent between their introduction in 1991 and August 1994 (*Mercado de Valores*, November–December 1994: 31). See Figure 4.4.

Given the opportunities for spectacular profits, the only calculation an investment bank or money management firm needed to make was the likelihood of default. For several years, the efforts of the Salinas administration succeeded in instilling confidence in the international financial community. "The great advantage of the money market is its security. No matter what, if you invest in it you get an assured yield, maybe not as high as you could get in the stock market, but a good yield. . . . And it's all done under the administration of experts, while the investor scratches his stomach and dedicates his energies to other things" (*Expansión*, November 21, 1990: 59).

At the end of 1993, economist Laura Carlsen succinctly described the role played by foreign investment in Mexico's economic model: "The importance of attracting foreign capital in the *bolsa* cannot be underestimated. Currently it represents the only support for the monetary policy of overv-

**Figure 4.4**
**Breakdown of Mexican Internal Debt (1989–1994)**

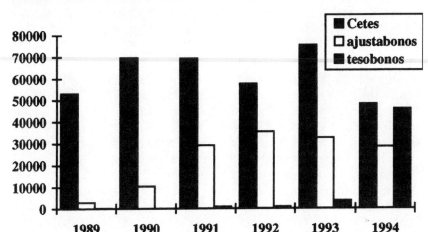

*Source:* SHCP (cited in Salinas de Gotari 1994: 100).

aluation of the peso and the current account deficit that had grown enormously during the *sexenio*" (Carlsen 1993: 112). As two Mexican economists observed in 1992, "The American citizen that walks the streets of New York, Chicago and Los Angeles doesn't know it, but the Mexican economy has been kept stable in recent years, thanks to him. . . . Without [foreign] money coming into Mexican financial markets, our finances would have been in crisis several months ago, since it would not have possible to finance the current account deficit" (Amador and Quintana 1992: 3–4).

*The Exchange Rate Trap*

During Salinas's first month as president, the fixed exchange rate inherited from the inflationary 1980s was relaxed somewhat when the central bank established a so-called 'crawling peg,' within which the peso could fluctuate relative to the dollar on a daily basis. Although this "restricted band" allowed moderate nominal devaluation of the peso, because the amount the currency could slide was far less than the difference between the inflation rates of Mexico and the United States, the result was cumulative overvaluation.

Notwithstanding the enthusiastic reception of Mexican debt issues among the foreign investment community, the relationship between the trade deficit and the exchange rate represented a vicious circle in Mexico's macroeconomic model. (See Figure 4.5.) Because the crawling peg continued to inflate the peso, imports became more affordable, further increasing the current account deficit. In order to cover the gap, the central bank had to acquire massive amounts of dollars from abroad, which in turn required the state to open the securities market to foreign investors to sustain the peso's value. However, because the strong currency made imports cheaper, the trade deficit grew ever larger and had to be covered with increasing inflows of foreign capital.

In such a precarious environment, any event that interfered with increased capital inflows would render this dynamic unsustainable. That event came in the form of increased U.S. interest rates in 1994. Fear of inflation following moderate U.S. growth led the Federal Reserve to almost double interest rates in 1994, from 3 percent to 5.5 percent. As a consequence, the rate of return on most U.S. securities rose, making these highly secure investments far more financially attractive relative to those issued in any developing country, including Mexico.

In the second trimester of 1994, as a result of increased interest rates in the United States and the perception of social instability in Mexico following political assassinations and the Chiapas uprising, foreign capital inflows dropped by 75 percent. The government's scramble to adjust interest rates to bring back skeptical investors demonstrated "the structural incapacity of the private sector to generate the foreign exchange needed to finance its own development" (*El Financiero* December 5, 1994: 4). In a desperate

**Figure 4.5**
**Relationship Between Exchange Rate and Capital Inflows**

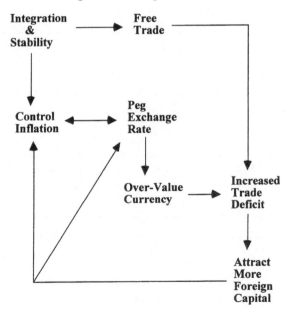

effort to defend the peso, the Salinas administration depleted foreign exchange reserves from a high of $30 billion to just $6 billion by the end of the year. In December alone, between $4 and $6 billion left the country.

In July 1994, an influential business newsletter published data showing that between August 4 and December 29 the Mexican government would amortize $20.4 billion in *tesobonos*, then the equivalent of 78 percent of international reserves (*El Inversionista Mexicano*, July 25, 1994). Even more ominously, data gathered from the BMV confirmed N$26.7 billion in *tesobonos* circulating by the end of 1993, which was almost five times the amount stated in the official economic report of the Finance Ministry's third trimester economic report. By March 1994, the sum had reached N$48.2 billion, over eight times the Finance Ministry figure. Incredibly, just two months later, *tesobonos* valued at over N$100 billion—almost US $30 billion—had become part of Mexico's public debt. A year-end report by the Finance Ministry revealed that after growing almost 20 percent in 1993, the amount of government securities in circulation, bloated by the massive issue of *tesobonos*, soared by 72 percent in 1994 (*El Financiero*, November 3, 1994: 3A).

On December 20, 1994, just three weeks into the Zedillo administration, the exchange rate band was widened by 15.3 percent. Investors panicked immediately and made a run on the peso. The next day, the Finance Ministry announced that the peso would float freely against the dollar. Its value plummeted to half its nominal value, and Mexico plunged immediately into a depression.

### The Politics of Overvaluation

Why did the highly ideological group of neoliberal economists that ran Mexican policy insist on distorting foreign exchange markets, particularly given the unsustainable dynamic of the crawling peg? Part of the reason for the government's stubbornness was the damage that devaluation had already done to the legitimacy and credibility of the ruling party. Each of the three previous presidents had allowed the peso to collapse. President López Portillo, who declared that "the president who devalues is devalued," would regret that he publicly vowed to defend the peso "like a dog" shortly before he was forced to let the peso collapse in 1982. Salinas's predecessor, Miguel de la Madrid, had been unable to tame triple-digit inflation for most of his term. Mexicans had come to equate a weakening currency not only with high inflation, recession, and economic incompetence, but also with national humiliation. As a leading Mexican business columnist observed, among the Mexican policy-making elite, "To pronounce the word devaluation is heresy and provokes [political] ex-communication and punishment" (*Proceso*, March 1, 1994: 34).

Yet the legacy of devaluation cannot explain the Salinas administration's refusal to simply slow the overvaluation of the currency. In the early 1990s, a modest expansion of the exchange rate band would have eased the trade deficit and stabilized the peso's value relative to the dollar, at a time when Mexico's inflation rate was the lowest in Latin America. Economists and investment counselors had been showing increasing anxiety over the valuation of the peso (Dornbusch and Werner 1994: 253; Hanke and Walters 1994: 161; Vidal 1994: 1062, *Mexico Insight*, May 1, 1994: 19). If free markets provided the optimal degree of efficiency and distribution of capital, why not let foreign exchange markets decide how much the peso should be worth, or at least widen the band significantly?

Part of the reason for Salinas's resistance to changing the exchange rate may have been his desire to successfully negotiate the North American Free Trade Agreement (NAFTA). Some observers argued that Mexico's current account deficit with its northern neighbor was helping convince legislators who feared American job losses that integration would be a boon to the economy. The American trade surplus was evidence that Mexico was creating more employment than it was taking away. The Mexicans might have been concerned that a weaker peso could undermine support for the treaty in the U.S. Congress.

NAFTA may have been an added incentive to maintain the exchange rate peg, but it was doubtfully decisive. The political salience of Mexico's crawling peg band width was negligible—few Americans even knew what it was or why it was potentially important—especially compared to headline-grabbing issues like labor and environmental standards. Moreover, while loosening the band in 1992 or early 1993 probably would have diminished the U.S. trade surplus somewhat, it also would have earned the Mexican government high marks from leading international economists who feared the fixed rate was unsustainable. In short, the technical debate over whether devaluation was good or bad would most likely have been a political wash.

The primary reason for Salinas's apparently deliberate strategy to overvalue the peso was that virtually all of the domestic interests that exercised influence over the PRI's political future were united, either implicitly or explicitly, in their support of the status quo. For bankers and large industrialists, the middle class, and workers, Mexico's crawling peg provided important economic benefits. Searching for a way to satisfy such disparate groups, the ruling party found itself under intense pressure to maintain an increasingly unsustainable "please all" exchange rate policy. What is remarkable about overvaluation is that it had virtually no detractors. In effect, as long as the illusion of currency stability could be maintained, the pegged exchange rate created no losers.

### The Legacy of Inflation

Because inflation had run out of control for so long, the containment of price increases became the most immediate source of concern among the business community. In fact, inflation fighting was such a high priority that the state managed to stifle business opposition to the acceleration of trade liberalization in the late 1980s by tying the economic opening to the renewal of negotiations for a price stability agreement with unions (Kaufman et al. 1992: 43). Private sector leaders routinely argued that the benefits of maintaining confidence and a stable currency outweighed the dangers of overvaluation.[24] In May 1990, the Center for Private Sector Economic Studies maintained that the elimination of inflation was the number one priority for business and that the fixed exchange rate was the key to its achievement (*El Financiero*, May 24, 1990: 3). Three years later, Grupo Moneda, one of Mexico's leading private sector think tanks, called the exchange rate "the principal thermometer of the success of president Salinas' economic policy" and argued that the high peso/dollar parity was necessary to keep inflation under control (*Reforma*, December 16, 1993; *Excelsior*, November 24, 1993).

Even those industrial interests that might have been expected to gain competitiveness through a devaluation supported the peg. Because so much of the value-added in Mexican manufacturing came from foreign inputs, a weakened peso would result in higher production costs. In 1992, Canacintra's president contended: "The peso is in better shape than the dollar . . . it benefits importers, above all in capital and intermediate goods." He added, "If we devalue without a doubt it will provoke inflationary pressures" (*El Norte*, September 29, 1992). In 1993, the National Council of Foreign Commerce acknowledged that overvaluation was a drag on competitiveness, yet insisted that a devaluation was not the strategy to increase exports or reduce the commercial deficit (*El Norte*, April 3, 1993).

### Big Business and Foreign Debt

The crawling peg also provided specific economic benefits for Mexico's most influential private sector actors. Just as a strong peso subsidized foreign goods, it also reduced the costs of credit obtained on international capital markets, making it much cheaper for Mexican corporations to borrow.

The devaluations of the 1980s had left the largest Mexican businesses exposed to a catastrophic increase in the level of real foreign debt. By the end of the de la Madrid administration, the age of the sliding peso appeared to have come to an end. A Mexican business journalist observed that the financial burden of business debt was reduced in large part due to the "freezing of the exchange rate, in that the value of debt contracted in dollars has reduced its burden in national currency for those enterprises that assumed these obligations" (Stein Velasco 1988: 15).

Significantly, the government led the way back to foreign capital markets. In June 1989, Banco de Comercio Exterior (Bancomext) issued a $100 million Eurobond issue, while Petroleros de Mexico (Pemex) and Nafin tapped the U.S. market in 1991. An IMF economist stated: "These issues . . . were particularly important, in that they established a complete yield curve for Mexican credit, which constitutes an important benchmark for future bond issues." He added that "it is accepted generally that the private sector has benefited from the leadership of the public sector in this regard" (Szymczak 1992: 66,70).

Although Mexico's largest firms enjoyed the most access to domestic credit, Mexican banks were unable to supply either sufficient quantities or competitive interest rates. As Mexico's director of public credit conceded in 1993, "Many Mexican companies want to raise funds in dollars. The difference between Mexican and U.S. interest rates is too attractive to pass up" (*LatinFinance*, March 1993: 67). A Salomon Brothers analyst working in Mexico discovered "a completely new mentality—a new, more savvy CFO. . . . I remember going on early sales trips with the corporate finance people when you'd have to sit down and explain to the CFO what equity was. Now the same guys expect us to offer them collared swaps" (House 1994: 53–54).

When large firms re-entered global capital markets in the 1990s, they did so in a big way (see Figure 4.6). Among the largest fifty-nine economic groups, dollar-denominated debt doubled between 1988 and 1991, reaching over half total liabilities (Garrido 1994). By 1991, Mexico accounted for 90

**Figure 4.6**
**Foreign Debt Placements by Mexican Entities (1988–1993)***

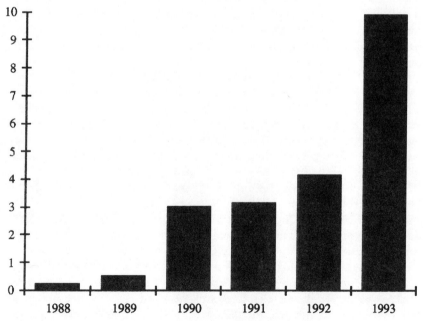

*Note:* *Billions of dollars

*Source:* CNV, *Annual Report.*

percent of the volume of total Latin American international bond issues (*LatinFinance*, May 1991: 19). At the beginning of 1993, *LatinFinance* chose Mexico as "this year's top bet for [international finance] business out of Latin America."

While the government actively promoted capital inflow as a key part of its efforts to take advantage of financial integration, it remained keenly aware that its success was made possible largely because of a semi-fixed exchange rate. When the government tightened the crawling peg from forty to twenty centavos per day at the end of 1991, it justified its action in large measure as a benefit to large Mexican firms: "The slower exchange rate crawl would avoid price increases on imported inputs and machinery, as well as financial costs for sectors indebted in dollars" (*El Financiero*, November 25, 1991: 87).

### Courting the Middle Class

One of the greatest political assets of a strong peso was greater purchasing power. The peg acted as a subsidy on goods and services from abroad. For middle class consumers, the fixed exchange rate reduced the price of imported groceries and department store luxury items, consumer durables, foreign travel, and domestic manufactures made with foreign inputs. Many of these goods became important cultural symbols of prestige, sophistication, and cosmopolitanism. The strong currency thus provided highly valued economic goods to a pivotal group whose electoral support the PRI had to regain. The Mexican middle class had flirted dangerously with both opposition parties in 1988. Just a few years into Salinas's term, white-collar workers and professionals were becoming used to Levis, high status cars, and trips to Disneyland.

At the same time that an overvalued currency added purchasing power to middle class wallets, the cost of living in Mexico, particularly the major cities, had skyrocketed. Moreover, the vast majority of Mexican wage earners had not even come close to recovering the real wages they had enjoyed before the 1982 debt crisis. With most Mexicans still complaining after over a decade of recession that their money bought too little, it was an unwise politician who argued that the peso was worth too much!

For this reason, political opposition to the maintenance of the exchange rate was extremely limited. On the left, Revolutionary Democratic Party (PRD) presidential candidate Cuauhtémoc Cárdenas stated in April 1994 that because of the PRI's mismanagement of economic policy, "we are living a predevaluation scenario." However, Cárdenas refused to endorse any kind of exchange rate adjustment, explaining: "The government has to take measures for economic recovery and it's not taking them. I don't know if a devaluation really would be such a measure. I do not pronounce myself in favor of it; that's an affair for the Banco de México, which knows what it has to do. I am not recommending, I am only indicating" (*El Economista*, April 14, 1994: 48).

On the right, the free market-oriented National Action Party (PAN) also backed away from an open attack on government policy. The main opposition party declined to make the abstract and confusing policy area of exchange rates an issue. Indeed, not until after the election was over did PAN legislators press the government to stop defending the peso with reserves (*El Financiero*, December 6, 1994: 10). At no time during the course of the presidential campaign did PAN candidate Diego Fernandez make devaluation a policy issue. To have done so would have exposed his party to withering attacks from PRI politicians and their Ph.D.-wielding technocrats. With Mexican recovery finally within sight, the PAN would be accused of sapping purchasing power and inviting a new round of inflation. That position surely would have undermined support among PAN's main constituencies—small businessmen and import-consuming professionals.

*Keeping Labor on Board*

Although the PRI's strongest constituency had been organized labor since the 1930s, a number of measures widely perceived to undermine union strength and worker welfare had begun to expose the Salinas administration to increasing labor criticism. Even more disturbing than job loss resulting from trade liberalization and the jailing of corrupt (but popular) union leaders was the unchecked decline in workers' living standards. (*El Financiero*, November 25, 1994: 24).

Since 1987, the PRI had pursued macroeconomic stability through a series of social "pacts," official agreements that bound the government to fulfill spending, taxation and deficit promises, labor to refrain from wage demands, and business to contain price hikes. While the unions objected to the Salinas administration's strict monetarism, they coincided entirely with its manipulation of the currency to fight inflation and strongly supported the exchange rate peg. All pacts made through the end of the Salinas administration included the "crawling peg" provision, "the most essential element of the *pacto*" (Demirors 1994: 6).

The consensus remains that considerable purchasing power has been lost and labor was not about to accept an extension of wage and price controls that did not "guarantee" some additional controls on inflation. Labor certainly would not endorse a pact that would accelerate the devaluation of the peso as that would be an *ipso facto* endorsement of a bulge in prices. (*Mexico Business News*, June 1990: A7)

*Limits to State Authority*

Why was the ruling party willing to alienate its bases of social support with painful liberalization policies, but not willing to risk adjusting the popular but unsustainable exchange rate? Macroeconomic discipline since the mid-1980s had hurt labor, the party's core constituencies, while trade opening had fallen particularly hard on small businesses. Similarly, Salinas did not have second thoughts about eliminating the communal *ejido* farms that had formed the basis for small-holder agricultural production since the 1930s.

The PRI's uneven level of policy autonomy is largely explained by the way its policies were evaluated by a skeptical electorate. The market-based development model would have been impossible without adopting basic liberalization policies that undermined the interests of workers, entrepreneurs, and peasants. The party plausibly declared that such measures were necessary in order to restore stability and make the economy competitive. Moreover, given the abject failure of statism since the 1970s, such arguments were broadly, if grudgingly accepted by diverse economic interests weary of stagnation and crisis.

However, to these constituencies, a solid currency represented the cornerstone of the new model. Steadily falling inflation and increased buying power were evidence that the model was working. By the final years of Salinas's term, the ruling party's own criteria for economic success had been widely accepted by voters who now had real electoral choices. Notwithstanding growing trade deficits and volatile capital inflows, the Mexican government had very little political room to maneuver on currency policy. While the PRI was able to sell difficult economic reforms as the key stability and growth, the exchange rate became the indicator upon which the government's economic performance would be judged.

## CONCLUSION: EVALUATING DOMESTIC AND INTERNATIONAL CAUSES OF THE CRASH

In the wake of devaluations in East Asia, Russia, and Brazil, there has been increasing recognition of the role played by international capital markets in precipitating domestic currency crises. The volatility of "hot money"—portfolio capital that can be quickly invested and withdrawn—has been identified as a major constraint on the ability of governments in emerging markets to take any action that might undermine confidence among foreign investors with an extremely short time horizon.

Although the influence of international capital over national policy is typically generated implicitly through market signals, in Mexico such pressure was quite direct. The Weston Forum, an international consortium of financial institutions, made very large investments in Mexican government securities during the early 1990s. It included some of the world's premier investment enterprises, including Fidelity Investment Company, Oppenheimer Management Corporation, Putnam Funds Management, Soros Fund Management, Salomon Brothers, Nomura Securities, and the Weston Group. In April 1994, following a slide in the peso's value relative to the dollar, the Forum met in secret meetings with then deputy finance minister

Guillermo Ortiz and central bank administrators to offer "advice" on the direction on Mexican economic policy.

According to a *Wall Street Journal* report, "the suggestions were aggressive." The financiers asked the Mexican officials to refrain from the small daily devaluations permitted under the crawling peg, that the Mexican government assume losses incurred on exchange rate fluctuations beyond the current band, and permission to increase their level of dollar-denominated portfolio investments. Moreover, they suggested that upon adoption of these measures Mexico would receive up to $17 billion in new investments from the consortium and its associates (June 14, 1994: A6). As journalist Douglas Payne concluded, "In effect, the forum wanted Mexico to further overvalue the peso and assume the risk . . . [Weston Forum pressures] explain in significant part why the Mexican government adopted policies that led to the [peso] meltdown" (1995: 22).

Because of such strong arm tactics, as well as more subtle pressures exerted continually by capital markets, some have argued that the international investment community held the Mexican exchange rate hostage. Because the profitability of peso-denominated financial instruments depended directly on currency strength, Mexican technocrats found themselves caught in a "Catch 22"—they could only prevent capital flight by maintaining an exchange rate policy that was ultimately unsustainable. Clearly, the external economic environment mattered.

Yet the pressure exerted by global investors upon the Mexican government presupposes the fact that "hot money" only entered the country as a result of domestic policy decisions in the securities market and exchange rate regime. The internationalization of Mexico's equity and debt markets was not the inevitable result of technology, information, and investor preference; it was the product of government action that opened capital markets quickly and deeply. Mexico's capital market and currency policies under Salinas were conditioned by both economic ideology and the global economic environment. However, the combination, scope and timing of those policies were also based, in large measure, on domestic political opportunities and constraints.

## NOTES

1. On labor relations, see Collier (1992) and de la Garza Toleda (1994). On agricultural relations, see Fox (1994b).

2. See Molinar and Weldon (1990), Camp (1993), and Peritore and Peritore (1993).

3. Author interview with Alonso Lujambio, December 10, 1998, Mexico City.

4. For example, J. P. Morgan floated a $1 billion bridge loan to the group that successfully bid on Bancomer, Mexico's second largest bank. See "The High Price of Bank Sell-Offs," *Euromoney Supplement* (January 1992), 20.

5. A major reason was that the banks had primarily invested in high yield, low-risk government securities. See *Economía Mexicana* (1986): 56–57.

6. See "Banca '93. Impulsarán nuevos bancos competencia," *El Norte*, September 6, 1993.

7. By comparison, charter minimums for American banks are between $1 and $5 million.

8. Author interview with Julio Alfredo Genel, November 28, 1994, Mexico City.

9. Author interview with David Vargas, March 10, 1995, Cámara de Diputados, Mexico City.

10. See especially Suárez Dávila (1994).

11. Author interview, on condition of anonymity, April 4, 1994, Mexico City.

12. See Dresser (1991), Cornelius et al. (1994), and Bruhn (1996).

13. While they concur with critics that Pronasol was politically motivated, the authors of the study do not characterize the program as clientelist, but rather as a classic example of pork-barrel politics. Accordingly, they suggest that Mexico's leaders were simply becoming more responsive to the needs of citizens whose vote actually mattered. Far from being a mechanism to maintain authoritarianism, they conclude, Pronasol was an indicator of democratization.

14. Matt Moffett, "Barrio Brigades," *Wall Street Juornal*, January 8, 1993, A1, A7.

15. In 1992, number two Bancomer enjoyed 108 percent profit growth, while number one Banamex surged 84 percent (Marray 1992: 148–150); In the extensive coverage of high Mexican bank profits, see Smith and Zellner (1993) and Girón (1994: 1074).

16. To be sure, before the nationalization, risk analysis was not a highly developed skill in the Mexican banking sector.

17. Author interview with Alejandro Díaz de Leon, August 10, 1996, Mexico City.

18. Because Mexico used extremely soft accounting standards, these figures significantly underestimate the actual level of bad loans. See Canavan and Pastor (1990).

19. In 1992, banks charged businesses real interest rates over 20 percent, three to four times higher than U.S. levels (*Proceso*, July 13, 1992: 9). Over two years after reprivatization, Mexican medium-size firms paid 25 percent interest and had difficulty obtaining loans longer than six months (*Los Angeles Times*, December 13, 1993: D1).

20. Author interview with PAN Diputado David Vargas, March 10, 1995, Mexico City.

21. For a summary of foreign investment options see AMCB (1991: 12–15).

22. Statement by Alejandra Cullen at public forum on Mexican economy, Berkeley, California, April 29, 1997.

23. *Ajustabonos* offered real interest after covering for inflation, while *tesobonos* guaranteed payment indexed to the exchange rate. For an explanation of how the yields were calculated, see Ana Laura de Coss, "Instrumentos de Inversión que Ofrecen Protección Cambiaria," *El Economista*, October 7, 1994, p. F16.

24. See Alejandro Márquez, "Tipo de Cambio: No Lo Toques, Por Favor," *Expansión*, June 1993; *Gobierno Mexicano*, April 1991, p. 39.

# 5

## After the Fall (1995–1999): The Bank Rescue and the Assertion of Legislative Power

For most of the century, the Institutional Revolutionary Party (PRI) was the exclusive arena for negotiation among diverse economic interests. Since the Revolution, Mexican presidents had mediated conflict among groups that derived their influence through corporatist linkages to the party. The politics of banking regulation and exchange rate policy under President Salinas, while shaped by the rise of viable opposition parties, was about recovering the support of those traditional constituencies. In contrast, the politics of the banking bailout under President Ernesto Zedillo was driven by parties themselves.

In the years following the 1994 peso meltdown, Mexico embarked on a political transformation that owes much to the continued mismanagement of the national banking system. Whereas the previous *sexenio* was about holding on to political power in the face of first serious electoral threat, Zedillo's presidential term would be about holding on to policy-making power even after the opposition's electoral victory. The Democratic Revolution Party (PRD) and National Action Party (PAN) succeeded in taking away the authority of PRI policy makers long accustomed to a legislative rubber stamp, and much of that transformation occurred in the banking system. Indeed, the politicization of banking policy accelerated the process of democratization in Mexico.

### LOSING POLITICAL CONTROL

At the beginning of Zedillo's term, even as the country staggered through possibly the most severe economic reversal of the century, the president and his party seemed to enjoy renewed legitimacy and had managed to distance themselves from the now-disgraced Salinas. Perhaps the most important result of the 1994 election was to prove that the PRI could win without fraud. The widely observed transparency of the election, the independence of the Federal Election Institute, and the pervasive presence of foreign observers gave the PRI a new level of legitimacy (Scherlen 1998: 19–28). Consequently, during 1995 and 1996, financial regulators and economic policy makers enjoyed virtually the same degree of autonomy they had enjoyed for most of the century.

However, while 1997 represented a turning point in the economic crisis, the dawn of recovery had done little to improve the living standards of most Mexicans, who punished the PRI at the polls as never before. On July 6, the PRI lost control of Congress for the first time. Opposition parties won 261 of 500 seats of the lower house. Although the opposition was split ideologically, it united to form a solid majority to take away PRI's control of the Congress. While all 239 PRI representatives boycotted the first session, the PAN and PRD appointed leaders to key committees and installed themselves as the new leaders of the legislature. This event fundamentally reshaped Mexican politics.

Aside from the basic power to pass and block laws, the new majority wielded the important new power to investigate. As one observer of Mexican electoral politics presciently observed shortly before the bank rescue scandal broke open, the loss of a majority removed the PRI's ability to quash formal congressional inquiries (Klesner 1997: 704). While this power threatened individual patronage relationships, its more important function would be to provide the opposition with the forum, legitimacy, and resources to subject the ruling party's economic policies to highly embarrassing public scrutiny.

Prior to the shocking defeat, focusing exclusively on the PRI had been a legitimate way to study economic policy making: The party's remarkable combination of authoritarianism, social inclusiveness, and patronage typically covered the full range of Mexican political actors and pressures. Social strains and political protest in Mexico were worked out within the party, as it reinvented itself on multiple occasions. However, when the PRD and PAN took over the *cámara de diputados* (lower house of Congress), PRI leaders and technocrats lost control of the policy-making process. Almost overnight economic reform became the product of struggle within a robust multiparty system. As Denise Dresser concluded, "In the past, in order to decipher Mexico, Americans focused on the presidency and the PRI. In the future, the spotlight will shift to Congress" (Dresser 1998: 60).

### Financial Aftermath of the Peso Crisis

The year 1995 was desperate. Just three months after the devaluation, the Mexican economy was unrecognizable, with consumption down by half. Automobile sales fell over 60 percent between January and February 1995, while restaurant sales went down between 20 and 40 percent. Hospitals and private medical services fell by 40 percent, while luxuries such as international airline tickets plummeted by 75 percent (*Proceso*, March 27, 1995: 8).

The United States government undertook unprecedented measures in an attempt to restore economic stability in Mexico. In March 1995, over the strenuous objections of the Republican Congress, the Clinton administration orchestrated a $50 billion rescue package with the IMF and other donor countries. Government officials cited Mexico's rapidly deteriorating economy, the likelihood of default on almost $30 billion in *tesobonos* that would come due in 1995, the potential loss of U.S. jobs resulting from a Mexican collapse, as well as concerns about social stability and immigration. Since U.S. legislators threatened to reject Clinton's proposal to provide a large capital infusion to bolster Mexico's financial solvency, the Treasury Department utilized its rarely-used Exchange Stabilization Fund (ESF) to make a $20 billion credit line available to the Banco de México without the need for Congressional approval.

Officials from all three North American governments, the IMF, and World Bank maintained that the financial package was instrumental in restoring macroeconomic stability and international financial credibility.[1] The plan, however, was assailed by political and academic critics from both countries and on both sides of the political spectrum. Mexican progressives argued that bailout punished the innocent and vulnerable, because harsh budget cutbacks required by the IMF fell disproportionately on the poor (NCD 1995). Conservatives in the United States argued that the bailout rewarded the guilty and the rich, ensuring repayment to wealthy foreign investors who had gambled in the risky Mexican securities market at the expense of U.S. and Mexican taxpayers (e.g., Hoskins and Coons 1995; Schwartz 1998).

Both groups of critics enjoyed considerable political support in their respective countries, from populists to neoliberal reformers; however, neither was able to put a stop to the deal made directly between two presidents. Clinton was able to take recourse in a depression-era law that enabled the Treasury Department to channel funds without Congressional approval and in secrecy in order to hide its interventions in foreign exchange markets. Zedillo presided over a congress still firmly controlled by his own party.

While the bailout contributed to the rapid recovery of macroeconomic stability and the return of global capital, it did little to restore the living standards of millions of Mexicans whose currency had lost half its value. In terms of longer term challenges to Mexican economic stability, Washington's rescue package did nothing to address the vulnerability of Mexico's banking system. Even as inflation fell and foreign investors resumed lending, recession and default brought the banks to the brink.

As the simmering financial crisis boiled over, the banks contributed to their own demise in a desperate and misguided attempt to increase profits.

Raising interest rates from about 18 percent to as much as 120 percent, they made loan repayment an irrational act for most borrowers. Using U.S. accounting standards, over one-third of all Mexican loans were nonperforming by the beginning of 1996 (Smith 1996: 80). At the same time, antiquated bankruptcy laws and an inefficient judicial system made it virtually impossible to collect collateral from nonpaying debtors. As of the summer of 1998, Moody's Investor Services had given Mexican banks an average financial strength rating of E+, the lowest in Latin America and even worse than those in crisis-ridden South Korea (Caplen 1998: 44).

In the environment of political opening and economic crisis, everyday Mexicans found it possible to organize independently, express grievances, and press demands. In 1995, a small group of rural debtors called *El Barzón*[2] exploded onto the national stage and quickly grew into a two million-member urban movement of middle class and business debtors who refused to pay the banks' usurious rates. The organization offered advice and legal resources that enabled many debtors to confront and negotiate with the banks. Threatening a national moratorium on bank payments that exceeded 50 percent real interest, they forced the government to address debt relief.

Under the motto *debo no niego, pero pago lo justo* (I don't deny that I owe, but I'll pay what's fair), the group's militancy, high degree of organization and well-executed publicity campaign earned *El Barzón* legitimacy among the public and respect as a potent political force among startled officials in the Finance Ministry. The financial collapse allowed what had been a minor social movement located in the countryside to become a genuine threat to the nation's financial stability.

The government responded with a series of debt relief schemes designed to slow the populist momentum for mass default. Shortly after the peso crisis, the government offered hundreds of thousands of debtors relief by converting their debts into a new, inflation-indexed financial instrument called the *Unidad de Inversión* (Udi), or Investment Unit.[3] Although debtors would pay more total interest on a loan over the long term under the restructuring program, the advantage of denominating debts in Udis was that the borrower paid much less during the first few years than with typical repayment schedules. In other words, the plan was designed to provide liquidity to viable companies that suffered serious cash flow problems as a result of the recession and increased interest burden.

Since the real exchange rate would be kept in check, borrowers would be spared further abuses by private banks. The plan was to restructure consumer and commercial debt by denominating them in Udis, which would automatically adjust for inflation and cap the real interest rate at 12 percent. Part of the attractiveness of the plan was that it allowed banks to set up a new department to administer Udi-denominated debts, so they could actually take these bad debts off their balance sheets (*The Banker*, May 1995: 59).

Udis had limited success. Because of confusion about the program, worries over future economic growth, and uncertainty over the calculation of the inflation rate, the government was able to restructure only a fraction of the debt (Levin 1995a). However, in the two years after their introduction in April 1995, the nominal value of Udis rose by 84 percent, while inflation had only gone up 66 percent. Worse still, in the same period salaries had only risen by 44 percent (*El Universal*, April 26, 1997).

While Zedillo's economic team directed numerous reforms toward debtors, most of its financial initiatives were directed toward the banks. Beginning in 1995, in the effort to stabilize the banking industry, the government imposed tougher capitalization requirements. Since few banks could meet those standards, the government provided the necessary capital, taking possession of bank stock as collateral. In effect, the Zedillo administration virtually renationalized much of the banking system through a massive bailout effort. Although virtually every bank turned to the government for assistance, twelve of them failed outright. Their shareholders lost their entire investment, equal to about $1.5 billion (*New York Times,* July 31, 1998: A1).

Far more consequential than the capitalization scheme was the government's assimilation of nonperforming loans. With real default rates hovering at nearly one-third of all loans, most banks were in danger of insolvency, raising the prospect of depositor panic and a run on all the banks, healthy or not. Because the government was in no position to shell out cash, it crafted the bailout in a way that did not require the immediate expenditure of scarce reserves. The institution it used to reduce the banks' level of bad debts was the Bank Deposit Protection Fund, a small agency set up during the Salinas administration and patterned roughly on the U.S. Federal Deposit Insurance Corporation. Known in Mexico by its Spanish acronym, Fobaproa discreetly began to absorb private bank debt in 1995.

For Fobaproa to take a nonperforming loan off the books, a bank had to agree to write off 25 percent of its value. In exchange, it received a zero coupon bond[4] for 75 percent of the asset's value. "With the stroke of a pen, a million-peso loan that had no chance of being collected in full was transformed at 75 percent of book value into an instrument backed by the government" (Willoughby and Conger 1998: 68). Not surprisingly, virtually every bank participated.[5]

The extent of the crisis was truly alarming. By 1998, Fobaproa had accumulated about $65 billion in liabilities. Yet most experts estimated that only about a third of that total would ever be recovered. Mexico's eleven largest banks accounted for about half of Fobaproa's liabilities. Since they had to pay a quarter of the losses, they were exposed to a loss of over $5 billion. Worse still, they could lose billions more on bad loans not covered by Fobaproa. These figures rivaled the banks' total net worth. According to Boston College finance professor Edward Kane, "If we write down assets for reasonably predictable losses, there is virtually no owner's equity left. The system is being kept afloat by the black magic of perceived government guarantees. This is virtually a zombie system" (Willoughby and Conger 1998: 64).

### Opposition Politics and Financial Reform

The bank rescue was a political time bomb that neither the PRI nor the opposition realized was ticking until the middle of 1998. The opposition lay dormant because it simply did not understand the issue and had not envisioned how to make further political use of the economic crisis for which it had already lambasted the PRI. The PRI failed to realize the extent of the problem for two reasons: it underestimated the degree of fiscal loss from the bailout, and severely underestimated the opposition's ability to mobilize, cooperate and set the political agenda. Significantly, when Zedillo's technocrats launched the bailout, the opposition did not have a majority opposition in Congress. In short, the opposition had not yet figured out how to use its power, while the PRI's economic leadership had no experience in dealing with assertive and autonomous Congress legislators whose primary goal was political advancement.

In April 1998, President Zedillo sent Congress a package of banking reforms to guide Mexico out of its financial wilderness. The legislation actually consisted of several different reforms, a number of which addressed improved prudential regulation (*The Banker*, May 1998: 101). Government initiatives that received less publicity and were subject to less political controversy sought to do the following:

- *Empower regulators* by increasing the autonomy of the National Banking and Securities Commission (CNBV) and coordinating its oversight functions with the Banco de México. The measure was designed to improve the government's monitoring capabilities and decrease the influence of the more politically susceptible Ministry of Finance.
- *Reduce moral hazard* incentives by creating a new bank deposit insurance fund. The new institution, called Fogade, would gradually roll back the 100 percent deposit guarantee established when the banks were reprivatized to $120,000.
- *Enforce debt payment* by making it easier and faster for banks to collect payment or take control of collateral. In addition to the impact of the recession and the difficulty of paying extremely high interest rates, the increase of nonperforming loans was due, in part, to poorly defined and enforced property and a judicial system that was often unresponsive to lenders seeking to claim assets from defaulting debtors.

Zedillo's reform package included three controversial provisions. Although they addressed different aspects of financial regulation, they all provided opposition legislators with politically salient issues that could be effectively communicated to the press and to constituents.

The first of the contested provisions gave the Banco de México exclusive authority to intervene in the exchange rate. Although only a few countries in the world give their central banks this kind of authority, the idea of technocratic control was not the main source of congressional concern. The complexities of the issue simply held little salience for most constituents. Moreover, since Mexico had floated the peso in December 1994, this power was essentially limited to open market operations. From a political perspective, given that the government had grossly mismanaged the exchange rate on at least three occasions over the last twenty-five years, it would have been odd for the opposition to insist that the rate remain subject to the discretion of political authorities.

Nevertheless, while few attacked the premise of depoliticizing control over the exchange rate, critics of the measure argued that the central bank was not truly autonomous. Notwithstanding legislation passed by Salinas granting the central bank complete administrative independence from the executive branch, Bank governor Miguel Mancera had walked in lock step with every one of the president's proposals and pronouncements, never once questioning the sustainability of the pegged exchange rate that led to the devaluation. Worse still, the new governor was now Guillermo Ortiz, author of the bank sale and bailout and Zedillo's former minister of finance. Opposition congressmen routinely called for the resignation of the technocrat they regarded as beholden to the PRI leadership.

The second provision removed remaining barriers to foreign ownership of the Mexican banking system. Zedillo proposed to do away with the 1995 ceiling preventing any foreign company from owning more than 20 percent of a Mexican bank whose assets amounted to more than 6 percent of total banking capital—a law specifically designed to keep the top three banks, Bancomer, Banamex and Serfín, in national hands. One of Fobaproa's missions was now to lure foreign capital and expertise to the country's troubled financial system.

To help bolster the solvency of the local and regional institutions, in 1995 the government raised the ceilings on foreign ownership. Ironically, smaller foreign banks, which had been virtually shut out of the domestic market, stepped in with capital and technical expertise to help nurse the industry back to health. As a result, a significant portion of Mexico's banking system fell under foreign control (Marichal 1997). Spain's Banco Bilbao Vizcaya led the way, buying out the crippled GF Mercantil Probursa and snapping up branch offices of two smaller banks. Santander, another Spanish bank, bought three-quarters of Banco Mexicano and purchased GF Invermex outright in October 1996, providing it instantly with the market penetration of 250 outlets. After revealing alarming levels of nonperforming loans, fourth-ranked Inverlat turned over 50 percent of its equity to the Bank of Nova

Scotia. By May 1996, about a quarter of Banorte was owned by thirty-five U.S. and British mutual funds. Even second ranked Bancomer sold 16 percent of its shares to the Bank of Montreal in March 1996, while number three Serfín sold as much as a quarter of its equity to Hong Kong's HSBC.

What cost the government politically was not so much the extent of the banking system put in private hands—although PRD members occasionally grumbled about the loss of Mexico's "national patrimony"—but rather the inconsistent manner in which Fobaproa conducted numerous foreign sales. The agency was taken to task for offering inappropriate concessions for investors to take over ailing banks. The most publicized example was the case of Banco Confia, a mid-size bank sold to Citibank for a paltry $200 million, which was not much more than its book value (*Wall Street Journal*, May 12, 1998: A15). To seal the deal, not only was three-quarters of Confia's $4 billion loan portfolio absorbed by Fobaproa, but if those loans were sold at a loss, Confia would not be charged with the 25 percent write-off. In addition, the government sweetened some deals with larger banks. For example, foreign institutions that bought shares of Serfín and Banco Mexicano negotiated with regulators to obtain treasury bills that actually bore interest, unlike the zero coupon bonds held by other banks (Caplen 1998: 46; Willoughby and Conger 1998: 70).

According to a banking analyst at a Mexican brokerage firm, foreign banks quickly moved beyond corporate financing and into traditional consumer financial services. "A lot of Mexican banks have begun to get worried, especially banks like Banamex and Bancomer that are very strong in this sector." Laura Berdeja, director of financial analysis at Santander Investment, noted, "We're now seeing that retail banking is also being strongly attacked by foreigners. It had been anticipated that foreign banks would focus exclusively on competing in the corporate area, but that's not what has happened" (*Reuters World Report*, December 12, 1996).

While these regulatory issues of Zedillo's reform package generated spirited debate among the opposition, it was the third provision of the reform package—the incorporation of Fobaproa liabilities into public sector debt—that sparked a firestorm in Congress. While the government argued that the measure was needed to strengthen the banking system and protect innocent savers who held their deposits at troubled banks, the opposition accused the PRI of underwriting the debts of its wealthy and corrupt allies with taxpayers' money.

While it was true that the reform technically was a deposit protection plan, it was equally true that the plan benefited many of Mexico's wealthy and unscrupulous entrepreneurs. Even before the bank rescue became a national scandal, the practice of buying up the private sector's bad loans with public resources had been questioned by those in the financial community. When Fobaproa first began to recapitalize the banks, Zedillo justified the program as helping regular people. During the March 1995

Mexican Bankers Association convention in Cancún, he promised his audience that the government would not let the banks fail, adding, "Supporting the financial system doesn't mean saving the wealth of the shareholders nor making them richer [but rather] protecting those who deposit and invest their savings or obtain credit for productive projects or to satisfy the needs of their families" (*Proceso*, May 6, 1996: 8–9). Over two years later, in the midst of the unfolding Fobaproa debacle, he observed, "The common man on the street says: 'Why are we going to avoid the bankruptcy of the banking industry? What they think is that the government is channeling resources to save the bankers, which isn't true. . . . Above all, we are avoiding a chain reaction that would begin in the financial system and move to other sectors of the economy" (*Wall Street Journal*, December 9, 1997: A11).

Zedillo's characterization of the average Mexican's perspective was accurate. A June 1998 survey indicated that only 27 percent of those polled believed the rescue package strengthened the banking system, while 55 percent believed it benefited the bank owners. As one of Mexico's most prolific political commentators remarked, "Although most people don't fully understand the subject, it's easy [for the opposition] to say the government rescued the banks for the bankers and gave them $65 billion" (*Wall Street Journal*, June 3, 1998: A11).

## THE BANK RESCUE

The PRI's solution was economically expedient but politically ill-conceived. Although the mechanics of the rescue effort were hardly surprising and closely patterned after the U.S. savings and loan bailout, the attempt to formally covert the financial obligations incurred by the bank deposit fund into government obligations led to unprecedented congressional outrage. By the middle of 1998, the bank rescue had been transformed from a highly technical issue of bureaucratic management to the most blistering political attack ever staged by Mexico's political opposition.

The financial scope of bailout was breathtaking. Fobaproa's $65 billion portfolio approached 15 percent of Mexico's gross domestic product. According to the Mexican Bankers Association, this amount was equal to almost one-third of total assets of the banking system and far more than the banks' total capital (*New York Times*, July 31, 1998: A1). The proposal represented the largest increase in the internal debt in Mexico's history, from about 28 percent of GDP to 42 percent (*Financial Times*, April 27, 1998: 14A).

Ironically, for all the howls of protests in Congress, nobody argued against the principle of conferring public debt status on Fobaproa obligations. Three reasons stood out: First, without taking clear steps to ensure deposits, savers might lose confidence in the system and put their money elsewhere. Second, converting the bank fund's portfolio to public debt would allow the government to restructure and repackage those assets through standard financial instruments, such as securitization, which would, in turn, enable the Ministry of Finance to significantly reduce the overall fiscal impact over the long term. Finally, part of the provision would let banks use their zero coupon bonds on financial markets to make new loans, helping to ease Mexico's credit crunch and stimulate economic growth.

The judgment of Eduardo Cepeda, managing director of JP Morgan's executive office was typical: "We have to separate the economic handling of the banking crisis from the political deadlock. Congress understands that the banking system had to be rescued, understands that public debt [Fobaproa's liabilities] is public debt, and that the reforms have to be passed. But they want a political price for it" (Caplen 1998: 44). As Mexican business leader Roberto Salinas León maintained, while Fobaproa may have badly mismanaged bank rescue, "the government is right that, without formally recognizing the liabilities of the fund as public debt, a bank run remains possible" (*El Economista*, June 25, 1998). Financial economist Jonathan Heath concluded, "The government gave the opposition a golden opportunity. . . . The Fobaproa controversy is 99 percent about politics, not economics."[6]

Government officials admonished the Congress not to play politics with the country's economic well-being. Undersecretary of Finance Martin Werner, observing that Congress had the choice between "governing for the future or settling old scores" (*Wall Street Journal*, June 3, 1998: A11), insisted that the plan was the key to avoiding further financial chaos. Referring baldly to the instability traditional during *sexenio* changeovers, he stated, "If we want an orderly transition with fewer economic risks, we must have a strong banking sector," adding ominously, "we've already seen what is happening in Asia" (*El Financiero*, July 13, 1998: 6). As economist Rogelio Ramirez warned, "Without the approval of Congress, the government bonds which comprise a large portion of the healthy assets of Mexican banks will become worthless pieces of paper" (*Financial Times*, June 18, 1998: 6). At the end of April, President Zedillo declared that the banking system's problems were so severe that he asked Congress to hold a special session in August to discuss and approve the Fobaproa debt plan.

Not only did the lower house refuse, it redoubled its efforts to discredit the proposal. Indeed, it is no exaggeration that the Zedillo bank rescue scheme succeeded in uniting at least monetarily the ideologically divided opposition parties. Both the right-wing PAN and left-wing PRD maintained that the bank rescue violated the constitution, indeed, that Guillermo Ortiz and Miguel Mancera had acted illegally in rescuing the banks because Fobaproa's liabilities were never authorized by Congress (*Reforma*, June 2, 1998: 1).[7] As PAN representative Carlos Plascencia stated, "Fobaproa isn't a matter of yes or no; this proposal only offends us because it's about an aspect of legality, not negotiation" (*El Financiero*, June 11, 1998). PRD leader Muñoz Ledo concurred: "Congress will not be cowered or rushed into approving Mr. Zedillo's finance bills. We will get to the bottom of Fobaproa because the stability of Mexico's financial system depends on it." Not forgetting he was on the political stage, he added, "All the dirty deals will be uncovered" (*Financial Times*, June 18, 1998: 6).

### Mismanagement

Even more controversial than the sheer quantity of debt that Fobaproa had accumulated was the incompetent manner in which it had taken on the assets of Mexico's troubled banks. One serious shortcoming in Fobaproa's operations was limited information. The agency clearly lacked essential data about the loans for which it had willingly taken responsibility. A major reason was the government's mandate to act quickly and the urgency to save a financial system that many feared was on the brink of collapse. "Under pressure to keep banks afloat, Fobaproa did not have the time, or the inclination, to look into the loans it was buying" (*The Economist*, July 25, 1998: 73). Perhaps even more problematic, the untested Fobaproa staff was charged with liquidating loans made by inexperienced and highly uncooperative financial institutions. Loan documentation was thin and often lacked information about the borrower. "Accurate valuation of acquired [Fobaproa] assets has proven maddeningly problematic." (*The Banker*, May 1998: 101).

The major result of insufficient information was the inability to sell off the banks' troubled assets. Unable to obtain proper credit histories of the debtors, potential purchasers understandably either chose to abstain or pay only a small fraction of the face value of the assets. Worse still, the conditions of the bailout may have induced the banks to make some assets as unattractive as possible. "The banks didn't really want those loans sold. They had no incentive to gather the necessary paperwork and data that would enable Fobaproa to find buyers. Why take a write-off if it can be avoided?" (Willoughby and Conger 1998: 70). According to Luis Rubio, "In most cases, once a loan was transferred to Fobaproa, it ceased to be managed by the bank, so nobody had an interest in recovering the loan" (*Los Angeles Times*, July 13, 1998: A11).

Aside from technical problems with the loan buy-out, Fobaproa's great flaw was its fostering of moral hazard. In the context of an extremely slow and weak judicial system and tremendous economic hardship, many business debtors simply gave up trying to repay, regardless of their solvency. "When borrowers discover that their loans come under Fobaproa, as most have, they are even more reluctant to repay, believing the government will eventually let them off" (Caplen 1998: 45).

Fobaproa had modeled itself after the U.S. Resolution Trust Corporation, which liquidated almost $200 billion of savings and loan debt over just a few years at up to sixty cents on the dollar. Yet after three years of managing its portfolio, Fobaproa had managed to sell less than one billion dollars and had not come close to recovering even half the value of the loans. In fact, the asset recovery agency created to liquidate the debt was itself liquidated following its disastrous July 1997 sale of $17 million of performing loans for barely half of face value (*Wall Street Journal*, December 9, 1997: A1). Most experts estimated that the government would only recover about 30 percent of the debt, which, even if the banks could pay their 25 percent share of the burden, would still represent loss of over $30 billion, nearly 8 percent of GDP.

In addition to attacking the government for poor technical execution, the political opposition argued that the size of Fobaproa's liabilities and the agency's inability to sell off the assets was the result of the PRI's misplaced priorities. The PRD suggested that the ruling party considered the welfare of Mexican citizens less important than preserving positive economic relations with external creditors, accusing Finance Subsecretary Martin Werner of neglecting the liquidation of Fobaproa obligations because he was more interested in paying off the $12.5 billion owed to the U.S. Treasury. Zedillo had chosen to pay off of the American debt ahead of schedule (largely by replacing it with longer term debt in overseas markets) in order to ease criticism in the U.S. Congress and to improve Mexico's international credit rating. However, PRD representative Pedro Salcedo, chairman of the Industrial Promotion Committee, accused the Mexican government of satisfying international lenders and IMF, while allowing Fobaproa liabilities to grow irresponsibly (*El Financiero*, June 11, 1998).

### Favoritism

Even more politically explosive than poor execution were accusations and evidence of favoritism. Opposition politicians, relying on the banks' own financial data and the testimony of known financial criminals, uncovered what appeared to be sweet deals offered to some of the country's wealthiest entrepreneurs and long-time contributors to the PRI. Critics charged that the agency had assimilated debts of solvent borrowers and, worst still, had done so largely to reward wealthy allies of the government. According to Manuel Espinosa Yglesias, principal shareholder of Bancomer before the 1982 nationalization, "It's disingenuous to say that [the government bailout] doesn't help the bankers. The purchase of non-performing loans is ridiculous, it is money lost and that helps the bankers" (*Proceso*, May 6, 1996: 9). As information about the bank rescue came to light, even the government could not deny the dubious circumstances surrounding many of the fund's operations. As former Finance Minister Guillero Ortiz admitted, "There were loans made that everyone knew were made by some banks, in conditions under which they should not have been loaned" (*El Financiero*, May 27, 1998).

Beginning in the summer of 1998, the press was transformed into a mine-field of embarrassing exposés and a vehicle for opposition criticism. An editorial by Democratic Centrist Party representative Marcelo Ebrard was typical:

Why do 90 million Mexicans have to pay the obligations incurred by 440 thousand insolvent large debtors, of which only 604 make up half that amount? Why was everything decided without asking authorization in Congress, without registering the huge guarantees, without publicizing the decisions, without explaining them to anyone but themselves? Everything was done in secret and with vast discretion. As if the law and the principles of the Republic had been suspended. (*Reforma*, June 10, 1998)

PAN leader Vicente Fox, one of the leading candidates for the presidential race in the year 2000, observed, "The Fobaproa case is one more instance where federal authorities want to spread the costs among 94 million Mexicans, their children, and their children's children." (Willoughby and Conger 1998: 63). As political pundit Enrique Semo lamented, "As has happened so many times in our history, a small group of governmental authorities made use of our wealth with impunity, without having to account to anybody" (*Proceso*, July 5, 1998).

The recapitalization program of 1995–1996 came under suspicion. Officially, Fobaproa's first mission was to strengthen banks with inadequate capital reserves, primarily by contributing two pesos for every one that shareholders added. However, tremendous discretionality in the actual administration of the program was more the norm. "In reality, the ratio of bank assistance depended on the judgment of the Finance Ministry, and in this way some banks benefited much more. . . . The ratio went from three to one, five to one, to as much as nine to one as is the case of Banco Santander Mexicano. With this mechanism, bankers had the opportunity to maintain control of their institutions" (Vargas Medina 1998: 13).

But the most serious allegations of favoritism concerned the absorption of private debt from known criminals and solvent businesses. While all Mexican taxpayers would eventually have to pay for the bank bailout, Congress gathered documentation indicating rich and well-connected businessmen would have huge financial obligations erased by the plan. As PRD representative Carlos Heredia declared, "The portfolio bought by Fobaproa was acquired with discretionary powers of government officials and coziness between bank owners and government officials" (Willoughby and Conger 1998: 73).

PAN and PRD legislators joined forces to demand the names of the borrowers whose debts appeared in Fobaproa's portfolio. PRD leader Porfirio Muñoz Ledo stated that the least Ortiz should do is provide the names of the big businessmen who had racked up millions in bank debt and received "illegitimate benefits" from Fobaproa and who still live "in super-luxury and with high living standards" (*El Financiero*, May 28, 1998: 53).

Preliminary documents obtained by the opposition in late July from Fobaproa suggested that just 604 loans made to some of Mexico's wealthiest entrepreneurs represented almost half of the agency's total liabilities (*New York Times*, July 31, 1998: A1). A week later, the PRD revealed a list of the top 310 names of businesses and people whose defaulted loans had been assimilated by Fobaproa. The list included the most notorious names associated with fraud and several major Mexican corporations.[8] While the PRD could not prove political malfeasance, PRD representative Dolores Padierna concluded, "The bottom line is that big business and government officials reached an agreement at the highest levels to pass their losses onto taxpayers" (*Financial Times*, August 10, 1998: 4).

The government had tried to prevent the release of such a list by citing the Banking Secrecy Law, legislation which supposedly protected borrowers from public exposure and shielded lenders from demands to make their account information public. Predictably, the opposition responded that this was merely an artifice to shield the PRI's wealthy allies. PRD president Manuel López Obrador defended the public disclosure, characterizing the legal argument as "a pretext that can never be above the public interest" (*El Economista*, August 4, 1998: 1).

Having pieced together the list from numerous collaborators within individual banks, López Obrador explained: "If this was a matter between two private parties, where one owes and the other is trying to collect, we wouldn't care about knowing secrets. But any attempt to make the debt of a handful of private people public makes full information indispensable" (*New York Times*, August 7, 1998: A7). While Fobaproa officials immediately reputed the accuracy of the list, the PRD had scored a political victory and further established itself as the citizens' main source of independent investigation.

Members of the opposition argued not only that bank regulators chose to ignore what they knew were improper credit arrangements, but actually directed Fobaproa to acquire suspicious loans made by some of Mexico's most unscrupulous businessmen (*Wall Street Journal*, July 31, 1998: A9). One of the most notorious names appearing on the list was Carlos Cabal Peniche. After sacking Banco Union and Cremi for several hundred millions of dollars, he went into permanent hiding. Cremi was one of the first banks taken over by the government, even before the peso devaluation occurred.

Angel "El Divino" Rodriguez, owner of troubled Banpais, allegedly pillaged his bank by lending himself $400 million—loans that eventually found their way onto Fobaproa's books. Fleeing the country in 1996 after Banpais went broke, Rodriguez was extradited from Spain in June 1998 to face charges of fraud and embezzlement. Much to the chagrin of financial regulators, the banker became loquacious when reporters were present: He publicly stated that National Bank and Securities Commission president Eduardo Fernández had been "extraordinarily generous" to selected bankers and businessmen. From his jail cell, he told journalists that Fobaproa had absorbed debts from some of Mexico's largest firms, such as Alfa, Bancomer, Vitro, and Mexicana, even though the companies were completely solvent (*El Financiero*, May 28, 1998: 53).

Jorge Lankenau, ex-president of Banco Confia, concurred. Jailed at the end of 1997 for racketeering, he declared that the bank deposit fund had used egregious criteria for accepting new loans. Noting that 5 percent of Fobaproa's liabilities were from his bank, he playfully asked a reporter, "So where are the other $62 billion from? My other banking partners. Why aren't they with me? I miss my partners" (*El Universal*, July 13, 1998).

The opposition majority had found the ideal issue to discredit the ruling party and establish its own credentials. It dedicated most of its efforts to investigating Fobaproa's records, publicly tormenting government policy makers, and assessing blame. The Congressional Committee on Technical Contracting demanded and authorized an in-depth audit of the deposit agency. To prevent collusion with Mexican financial authorities, and to ensure transparency and impartiality, it insisted that the auditing team be composed entirely of foreigners—a surprising demand from a legislature that had been outspoken about defending national sovereignty.

At the beginning of August, fifteen of Mexico's most powerful economic administrators and bankers were "invited" to discuss what they knew about the bailout with legislators. In fact, no less than the likes of central bank governor Ortiz, former finance ministers Pedro Aspe and Jaime Serra Puche, former central bank governor Miguel Mancera, banking commission president Eduardo Fernandez, and former presidential chief-of-staff Jose Córdoba Montoya were hauled before the Subcommittee for the Investigation of Financial Reform Programs. Humiliated, the Zedillo administration had no choice but to cooperate. Given that the administration still had to convince the testy Congress to pass the reform package, it was in no position to stonewall the committee that would largely decide the fate of the legislation.

### Party Politics and the Bailout Deal

A logic of multiparty competition emerged during the Fobaproa debate. As the still-dominant party with the broadest social base, the PRI centered its efforts on forging a compromise. Burdened with blame for the crisis, it could adopt a highly flexible and conciliatory posture without further political damage. As the voice of economic sobriety, the PAN found itself in a difficult position: On one hand, its core business constituency demanded some resolution to a financial crisis that was threatening to spin out of control. On the other hand, the Left could easily portray any cooperation with the ruling party as a sellout, endangering the PAN's ability to broaden its appeal among popular sectors. The PRD thus cast itself as the sole protector of social justice. As Luis Rubio explained: "PAN recognizes the need to approve the government's debt increase bill, but does not want to pay a hefty political price for doing so. PRD has stolen the legislative agenda from the other parties and is doing everything is can to enhance the political cost of the whole deal" (*Los Angeles Times*, July 13, 1998: A11).

As a result of relentless attacks from both the Left and the Right, the PRI became concerned over the possibility that the bank rescue could sink the party at the polls. According to PRI representative Carlos Jimenez Macias, "If we [in Congress] do not propose alternatives the risks are very high, and include putting at risk the presidential elections in 2000" (*Reuters World Report*, August 12, 1998). On August 13, PRI leaders proposed a thorough congressional investigation of bank records that would also address the Finance Ministry's concerns about protecting bank secrecy laws (*The Banker*, September 1998: 12).

The PRD leadership realized that the PAN-PRI cooperation could eventually lead to a political compromise. In late August, the party conducted a "national referendum" on the bailout in which over two million people participated. When it announced that 94 percent opposed the conversion of bad bank loans into public debt, the referendum was immediately dismissed as biased and deliberately provocative (*Financial Times*, September 1, 1998: 5). Characterizing the congressional talks as a sham, the PRD publicly announced its exit from the ongoing negotiations and dedicated itself to attacking any progress toward a resolution as antidemocratic and unconstitutional.

After several months of politically motivated acrimony, the PAN began to cooperate with the PRI in crafting an alternative proposal as a substitute for Zedillo's much-maligned financial reform package. The initiative included a number of provisions designed to provide political cover for Congress members seeking an end to the legislative brinkmanship. First, it withheld public outlays for coverage of loans exceeding five million pesos and included smaller credit card and mortgage obligations in Fobaproa. The compromise represented a way to deflect public criticism by making the banks responsible for the largest business debts. At the same time, because of securitization and lower administrative costs, corporate loans were considered more collectible for the banks. The price of the political deal may have been to increase moral hazard and eventually burden taxpayers with unpaid small debts. As Deutche Bank Securities analyst Susana Ornelas remarked, "People might say: 'If the government's paying for my mortgage, why should I pay?'" (*LatinFinance*, November 1998: 39).

Second, the new package provided aid for smaller debtors who had continued servicing their loans throughout the crisis. It was targeted specifically at small and medium-size businesses, farmers and home owners (*SourceMex*, December 16, 1998). The political value of these constituencies—urban middle class and rural landowners—clearly facilitated the compromise between the PAN and PRI.

Finally, the legislation incorporated the PAN demand to eliminate Fobaproa and relocate its portfolio to a new agency, the Bank Deposit Insurance Institute (IPAB). Through a series of legal changes, IPAB would not officially transfer its obligations to the public debt. However, as critics immediately pointed out, because its obligations would be financed from a special allocation of the federal budget, the change amounted to a legal fiction that essentially repackaged Zedillo's original proposal. The provision also prohibited any public officials who had participated in the 1995 bailout from serving on IPAB's board. Since the PAN had given up its longtime demand for Guillermo Ortiz's resignation, at least it could claim that it had prevented the vilified central banker from meddling further with the bank rescue.[9]

On December 12, the PAN and PRI overwhelmingly approved the reform package.[10] Although the long-term budget implications of the bailout were extremely disturbing, both the PAN and PRI publicly congratulated themselves for rising above politics and saving the country's economy. PRD members were rabid, calling the Congress "traitors to the fatherland" and characterizing right-wing legislators with whom they had recently cooperated as "goddam panista whores." Party leader Porfirio Muñoz Ledo declared in a live radio broadcast following the vote, "It wasn't a negotiation; it was sex" (*Boletín Mexicano de la Crisis*, December 19–25, 1998: 10). Protesters from El Barzón muscled their way onto the legislative floor and pelted PAN and PRI members with flour and tomatoes.

While the PRD had reveled in its role as political spoiler, it gave the other two parties the opportunity to isolate it from the moderate, mainstream electorate. As PRI representative Carlos Jimenez stated during the debate, "The PRD is radicalizing [the debate] in order to capitalize politically. We have come to the conclusion that the PRD has taken an irreversible path. We are looking for points where we coincide with the PAN" (*Reuters World Report*, August 12, 1998). The PAN also characterized the PRD as a force that, given real power, would destroy the financial system. Following the approval of the package, one panista legislator declared that his party was "the deciding factor in saving Mexico from crisis" (*The Economist*, December 19, 1998: 46).

## CONCLUSION: POLITICS AND POLICY MAKING IN A COMPETITIVE PARTY SYSTEM

The bank rescue offers a case study in how parties in a democratic environment develop political priorities. Scholars who have studied Mexican politics have understandably focused primarily on the PRI. While far from democratic, Mexico's ruling party functioned as the forum in which the major social groups articulated demands, found representation, and received concessions. This book describes how the party responded to threats to its dominance during a series of social, economic, and political crises. Yet the events at the close of the century suggest that future books about Mexico will focus on how politicians in a competitive political system respond to an increasingly sophisticated electorate to win votes.

The PAN's disappointment is revealing. Election figures from 1994 suggested that PAN would become the main source of opposition. However, as its leadership bickered over the proper direction to lead the country, the "purist" branch associated with devout Catholicism and social conservatism weakened the party significantly. Party leader Carlos Castillo Peraza, widely perceived as arrogant and distant, came in a distant third in the race to be Mexico City's first elected mayor, even though he began with a commanding lead over both other parties. Worst of all for the PAN was its close identification with Zedillo's major policy proposals. Most observers agreed that "the PAN's dismal performance in 1997 is in part due to perceptions that it has been the PRI's junior partner" (Klesner 1997: 709). As a result of PAN efforts to appeal to the mass electorate, the pragmatist faction, led by presidential candidate and popular Guanajuato governor Vicente Fox focused his campaign more on political necessity than ideology.

Notwithstanding the boldness of new challengers, however, the PRI remains the strongest, richest, largest, and most experienced party in Mexico. It is the only truly national party, with strong organization in every state and in virtually every locality. While the worst vestiges of fraud have been done away with, the PRI still enjoys advantages in financial resources and access to the media, particularly television.

In addition, under Zedillo the PRI began to adopt new political strategies. Significantly, the weakening of the executive came not only from the opposition, but also from within the ruling party. As Mexican political scientist Denise Dresser observed, "Now the president must come to terms with a resentful and undisciplined party that feels it is paying at the polls for his economic policy. The PRI will have few incentives to toe the presidential line on legislative issues, and its loyalty to neoliberal economic reform will be tenuous at best" (1998: 56).

The party that succeeded in reinventing its ideology on multiple occasions is now in the process of reinventing itself. One of its most interesting responses, at least at the state level, has been internal democratization. In the face of the Fobaproa debacle, the PRI wisely opted not to shoot it out against superior firepower on the floor of Congress. Rather, recognizing the catastrophic potential of losing several governorships before the 2000 elections, the party directed its energies toward winning local elections.

In the past, party bosses had traditionally hand-picked candidates who had been loyal to the local machine. This kept politicians loyal to the party and, apart from distributing patronage resources, indifferent to the concerns of voters who had no real choice. Losing governorships in five states demonstrated that the electorate now had alternatives and convinced party leaders in several states that they had to find a way to pick candidates who were popular with voters.

The most innovative response to the need to appeal to voters was the primary election. A series of state elections in July 1998 revealed the success of the new strategy. In the economically thriving state of Chihuahua, the PRI accomplished a first by retaking the governorship from the popular PAN. The campaign was a tough, issue-oriented barrage against the complacent PAN governor, which "reminiscent of U.S.-style campaigns, featured heavy spending for slickly produced radio and TV commercials and pointed criticism of the opposition's failure to solve social problems like crime and education" (*Dallas Morning News*, July 7, 1998).

But before the PRI candidate won the state election, he had to win the party's open primary. A popular businessman named Patricio Martinez easily defeated a local PRI dinosaur, Artemio Yglesias. PRI president Mariano Palacios reflected on the implications of the new strategy: "The primaries have given the party an enormous activism and produced candidates with greater political force and legitimacy" (*New York Times*, July 22, 1998: A1). As political scientist Peter Ward put it, "The party realized it had to put up a credible candidate with strong local roots if it wanted to win back the state" (*Financial Times*, July 8, 1998: A4).

Equally revealing was a disastrous PRI defeat in Zacatecas. Congressional representative Ricardo Monreal sought and lost a bid to become the PRI candidate to local machine politician Antonio Olvera. He responded by publicly attacking his own party's top-down control, defecting to the PRD, and soundly winning the governorship.

The experience with primaries promises to force a show-down between traditionalists and reformists for the 2000 election. Indeed, the success of the Chihuahua primary has led to soul-searching and genuine debate about adopting the format even in safe localities (*El Financiero*, August 4, 1998: 49). President Zedillo, whose political clout within the party is far less than that of previous presidents, seems to favor more primaries and openness, while the traditional bosses, such as Puebla governor and presidential hopeful Manuel Bartlett, insist that the party leadership must select candidates. The summer of 1999 featured an unprecedented gloves-off fight between two PRI politicians seeking to become their party's presidential candidate. Although Francisco Labastida was considered Zedillo's choice and had most of the PRI machine behind him, populist Tabasco governor Roberto Madrazo, a party veteran with a reputation for corruption and rejection of the PRI's neoliberal agenda, led in public opinion polls during August 1999.

Mexican politics is suddenly party politics. More than any other issue, Fobaproa redefined the way politics is practiced in Mexico. The struggle over approving Zedillo's reform package was the death-knell of the PRI's policy-making hegemony. The most stunning aspect of Zedillo's financial reform package of 1998 was its initial failure in the legislature. As political pundit Alejandro Ramos quipped, "How easy it would have been for the government to send the Fobaproa initiative when the PRI had the majority in Congress. One vote and it's done" (*El Financiero*, July 31, 1998: 54). In previous decades, policies that had fundamentally reshaped the financial landscape of Mexico—the creation of treasury notes in the 1970s, the nationalization of the banks in the 1980s, the deregulation and reprivatization and rescue of the banks in the 1990s—all began as an idea conceived in Los Pinos and were approved after minimal debate by a pliant Congress of fellow *priistas*.

The clumsy and detached manner in which the Zedillo administration attempted to push the reforms through an unwilling Congress demonstrated how out of touch the Mexico's political leadership was with rapidly changing political realities. As Miguel Angel Grenados put it, "Nobody doubts the intelligence and academic preparation of these four, but what is surprising is their lack of comprehension of the public reaction to the matter, because they proceeded under an assumption that no longer holds true today; they acted without imagining that one day they would be held accountable and they were unprepared for this" (*Reforma*, June 25, 1998: 11).

The PRI remains the most formidable party in Mexico. Moreover, as the Fobaproa compromise between the PRI and PAN suggests, back-room deals are unlikely to disappear as a feature of Mexican politics. However, if Mexico's system of representation is still far from transparent, it is becoming more robust and inclusive. The PRI can no longer take elections for granted at the local or national level. Even the authority of the Mexican president was severely eroded. Elections in the late 1990s have been characterized by intense local struggles all over the country. As Georgetown professor John Bailey concluded, "The old rules of presidential control are broken" (*New York Times*, July 22, 1998: A1). Accordingly, a stable three-party system may be emerging, each with a core group of loyal voters, but each unable to win elections without capturing a significant proportion of those without a firmly established party identity.

As the PRI loses its hegemony, the opposition is discovering the pleasures, pains, and responsibilities of wielding real power. Most members of the opposition are inexperienced in politics, and virtually all members of Congress are inexperienced in the art of creating and passing laws of their own initiative: "The parties have only begun what it means to oppose and to govern at the same time. . . . Legislators are learning to argue, to negotiate, and to reach agreements—in other words, to legislate" (Estudillo Rendón 1998: 20).

What kind of future can be expected from Mexico's increasingly democratic environment? On one hand, major economic policies are likely to be based more on political compromise and maneuvering than on sober technical analysis. On the other hand, Mexico's Ph.D.-wielding economic authorities were hardly free of political considerations and their bureaucratic fiat did not guarantee prudent economic management. While it remains to be seen whether elected legislators with little command of economics do any better than the technocrats, their performance is secondary to the larger issue of meaningful representation. After monopolizing power over the political system for most of the century, the PRI was held accountable for the bank bailout. Mexico's citizens submitted humbly to the ruling party during rapid development through the 1970s, endured economic crisis through the 1980s, and watched helplessly as PRI's reform program disintegrated into renewed crisis during the 1990s. They deserve a real voice in determining their economic future, which begins with the solvency of the banking system. That voice is being heard through Mexico's remarkably robust political opposition.

## NOTES

1. Mexico paid off the final installment on the $13.5 billion it had borrowed from the ESF in January 1997, three years ahead of schedule. The United States government earned over $500 million in interest from the loan. While the Mexican government technically liquidated its debt to the U.S., in effect it simply replaced that financial obligation with long term bonds issued in foreign capital markets.

2. The name comes from the title of a clever folk song about exploited peasants who find themselves forever indebted to an unscrupulous landowner. The group's official name, rarely used in the press, is the National Union of Agricultural, Industrial, Commercial Producers and Service Providers.

3. For an explanation of calculating payments and an evaluation of the Udi's usefulness for typical debtors, see Levin (1995b).

4. Although similar to Mexican treasury bills, these bonds do not bear any interest, cannot be bought or sold on any market, and cannot be used as collateral in financial transactions.

5. For a detailed account of Fobaproa's action in each bank, see "Fobaproa, banco por banco, peso por peso," *Epoca,* June 22, 1998, pp. 10–15.

6. Public forum on the Mexican economy, sponsored by the Center for Strategic and International Studies, Washington, D.C., July 13, 1998.

7. The basis for the accusation was Article Nine of the Public Debt Law, which states that Congress will authorize the amount of net internal and external debt necessary to finance the government and other federal public entities. However, according to Attorney General Ismael Gómez Gordillo, because Fobaproa's assets are private, the bank rescue was not subject to the same rules governing public debt. For an account of the debate over constitutionality of the Fobaproa, see Mónica Pérez, "Para el procurador fiscal, el Congreso no puede supervisar al Fobraproa porque no es una paraestatal . . . aunque lo parezca," *Proceso,* July 5, 1998; Francisco José Paoli, "La legalidad del Fobraproa," *El Universal,* August 7, 1998, p. 6.

8. For example, included in Fobaproa's portfolio was $424 million that the Mexican World Trade Center borrowed from Banco Mexicano and Banco Nacional de Comercio Exterior, $433 million borrowed from the airline Taesa, and $196 million from Autobuses Estrella Blanca. Critics dubbed the program "Barzón of the Rich," after the populist debt embargo movement. See Fernando Ortego Pizarro, "El Ucabe, 'barzon de los ricos'" *Proceso,* July 5, 1998.

9.  When IPAB held its first meeting on May 6, 1999, the seats for central bank governor Guillermo Ortiz and Banking and Securities Commission president Eduardo Fernandez remained empty.

10.  The vote was 325–159 in the lower house, with twelve *panistas* (PAN members) and seven *priistas* (PRI members) joining the opposition, and 93–10 in the PRI-dominated Senate.

# 6

---

# Financial Crisis in
# Comparative Perspective

In the wake of the East Asian devaluations, it became fashionable to blame global capital markets for financial crises that seemed to have become almost routine at the end of this century. There is certainly validity to the argument that high capital mobility and excess global liquidity were major factors in financial volatility. To use a metaphor from Massachusetts Institute of Technology economist Paul Krugman, when a certain road suddenly becomes littered with car accidents, it may be more sensible to examine the conditions of the road than the mistakes of the drivers (Krugman 1999). Nevertheless, the international environment did not lead to crisis in all emerging markets. The reason is that not all emerging markets adopted financial policies that made the health of the "real economy" hostage to global investor confidence.

Liberalization of capital markets and foreign currency transactions does not inevitably lead to massive capital flight. However, when yields are high and growth robust, it often motivates the global financial community to invest heavily in portfolio instruments, so-called 'hot money' that can be removed as quickly as it enters. As we saw in Mexico, massive capital inflows can become extremely dangerous when a country depends on their indefinite continuation for maintaining stability. The question is, why do some governments make their economies vulnerable to global forces over which they have virtually no control?

In order to explain why even the most powerful, stable, and competent of states make seemingly irrational policy decisions, we first need to know what makes them tick politically. The main premise of this chapter is that countries are shaped by a distinct *political settlement* that underlies social stability and regime legitimacy.[1] In order to explain why reformist governments undertake failing financial policies, it describes their political settlement and the political challenges they faced.

In the preceding chapters, I argued that Mexican financial policy is best understood as the ruling party's response to threats to a political settlement that had brought social peace and economic growth dating from the 1930s: a broad corporatist alliance among business and popular sector organizations. After economic growth faltered, the Institutional Revolutionary Party (PRI) attempted to hold that alliance together by using financial policy to allocate economic goods to economic interests it relied on to legitimize its political domination. That is, after 1970 the political settlement was based increasingly on *ad hoc* social redistribution.

However, Mexico is hardly a template for the rest of the developing world. Rather than attempting to construct a general theory of policy behavior within emerging markets, we can improve our understanding of policy choices by grounding our analysis in the political settlements of individual countries. In the remainder of this chapter, I will consider two other cases of financial crisis in the 1990s, South Korea and Russia, to suggest how domestic politics shaped and undermined reform efforts in other regions of the world.

## SOUTH KOREA

Perhaps only after Japan, South Korea is the classic "development state." One of the world's most successful developing countries, it rose from abysmal the poverty following its war with North Korea in the 1950s to become the eleventh largest economy by the mid-1990s. The key to its success was opening new markets around the world. Numerous studies of the Korean "miracle" have emphasized how a highly autonomous government used selective incentives to both target the private sector into priority industrial sectors and, equally importantly, to generate competitive advantage in more capital-intensive, technology-based production (Amsden 1989; Wade 1990).

Like Mexico, though much more cautiously, Korea began reforming what had been a state-led economy in the 1980s. As the economy matured and became more complex, state leaders relaxed investment guidance and relied less on sectoral credit. They also lowered long-standing trade barriers, such as tariffs and import quotas. Korea became part of the World Trade Organization (WTO) in 1995, and the following year joined Mexico as one of the world's few developing countries to become a member of the prestigious Organization for Economic Cooperation and Development (OECD). At the same time, Korea undertook financial liberalization. In the 1980s, the state ended direct control of commercial banks and deregulated interest rates.[2] In the 1990s it removed most capital controls on banks.

Korea was also becoming more democratic. Forming a strict authoritarian government following the war, Korea's military leaders had presided over the first stages of industrialization and growth. Yet by the end of the 1980s, student and labor mobilization had become routine political events. Notwithstanding several violent clashes with state police, Korean civil society deepened and matured, and the government gradually ceded to its demands for greater representation and accountability (Kim, Sunhyuk 1997). By 1997, a former political dissident was elected president in a fair election.

Korea thus resembled Mexico inasmuch as it was becoming more responsive to both domestic constituencies and international markets. As its economy grew more sophisticated and its civil society more robust, the state found itself with fewer tools to maintain either political or economic continuity. Many observers applauded free elections and economic liberalization as evidence that the overbearing Korean state was finally on the eclipse. Again, as in Mexico, that characterization hid deeper truths. Rather than relying on heavy-handed intervention, the Korean government turned to capital market liberalization in an attempt to defend the political settlement that had brought so much prosperity in such a short time.

### Financial Crash

South Korea's financial collapse was not the result of macroeconomic weakness. Its economic fundamentals were strong (Chang 1998: 1556). While Mexico's trade deficit had grown steadily since the early 1990s, Korea enjoyed a trade surplus until 1996, and its subsequent deficits were moderate. Korea's domestic savings rate was among the highest in the world, while Mexico's was quite low. Even more importantly, while most of Mexico's foreign capital inflows went toward consumption and intermediate inputs, most of Korea's went toward investment, presumably productive activity that would yield economic pay-offs in the future. Finally, the Korean won had not dangerously appreciated as the peso had prior to Mexico's devaluation.

While Mexico experienced a systemic crisis of solvency, Korea's crisis has been characterized as a liquidity problem, caused primarily by its private sector's tremendous reliance on short-term external debt.[3] Indeed, it was because Korea's fundamentals were so strong—its total external debt-to-GDP ratio and public sector debt were quite low by world standards—that lenders and ratings agencies were lulled into a sense of calm. The explosion of short-term liabilities did not ring alarm bells until much too late (Huhne 1998).

Korea had avoided the kind of consumer credit boom and asset price bubble seen in Mexico and other East Asian countries. A major reason was that the government had deregulated the financial sector quite slowly: "The cautious and gradual approach to financial liberalization hindered financial intermediaries from engaging in excessive loans to households or investments in asset markets" (Park 1996: 257). In fact, the Korean authorities were highly aware of risks of foreign capital inflows. The director of the Ministry of Finance and Economy openly expressed concern over "hot money from abroad," which he worried could inflict "very high damage if suddenly withdrawn. If that happens, we cannot maintain the soundness of markets. That's the reason why we are adopting a gradual opening in the bond and stock market" (McGill 1995: 374).

Notwithstanding the rhetoric of caution, however, it was precisely "hot money" that derailed the Korean miracle. Private foreign borrowing sky-rocketed in the mid 1990s. Whereas Korean firms borrowed an average of about 2.5 trillion won from 1991 to 1994, by 1996 that level reached 12 trillion won (Kim and Suh 1998: 61). Most of this amount was short-term.

Shortly after Thailand devalued the bhat, investors began re-evaluating risk throughout the region. Korea's highly leveraged corporate sector and short-term debt structure became a source of concern. As a senior investment economist observed, "Once confidence began to erode, investors ceased to focus on macroeconomic factors, such as budget deficits or ratios of debt to GDP, and concentrated instead on potential microeconomic risks, such as the volume of dollar debt maturing during the next twelve months or the debt/equity ratios of the corporate sector" (Hale 1998: 21).

With debt-to-equity ratios well over 400 percent, large Korean firms found it difficult to raise money on their own at favorable terms. By the middle of 1997, as it became increasingly clear how weak the financial situation had become, Korean banks found their international rating plummeting. A number of foreign creditors chose to limit their exposure only to short-term loans, while others simply terminated their credit (Lee 1997: 78). "They had to turn to foreign hot money, as foreign lenders began to recall their loans" (Cho, Dong-sung 1998: 21).

Between 1994 and 1996, the country received over $52 billion in net foreign inflows, more than triple that of the 1991–1993 period. On the brink of the crisis, Korea's net external debt of $160 billion was actually quite reasonable relative to its eleventh-ranked GDP. However, almost two-thirds of this amount matured in less than a year (Park 1998: 15–16). When foreign banks decided to call in their loans, Korean banks were unprepared.[4] By the beginning of 1998, over 100 creditors were negotiating ways to roll over short-term debt and convert most of it to long-term obligations. About $15 billion was coming due every month (Dean 1998: 57–58).

In addition, the highly publicized failure of several over-leveraged giant conglomerates eroded investor confidence. Giant steelmaker Hanbo went bankrupt in 1997 under a debt of over $6 billion, after which its chairman and his son were convicted of stealing hundreds of millions of dollars to buy the silence of both creditors and state regulators. Shortly after the Hanbo scandal, an even larger conglomerate, auto producer Kia Motors, collapsed under debts worth several times the value of the company. The prospect of bankruptcy threatened to sink one of Kia's main creditor, venerable Korea First Bank.

Beginning in 1997, many of the banks that had lent to indebted conglomerates had to write off huge quantities of bad debt, which led the government to stage a number of poorly executed financial rescues (*The Economist*, October 25, 1997: 82). But when international banks, startled out of their slumber by the Thai debacle and headline-grabbing Korean failures, started calling in their dollar- and yen-denominated debts, the won fell like a stone. The results were devastating. In just over a year, unemployment rose from less than 3 percent to almost 8 percent. During the first half of 1998, GDP shrank by over 5 percent, after growing over 6 percent during the first half of 1997. Small businesses were going bankrupt at twice the rate of the previous year.

There is broad consensus that Korea's debt profile was the main contributor to the capital flight that led to devaluation. The question is why a government that still retained significant economic power and was firmly committed to economic stability would allow, indeed promote, such a dangerous build-up of private foreign debt.

### The Political Settlement: *Chaebol,* Labor, and Growth

Korea's political settlement is based on a development model that subordinates redistribution issues to economic growth. It reflects a highly successful industrial policy in which the government directed subsidies to strategic industrial sectors, deliberately "getting the prices wrong" in order to generate competitive advantage in high-value added production. The social consensus required to make that model work was largely rooted in Korea's perennial national security concerns. If political legitimacy in Mexico was based on corporatist inclusion, in South Korea it was based on uninterrupted industrial expansion and economic growth.

As we have seen throughout the preceding chapters, the key to understanding Mexican politics prior to the late 1990s was the PRI's hold on core social constituencies. The party sought to preserve its political hegemony by monitoring support among those groups and, when necessary, redistributing economic rewards to those defecting from the party. When Mexico liberalized, it could no longer do this with fiscal targeting and turned to financial reform.

Korea was different. Its leaders have not traditionally relied on populist symbols or policies to build political support. "To the extent that the centralized, authoritarian governments which have ruled Korea since 1961 have sought legitimacy for their actions, they have done so largely by appeals to the masses rather than by openly cultivating particular interest groups" (Dee 1986: 32). Largely as a result of regional security threats, Korean governments have been able to justify their control over economic decision making. With hostile North Korea and China nearby, one of Seoul's central policy objectives was to create the manufacturing capacity to fight a prolonged war independently.[5] In short, military advantage required competitive advantage. At the same time, in order to create a social consensus on development priorities, the Korean government promoted social policies such as land reform and full employment.

The key to Korea's development model is the *chaebol*, the huge, diversified industrial conglomerates whose production represents the bulk of the country's output, employment, foreign exchange earnings, and virtually all of its technological prowess. At the center of Korea's early efforts to increase military preparedness, the *chaebol* became virtually synonymous with industrialization. Even as the regional security threat diminished and the government was transformed from an authoritarian system into a democracy, the *chaebol* remained the most important contributors to development and, by extension, the most powerful actors in politics.

The *chaebol* came into their own during the 1970s under the Park regime, when they developed a symbiotic relationship with the state. The government transferred vast quantities of domestic savings to the *chaebol*, which received preferential credit based on export performance. Highly dependent upon the government for capital and protection, they willingly followed the state's development strategy, which broadly promoted heavy industry and technology. The state rewarded the *chaebol* not for profitability or even efficiency, but rather for heavy investment in priority sectors and the successful penetration of export markets.

Yet the state also relied on the conglomerates, whose economic performance validated both the regime's political authority and its development model. *Chaebol* growth not only enhanced national power in the global environment, but also fulfilled basic domestic goals, such as full employment and higher wages. As sociologist Peter Evans argued, "The Park regime was dependent on the *chaebol* to implement industrial transformation, which constituted the basis for its legitimacy" (1995: 53).

While the state's stewardship of the *chaebol* represented the economic component of the political settlement, stable labor relations was the social component. Beginning in the 1970s, the Korean government faced an increasingly radicalized labor force, whose strength and militancy it had promoted through successful industrialization. Although firing employees in Korea is difficult, labor flexibility was not a burning issue; the economy grew so rapidly that shedding workers was not a corporate priority. But as the economy matured and growth slowed, the *chaebol* found their hands tied in cost-cutting. During 1997, for example, unions carried out a series of general strikes to pressure the government to back away from a proposal to facilitate laying off workers (Ihlwan 1998: 102–103).

By the end of the century, domestic social discord had largely replaced the military threat as the central challenge to the state. Indeed, as Korea democratized throughout the 1980s and 1990s, the developmental component of the political settlement did not diminish but actually intensified. To preserve the business-labor peace that had been a pillar of the original settlement, Korean governments had to ensure the continuation of full employment and rising wages.

The problem was sustaining growth. Many sectors of Korea's economy had matured and competed directly with advanced countries for market share in heavy industry and high technology goods. "Sustaining the real wage increases that were possible during the transition from peasant agriculture to manufacturing jobs or during the initial movement to more capital- and technology-intensive forms of production is . . . difficult" (Evans 1995: 231).

Achieving this would require a new kind of investment strategy, one tailored to rapid changes in the world's most competitive markets. Increasing capacity was now less important than quality control, cutting edge research, and niche marketing. The state's traditional function of centrally guiding capital investment was becoming obsolete. At the same time, political liberalization severely limited the autonomy of the state vis-à-vis major organized interests.

The paradox of South Korean development was that the comprehensive development state was forced to reevaluate its *raison d'etre* upon tremendous success in attaining its goal. Contradictions inherent in the comprehensive development state, as well as the growth of the *chaebol* and labor into a powerful class and social group, respectively, put pressure on the state to reduce its control of the economy. This process of transformation from a comprehensive to a limited developmental state was challenged by a more dramatic breakdown of the authoritarian state. The ensuing democratic consolidation made the developmental state's transformation difficult, since the state was mandated to cater to the disparate demands of the *chaebol* and labor. (Eun Mee Kim 1997: 50)

Ironically, when the state decided to end indiscriminate industrial expansion, it was no longer capable of changing the *chaebol*'s behavior. Despite periodic bursts of public resentment over the *chaebol*'s privileged position, governments that have attacked them for political gain have been unable to mount a substantive challenge (Clifford 1990: 46–47). When Kim Young Sam became president in 1993, he promised to liberalize the economy and restructure Korean business and particularly to force the *chaebol* to specialize in industrial niches (Nakarmi 1995: 58). He failed.

Yet by deregulating the economy, the government had lost much of its discretionary power over private economic activity. On the heels of a dramatic export boom in 1995, "many *chaebol* [were] expanding their range of businesses, rather than concentrating on key industries." (*Christian Science Monitor,* June 15, 1995: 9). The scope of *chaebol* investment was breathtaking. Korea's number two conglomerate, Samsung, "promised to quadruple sales over six years; by 2001, it hoped to produce $200 billion worth of goods, more than the entire output of Sweden" (Mallaby 1997: 13).

The reform-minded government proved unable "to control and limit the influence of the *chaebol.* . . . The tremendous economic power amassed by the *chaebol* makes them almost invincible from the state's and society's will to restructure" (Eun Mee Kim 1997: 226). Indeed, direct confrontation presented the unacceptable prospect of economic disruption. "In a country where size is often equated with power, challenging the *chaebol* was considered tantamount to placing the country's economic future at risk" (Ungson et al. 1997: 17).

### Decline of the *Chaebol*

Internal investment behavior and external economic change collided to undermine Korean growth. The *chaebol* continued to rely on strategies that emphasized market share expansion, even when global conditions made that approach problematic. Exports and domestic revenue began to slow in the mid 1990s, with manufacturing sliding from 29.2 percent of GDP in 1990 to less than 27 percent in 1995 (Cho, Yoon-je 1998: 29). Along with short-term foreign debt, sluggish growth and plummeting profits contributed to investor apprehension that led to capital flight.

The *chaebol* borrowed extensively abroad to obtain the capital for increased investment. However, productivity gains in the markets dominated by the advanced economies were proving hard to come by.[6] Many firms poured money not only into research and development, but also into expanding market share. In the process, they increased capacity (and consequently supply) so much that export prices fell (Hale 1998: 20). Some of the most notorious of examples of market aggressiveness occurred in 1988 when Samsung and Hyundai (Korea's two largest *chaebol* and the country's largest exporting firms) both entered the petrochemicals industry—despite either of them having any experience in the sector—depressing prices worldwide (Su and Loubet Del Bayle 1996: 470). The *chaebol,* "habituated to competing for market share rather than for profits, were slow to adjust their production and investment" (Park 1998: 15).

Many critics instinctively blamed government meddling for the problem. "Bureaucrats chose to finance giant petrochemical plants and build millions of cars, even when markets clearly couldn't absorb the additional production" (Chanda 1998: 48). However, those who regarded Korean state coordination as an essential element of successful development pointed out that overcapacity became a serious problem only *after* government intervention ended. When President Kim Young Sam assumed office in 1993, he eliminated the Economic Planning Board and ended the government's role in guiding investment. "This made it easier for market failure to manifest itself in excess capacity in automobiles, shipbuilding, petrochemicals and semiconductors" (Wade 1998: 1539). Rather than pick which industries would enter new markets, the government now "allowed" new producers to compete, regardless of the impact on export prices and profitability (Chang 1998: 1559).

Still, the government's presence has been blamed for habituating the private sector to irresponsible investment behavior: "Industrialists had grown addicted to government guidance . . . the risk of failure had been dulled by the implicit promise of government rescue; the only restraint on the *chaebol*'s expansion had been a system of official permits. And so, whenever the government began to relax the permit system and let firms invest as they chose, the *chaebol* unleashed an investment boom that threatened to blow up" (Mallaby 1997: 13).

In addition to contributing to their own problems, the *chaebol* began to confront the challenges that come with successful development. Strong unions and full employment made Koreans among Asia's best paid workers. Rising labor costs were making traditional industrial producers far less competitive internationally (Kim and Suh 1998: 51). The stagnation of *chaebol* production did not stop the momentum of significant wage increases for workers, which had long been a routinized element of Korea's social stability. The higher wage bill further eroded the conglomerates' shrinking bottom line. Production was thus squeezed from both the high end and low end. Even as prices for computer chips and cars plummeted, comparative advantage in more labor intensive manufacturing had gone to the region's less developed economies. On the eve of the crisis, the *chaebol* were basically breaking even.

As long as traditional exports remained strong, the *chaebol* could easily finance their efforts to move up the technology ladder, even if results were discouraging. However, as those revenues began to dry up, "the low quality of investment tended to become a drag" that made it much more difficult to service short-term foreign debts that had been incurred in the frustrating attempt to improve productivity (Khatkhate 1998: 966).

Yet lending continued unabated. Domestic commercial and merchant banks borrowed heavily on international markets to acquire the capital demanded by the giant industrial groups (Kawai 1998: 169). During the mid-1990s, deregulation of interest rates made Korean rates double those on world markets, making it very attractive for local banks to obtain capital abroad. If expansionary investment decisions were questionable, they were only made possible because financial intermediaries failed to question them. "Korean banks lent (largely at the government's behest) to *chaebol* that were indifferent to the return on that borrowed capital" (Sender 1998: 59).

Korean financial institutions had no experience in credit analysis, while regulators had no experience in ensuring the soundness of banks. None of the institutional infrastructure needed for monitoring financial viability was in place. "Long relegated to the role of supporting manufacturing industries under the control of the government, banks and other financial institutions had become accustomed to accommodating the credit needs of the industrial conglomerates without necessarily checking their creditworthiness" (Park 1998: 16). According to the head of a major Korean securities firm, "The concept of risk analysis does not exist in the Korean banking system" (*Business Korea*, April 1998: 26). Banks also lent to *chaebol* subsidiaries because of the cross-industry loan guarantees that permeated the Korean financial system. As long as the parent guaranteed the loan, banks did not worry about the soundness of the subsidiary, much less the viability of its investment project (Cho, Yoon-je 1998: 33).

### Explaining *Chaebol* Investment

After the Korean crash, *chaebol* investment behavior was routinely characterized by policy makers and pundits as "crony capitalism." (Interestingly, admirers of Korean development had previously identified the close relationship between businessmen, bureaucrats, and politicians as the institutional basis of three decades of sustained growth.) In Korean politics, size does matter. The larger conglomerates generated the most jobs, foreign exchange, and technological development, making them indispensable to the government. When President Kim criticized *chaebol* privileges, the *Far Eastern Economic Review* remarked, "While his rhetoric is hostile, the conglomerates remain the economy's main vehicle for recovery and growth. As a result, the government's relationship with the *chaebol* is likely to be conciliatory rather than confrontational" (January 7, 1998: 22). Equally important, size provided protection against insolvency. Before the financial crisis, "the *chaebol* had become so large and participated in so many sectors of the economy that they were too big to fail" (Alexander 1998: 10). As a result of their close cooperation with state planners, "the risk of failure had been dulled by the implicit promise of government rescue" (Mallaby 1997: 13).

However, while "cronyism" may have sheltered the *chaebol* from political and economic storms, it does not explain the nature of their investment. Unlike some other Asian countries, Korea did not experience an asset price bubble in real estate or stocks. Credit flows went primarily to research, production, and capital goods, not to financial speculation or private consumption. This investment pattern had characterized Korea since the 1970s, and observers widely agreed that it was a basic element of the Korean "miracle."

Several reasons explain the *chaebol*'s atypical investment behavior. First, very high levels of investment and aggressive pursuit of market share had paid off extremely well. Decades of government promotion and preferential credit, which was contingent on growth and global export performance, had conditioned the *chaebol* to expand, regardless of profitability. One reason the *chaebol* borrowed fearlessly "was their long track record of success stories in the face of domestic and international skepticism" (Kim Chungsoo 1998: 46). Indeed, most of Korea's greatest industrial achievements, such as ships, semiconductors, and automobiles, required extraordinary levels of investment capital in capacity and research. They had been conceived and orchestrated by centralized government planners against the advice of mainstream economists.

Second, the *chaebol* feared falling behind competitors. The leading industrial and technology sectors are capital intensive. In the highest value-added products, success depends on innovation and research. Once a competitor loses ground in these markets, catching up becomes extremely difficult. Korean industrial policy had traditionally involved the promotion of investment for the importation of capital goods needed for technological and production improvements (Amsden and Euh 1993: 380).

Although the Koreans were world leaders in several manufacturing areas, they were painfully aware of their technological dependence on Japan, the United States, and parts of Europe (Kang 1988: 221). In fact, Korean firms had to make large investments just to remain viable *users* of technical advances generated elsewhere: "Significant expenditures on R & D are required to ensure that production units possess the requisite skills to continue to link their activities to the technological changes that are proceeding at prodigious speed in the centers of innovation of the global political economy" (Bernard and Ravenhill 1995: 193). As ING Baring's Seoul research director observed, the *chaebol* "have no big foundation of strong technology" (*Asian Business*, April 1997: 21).

Industrial exports such as memory chips and subcompact cars had practically become commodities. As a Korean economist explained two years before the crash, "To increase the volume of export, Korean firms and the government should promote the upgrading of Korea's industries toward continued product specialization in favor of higher value-added goods. These efforts are only possible by raising the level of technology" (Cho 1995: 478). Even after the financial crash, the leader of the *chaebol*'s main lobbying organization continued to defend the investment strategy (*The Economist*, August 29, 1998: 62).

Third, investment capital was critical for overseas expansion, which itself was a response to high and growing wages. Ironically, just as Korea had benefited from foreign direct investment when its labor costs were low, by the 1990s the *chaebol* were investing heavily in other emerging markets, relocating much of its production to low-wage countries such as China, Thailand, Indonesia, and Vietnam (Su and Loubet 1996: 477). But in order to achieve the benefits of long-term cost reduction, the *chaebol* needed short-term financing to create and expand their foreign subsidiaries. When the government attempted to slow the *chaebol*'s pace of international investment in 1995, business protested that its only way to grow was to tap global markets. Citing high labor costs, the chairman of Hyundai complained, "We can't do business anymore in Korea" (Nakarmi 1995: 58).

### Financial Liberalization

By the 1980s, the most direct forms of Korean government intervention began to end. As the *chaebol* began to produce highly sophisticated goods for increasingly competitive and changing global markets, central planners could no longer rely on traditional incentives for expanding production. The Korean bureaucracy gradually accepted that it could not effectively micromanage the private investment decisions of a large and complex economy.

Nevertheless, the state still retained significant discretion over private sector activity. Notwithstanding genuine moves toward the market, "the government did not change its basic attitude of treating private banks as instruments of state policy. Nor did it allow the *chaebol* to act as fully market-driven enterprises" (Alexander 1998: 10). After a decade of financial reform, a *World Development* study reported, "There has been some liberalization of financial markets in Korea, but the financial system continues to operate within the context of industrial policy" (Amsden and Euh 1993: 379).

One important change in Korea's development model, however, was that the source of investment capital shifted overseas. Ironically, Korea experienced massive capital inflows in the mid-1990s, in spite of widespread complaints that its financial system was too closed (*Asian Business*, April 1997: 38–40). Notwithstanding the central bank's declared concern over the destabilizing effects of "hot money," financial authorities liberalized and promoted capital markets significantly during the 1990s. "Especially in relation to foreign borrowing, an area which had been traditionally most tightly controlled by the government, liberalization was considerable, and now there was virtually no restriction" (Chang 1998: 1557–1558). While foreign countries pressured Korea to make these changes, especially given its successful petition to enter the OECD, a number of domestic considerations contributed to the government's decision to open up the financial system.

First, the state simply lacked the resources to provide credit directly. In the past, the *chaebol* had obtained much of their investment capital through government subsidies. The government, in turn, had acquired its capital from large quantities of U.S. aid in the 1950s and 1960s, and foreign loans in the 1970s and 1980s. (Foreign capital had thus long been a fundamental component of Korean growth.) But state resources were now extremely limited relative to the size of Korea's mature economy. Moreover, the state's priority of maintaining fiscal discipline precluded large budgetary outlays for industrial promotion.

Second, and more fundamentally, there was a consensus among both state and private sector leaders that productive investment must continue to drive the economy. As a Korean central bank economist explained, "If foreign money is spent on the manufacturing sector, it would do our economy good. But if it is speculative money flowing into the stockmarket, it would throw the economy into major chaos" (*Asian Business*, April 1997: 39). Although the domestic and international economy was changing, the time-tested strategies of expanding market share and generating competitive advantage remained largely intact. Since the levels of capital required to increase production capacity and move up the technology ladder could not be met through domestic savings, the state grudgingly ceded its credit allocation authority to overseas lenders.

The Korean government undertook several major reforms to increase the *chaebol*'s access to investment capital. Policy changes in the 1990s not only helped the *chaebol* raise capital abroad, but also helped banks tap foreign capital markets to lend to domestic firms. The president of the Korean Institute of Finance wrote, "As financial liberalization accelerated, domestic financial institutions were given greater freedom to manage their assets and liabilities, particularly to borrow from world financial markets" (Park 1998: 16).

*Internationalization*

One of the major reforms lifted restrictions on foreign currency transactions conducted by domestic banks. In 1993, the government significantly increased the foreign exchange positions banks were allowed to hold and eased documentation requirements for currency futures contracts (*Far Eastern Economic Review*, September 23, 1993: 94). In conjunction with the *chaebol*'s improved credit rating following OECD membership, the surge in foreign placement of corporate bonds in the Euro market was the direct result of capital account liberalization and the elimination of restrictions on foreign exchange operations (Kim and Suh 1998: 61).

Beginning in April 1993, the government undertook a series of reforms to increase the foreign presence in domestic finance. These measures included developing a sophisticated public trading database, inviting foreigners to invest in both the corporate and public sector bond market and moving toward a universal banking structure in which banks could underwrite securities (Doh 1996: 58–61). As two Korean economists explain, "Some globalized Korean firms such as multinationals in Daewoo group can now finance huge projects by issuing foreign-currency denominated bonds in the eurobond market with cheaper interest rates than those of domestic markets" (Kim and Suh 1998: 41). In addition, the state ended the system of strict quarterly emissions of foreign convertible bonds that constrained business borrowing. Samsung's director of international finance beamed: "Now we can issue when we want, when the market is right" (Marriott 1997: 35).

Beginning in 1994, Korea converted short-term finance companies into investment banks and introduced numerous new financial instruments such as offshore investment funds and derivatives. These innovations "effectively created a commercial paper market and provided new sources of foreign borrowing" (Kregal 1998: 7–8). In 1995, Korea developed a short-term money market and allowed foreign participation in the primary bond market (Park 1996: 252).

The Korean government also opened up the domestic banking sector, largely to enable smaller *chaebol* to increase investment levels vis-à-vis the larger ones. In April 1996, in an effort to increase the international competitiveness of mid-sized industrial firms, the Finance Ministry eliminated foreign credit quotas on all but the top ten *chaebol*. The remaining domestic restrictions reflected the fact that the largest conglomerates had been able to get credit on foreign markets, and the Finance Ministry's concern that smaller competitors not be squeezed out of the credit market (*Wall Street Journal*, April 29, 1996: A19). Thus, while the state continued to manage industrial credit allocation, it now did so by targeting financial liberalization policies and selectively opening credit markets.

### Merchant Banks

One of the major contributors to the explosion of *chaebol* debt was a little known but far-reaching innovation of Kim Young Sam's government: the expansion of merchant banks. Merchant banks were officially created in 1972 under the Park Chung Hee administration, when several private loan sharks catering to the small business sector were converted into formal credit institutions and brought under the authority of financial regulators. Although the entrepreneurial newcomers did extremely well, their number was limited by government restrictions. By 1993, Korea had only six merchant banks. However, following Kim's liberalization, the sector multiplied, reaching thirty by 1997. Of these, twenty-four engaged primarily in short-term lending, buying up three-month commercial paper. They gave credit "mainly to companies too frail to issue bonds or obtain loans from commercial banks" (*The Economist*, September 13, 1997: 74).

According to the Korean government's Board of Audit and Inspection, merchant bank debt soared by 60 percent *per year* between 1994 and 1996, from $7 billion to almost $19 billion. In addition, state regulators paid little attention to the dangerous pattern of debt maturity generated by the new and inexperienced banks. Of the $20 billion the merchant banks had borrowed on overseas capital markets, 64 percent was short-term debt, while 85 percent was lent on a long-term basis (Yoo, Chang, and Park 1998: 738–

739). As Korean economist Kim Kihwan complained, the conglomerates who controlled the merchant banks used them "literally as private coffers" (*Washington Post*, January 4, 1998: A1).

By 1997, struggling companies began offering commercial paper to merchant banks at discounts as steep as 14 percent just to maintain liquidity. Unbacked by collateral, defaults increased and destabilized the lucrative new sector. In April 1997, faced with the prospect of widespread corporate bankruptcies, the government ordered the merchant banks to give a repayment reprieve to insolvent borrowers. In exchange, the central bank dispersed hundreds of millions of dollars in heavily subsidized loans to the banks, providing them with new liquidity to continue buying paper from largely failing firms (*The Economist*, September 13, 1997: 77). The liberalization of merchant banks, promoted by the state to modernize corporate finance and provide greater competition, had merely increased the incentives for high risk lending and resulted in a traditional statist solution: a taxpayer financed bailout.

### Stock Market

In addition to increasing opportunities for borrowing, the Koreans also began to promote corporate equities, both as a lucrative alternative for savers and, more importantly, a debt-free vehicle for financing growth. The state assumed a central role in promoting the stock market. As many *chaebol* are family possessions, owners traditionally shunned equity financing, not only because credit was cheap, but also because they feared losing control of their companies. They preferred bank loans and became accustomed to very high debt-to-equity levels (Kim, Hyuk-rae 1988: 63–67; Su and Loubet Del Bayle 1996: 475).

Beginning in the mid 1980s, the Korean government began to actively pressure the *chaebol* to list more of their subsidiaries on the Korean stock exchange. Domestic bank investment in the stock market in 1991 was 8.2 percent of capital, while in May 1995 that level stood at 13.7 percent. Once again, however, market promotion went hand in hand with government intervention. Part of the reason for the Korean Stock Exchange's (KSE) performance was Finance Ministry pressure on the banks to invest in stocks even when share prices were falling (*Euromoney*, September 1995: 378). Domestic promotion quickly became international. In January 1992, the government allowed foreigners to buy Korean stocks for the first time.

The results of government promotion were impressive: The number of companies listed on the KSE increased from 355 in 1986 to 626 in 1989, while the level of new equity investment climbed from less a billion dollars to over $21 billion during the same period (Clifford 1990: 47). From 1975 to the end of 1994, the KSE index rose by a factor of sixteen (Henderson 1998: 21).

### Consequences of Financial Opening

It is revealing that critics have attacked Korea's leadership for both over-regulating the economy and under-regulating it. Predictably, economists, policy makers, and pundits have explained Korea's fall as the inevitable consequence of excessive state intervention and restrictions. Throughout 1998, they were giddy with tales of Korea's (and Japan's) economic woes, which offered proof that state-led development (and its evil twin "crony capitalism") was fatally flawed. Such commentaries routinely ignored the fact that this same model had led to decades of sustained growth and produced several of the world's most successful industrial competitors. They also failed to ask why other state-led countries, such as Taiwan, had not suffered a financial crash.

On the other side of the debate, financial liberalization is the culprit in Korea's collapse. If the *chaebol* borrowed far too much money for dubious investments, that money was available only because of relaxed capital market regulations: "The *chaebol* responded to tentative liberalization by investing at a crazy pace" (Mallaby 1997: 13). Moreover, the capital flight that crippled the Korean economy could not have occurred without equally massive capital inflows. Political scientist Robert Wade describes the general trend throughout Asia's crisis economies: "The deregulated financial systems enabled inexperienced private domestic banks and firms to take out large, dollar-denominated loans from foreign lenders and on-lend with generous spreads." In his view, "perhaps the single most irresponsible action the whole crisis was capital account liberalization without a framework of regulation (1998: 1539, 1545).

These contradictory criticisms are the result of a coherent policy response to defend Korea's political settlement. Foreigners and new domestic banks did not alter the long-standing model of investment in Korea. They simply replaced the state as main supplier of credit. As long as the financial system continued to channel capital into manufacturing technology and capacity, tapping overseas capital markets remained fully consistent with the prevailing development model. Equally important, it enabled both the state and the *chaebol* to avoid—albeit temporarily—the political challenges involve in adopting a new growth strategy.

Unfortunately, the same economic environment that made investment capital so plentiful would ultimately exact a high price. By the 1990s, Korea's venerable investment strategy, which now relied increasingly on private foreign borrowing, severely undermined investor confidence and led directly to the financial crash.

## RUSSIA

The prospect of the world's second military superpower undertaking the transformation to capitalist democracy sparked the imagination of the international policy-making community like no other country. With a highly educated workforce, a gigantic pool of scientific and technological talent, and natural resources rivaling those of the United States, Russia seemed to have all of the advantages needed to make political and economic liberalization work.

Russia's leadership appeared genuinely committed to reform. Russia became a formal democracy for the first time in its history. Members of the *duma* and the president assumed office through elections. The police state was dismantled, and citizens began to enjoy meaningful civil rights. The central government delegated power and allowed the redistribution of a significant amount of economic resources to regional governments. The country also undertook comprehensive economic liberalization. Russia went far beyond a rejection of communism and pursued far-reaching market reforms: reducing restrictions on trade and investment, privatizing state industries, and, of course, liberalizing the financial sector. In short, in an even more dramatic way than Mexico and South Korea, at the beginning of the 1990s, Russia was an emerging market with tremendous economic potential that was shaking off the shackles of government.

Yet by the mid-1990s, reformists were struggling against Fascists and Communists to prevent a return to statism or the triumph of even scarier ideas based on xenophobia and nationalism. While the history of Russia's transition is far from over, it is clear that the first decade fell far short of the success that so many had predicted. In hindsight, we can see that disappointment with Russia's economic performance had at least as much to do with unrealistic Western expectations as with domestic problems. Popular explanations for the Russian debacle have relied on simplistic notions of "corruption" and crude portrayals of "national character." However, serious scholars have begun to construct a more complex understanding of Russia's social and economic challenges. While the evolution of post-Soviet finance policy is only a small part of that story, it serves as a useful lens through which to view Russia's perplexing political environment. It also offers insight into why a country recently seen as a potential economic powerhouse fell into financial oblivion in just a few short years.

### Financial Crash

While President Mikhail Gorbachev made important strides in freeing the Soviet Union from completely centralized economic management, President Boris Yeltsin made Russia a formally capitalist nation. In his January 1992 reform initiative, most prices were freed, distribution and foreign trade were decentralized, and a voucher system to promote the privatization of public property was completed.

However, those achievements were undermined by the government's failure to establish macroeconomic stability, and the private sector's failure to adjust in any meaningful way to the challenges of an open economy.

Throughout the 1990s, inflation swung up and down wildly and unpredictably. Although foreign investment was welcomed, it came slowly, as cautious multinational firms rarely risked their capital outside of traditional extractive industries such as oil and minerals. Russian banks lent very little toward improving productive capacity. Not surprisingly, the widespread economic "rationalization" anticipated by naïve Western advisors never materialized. Although firms remained extremely inefficient, managers (often former Communist officials) and workers banded together to prevent downsizing and maintain state subsidies.

As a result, Russian output plummeted. GDP fell by over 10 percent in 1993 and 1994, with industrial output falling over 20 percent in the latter year. By the late 1990s, Russia's economy, long regarded as second only to the United States, was around the size of Switzerland's. Despite the artificial preservation of industrial jobs, unemployment skyrocketed and wages fell, forcing millions into the informal sector and second jobs. National mortality rates resembled those found in third world countries.

While Russian citizens were becoming increasingly used to economic misery, what got the world's attention was the country's financial freefall. Between 1994 and 1998, the Russian government had been a welcome newcomer on the world's capital markets, racking up $45 billion by selling securities, while private firms borrowed about $20 billion more. Yet during the same years, capital flight virtually canceled out those inflows, "indicating that Russian borrowers knew their country's ways better than foreign lenders did" (*The Economist*, December 19, 1998: 98). In July 1998, Russia worked out a deal with the IMF for a stabilization loan. However, just a month later, the Russian government stopped payment on its foreign obligations, instructed private debtors to do the same, and abandoned its defense of the ruble.

The meltdown was the result of relentless speculation against the currency, which was prompted by the Russian government's complete loss of credibility among foreign and domestic investors.[7] According to Brookings Institution scholar Jerry Hough, "As the system ran down at home, Yeltsin increasingly turned to foreigners for money. But it was a ponzi scheme in which foreign money received one month was used to pay high interest rates on last month's 30-day bonds. As the pyramid grew, so did the interest payments. As private investors, already shaken by events in Asia, increasingly refused to play in the game, it collapsed" (*Los Angeles Times*, August 18, 1998).

While the government has been routinely vilified as either corrupt, incompetent, or both, what are now recognized as blatant policy failures can also be interpreted as reasonable responses taken by political leaders to survive within an extremely constrained political space. The economic benefits of responsible reform might have been significant, but the government's ability to undertake a transparent and disciplined liberalization process was limited by the absence of organized and coherent bases of social support for such policies. In order to understand why the state chose to assume debt, ignore inflation, and satisfy the narrowest of rent-seeking interests, it is necessary to consider the challenge of ruling without a political settlement.

### Politics Without a Settlement

Not all governments in emerging markets are governed by long-standing, successful political settlements. Russia's financial experience during the 1990s suggests the extent to which the policy-making process can be hijacked by narrow interests in countries that lack well-established arrangements for negotiation and distribution among major social groups.

The absence of a recognizable political settlement in Russia is a legacy of Soviet domination. Since the Communist party had organized and dominated every major social, professional, and cultural group in Russia, there was no civil society waiting underneath to assert itself. As a former senior U.S. diplomat in Moscow observed, "While it may not be as atomistic as it was during the Soviet period, [Russian society] is paradoxically less well structured. There are no well-defined, self-conscious classes" (Graham 1995).

This does not mean that Russian society has no organization. Narrowly defined groups based on material self-interest are common. For example, managers and workers whose livelihoods depend on a particular factory or industrial sector—and public subsidies—are often well organized, as are pensioners whose income comes from the national budget. More broadly, there is a complex system of networks and alliances among local governments and private firms. Public-private cooperation at the regional level helps states and municipalities generate revenue, sustain employment and provide social services, and helps companies to stay profitable and evade federal taxes. However, such arrangements tend to promote narrow, particularistic or geographically defined goals, rather than broad-based economic interests. They have not created socially inclusive, programmatic parties or organizations that form the basis for pressuring government to adopt a coherent policy strategy.

Yeltsin's administration focused on radical economic reform at the neglect of political transformation. "Like their advisors from the West, the Russian team of economic technocrats saw politics and political reform as a nuisance and distraction from the more important task of creating a market economy" (McFaul 1995: 227). However, without a political base of support, economic failure made the reformers particularly vulnerable: declining living standards, unpaid wages, and an increasingly lawless society threatened to trigger mass mobilization, reactionary nationalism, and Communist resurgence.

Since the first decade of capitalism made more people worse off than better, Russia's weak and socially isolated government spent most of its energies on establishing political allies, rather than attempting to fashion a political settlement. Yeltsin did not even belong to an official party, but his many administrations tried to forge alliances with groups that claimed to support a capitalist agenda.

These groups included both Soviet-era public managers and new entrepreneurs. In many cases, ex-Communist officials used their power to take direct control of state assets after the Soviet Union crumbled. "Leading government officials began to set up independent companies with Western-style management, simply using their political clout to grab control of assets whose real ownership, with the collapse of the Soviet state, was in limbo" (*Forbes*, December 1, 1997: 149). In other cases, government officials sold their bureaucratic power and knowledge to private actors, facilitating private ownership of public assets or granting lucrative licenses.

In the absence of a political settlement, "the new elite sees its power based not on popular support, but on its control of political institutions and economic assets. . . . The most powerful among them share the same basic structure: they are centered on a major political figure . . . and linked to leading financial, trade and industrial structures" (Graham 1995). Indeed, politics in Russia during the 1990s consisted largely of competition among the large conglomerates known as financial-industrial groups (FIGs). As the leader of Russia's opposition Yabloko party claimed, "Russia has consolidated a semi-criminal oligarchy that was already largely in place under the old Soviet system. After communism's collapse, it merely changed its appearance, just as a snake sheds its skin" (Yavlinsky 1998: 69).

### Financial Policies for the Few

While characterizing Russia's financial elite as criminal may be subjective, if not partisan, there is little doubt that it became a major benefactor of rent-seeking opportunities created by the state. Although the Soviet Union was dead, the ironic result of pushing the reform agenda was the persistence of the Soviet way of doing business. Financial liberalization was at the center of these efforts. The remainder of this chapter analyzes bank chartering laws, public credit allocation, government securities, and private lending to the state. It describes how the government's efforts to establish and empower bases of support twisted those policies into schemes to enrich a small group of strategic allies.

#### Bank Chartering and Privatization

As part of his *glasnost* project, President Gorbachev began the liberalization of the Soviet banking system. However, because the private sector still did not exist as such, there was no influential constituency demanding greater control of credit institutions. At the time, maintaining internal support for reform was more important than actually implementing meaningful reform. Hailed at the time as a step toward free market capitalism, the

1988 Law on Financial Cooperatives actually ensured the continued domination of Communist party leaders. "As a condition of the 1988 legislation, the *nomenklatura* who planned on running the new private cooperatives demanded separate banking services of their own. . . . Factory heads and Party officials demanded authority to form their own banks" (McCoy 1997: 71).

Two years later, dissatisfied with the state banks' monopolization of credit, the former managers, now bank owners, demanded the liberalization of credit allocation. The result was two pieces of legislation, the 1990 Law on the Central Bank, which eliminated the Gosbank's control over credit; and the 1991 Law on Banks and Banking, which formally authorized the privatization of commercial banks. The 1990 law included no provisions on conflict of interest lending to bank shareholders. It was "specifically designed to elicit the support of the *nomenklatura* in return for the right to capture banks for use as private financing arms" (McCoy 1997: 77).

As a World Bank report explained, "Banks are also being privatized, in practice, as the state-owned enterprises that are their main shareholders become joint stock companies and are themselves privatized. . . . This ownership structure helps perpetuate the practice of connected and insider lending common in the Russian banking system" (Lamdany 1993: 13). As one scholar put it, the legislation on cooperatives "gave the state bureaucratic apparatus broad new avenues for becoming rich. Within major state enterprises, cooperatives began to be established through which the executives of the firms and the ministerial officials at the middle level worked out methods for amassing personal fortunes" (Rumer 1991: 20).

A revealing feature of early bank reform legislation was the remarkably low minimum capitalization requirement. In the early 1990s, as little as $100,000 was needed for chartering a new bank, so just about anyone with some government connections could legally dispense credit. "The establishment of a bank was a profitable undertaking for a great many enterprising people, since the minimal statutory capital was at times as small as the cost of a luxury car" (Aslund 1996: 496). Financial liberalization led to the rapid spread of thousands of "wildcat" banks, which were formed by both private firms and local governments.

Because banking was deregulated much faster than the rest of industry, "it became a haven of rent-seeking and arbitrage between the regulated state sector and the free market. The ultimate objective was to secure more or less interest-free loans or deposits from the state sector and put the money to work so that it kept pace with high rates of inflation" (Aslund 1996: 496). In other words, in order to get access to a lot of capital, all that was necessary was scraping together a little capital and giving a banking regulator the appropriate incentive to sign off on a new charter. Because requirements were minimal and the profitability potential of setting up a captive bank to loan to enterprises was great, "undercapitalized banks designed for short-term gain sprung up almost overnight" (Johnson 1996: 58).

By the late 1990s, capital adequacy standards had been raised to 4 percent capital/asset ratio, half of the international standard set by the Basle accord. However, because Russian accounting regulations allowed banks to significantly underestimate the degree of portfolio risk, even this low standard was typically not met (Bald and Nielsen 1998: 83). As a result, the number of banks exploded, reaching 2,500 by 1994 (*EIU Country Report: Russia* 1995: 36).[8]

Russian banking deregulation was remarkably fast and deep, making banking not only the most profitable of economic activities, but making bankers the most powerful of actors. Because the banks were liberalized early, "the individual components of the Russian banking system gained a great deal of autonomy from government organs, giving bankers themselves a key role in the process of institutional change" (Johnson 1996: 49). In pursuing a strategy to establish an influential private sector ally, the socially disconnected government had created an independent political force that would rival its own strength.

### Subsidized Credit and Lucrative Securities

The key to making banking liberalization so profitable for a privileged few was a thoroughly undisciplined monetary policy. Throughout the first half of the 1990s, the central bank distributed credit virtually without restraint. Because interest rates were generally much lower than inflation, those with access to the discount window could make a tidy profit just by borrowing rubles, converting them to a hard currency or asset, and holding on (Aslund 1996: 497). In an environment of hyperinflation, bankers with no financial experience became millionaires without lending a dime for productive investment. "In practice, the discount window serves almost solely as a channel for directed credit subsidies" (Lamdany 1993: 7).

Although credit allocation was formally under the control of the Russian Central Bank (RCB), the Law on the Central Bank actually made it subject to the duma's political demands to fund the deficit and provide subsidies. The Russian legislature installed the fiscally irreverent Viktor Garashchenko as head of the RCB, and gave him the authority to ignore Yeltsin's appeals for discipline. Because banking legislation also lacked any prohibitions on insider loans, the *nomenklatura* turned privatization into a channel for capturing rents from state. As one scholar explains, "The large majority of Russian banks practiced Soviet banking as usual, but in a new guise. That was the direct legacy of the ownership structure of most Russian commercial banks" (McCoy 1997: 74–82).

The persistence of credit subsidies was the result of a political compromise between reformers, who wanted liberalization, and old guard enterprise managers, whose constituency consisted entirely of the workers whose livelihood they controlled. Yeltsin's democratic government "rested on the support of workers dependent on public sector jobs . . . the Yeltsin government faced overwhelming pressure to avoid layoffs at all costs. . . . Subsidies to prop up inefficient enterprises had the obvious appeal of staving off immediate shutdown and unemployment without raising the government deficit" (McCoy 1997: 93, 95).

The labor movement was not a particularly important factor. Indeed, because of growing unemployment and strong dependence on public enterprises for economic survival, unions were quite weak. Far from making demands on management through collective action, workers and managers were united in a common cause of rent seeking. The main activity of the Federation of Independent Trade Unions of Russia, the largest organization, was to join forces with employer associations in demanding the continuation of cheap credit and subsidies.[9] "Without the realization of an effective independent labor movement, labor politics has not been a force for social democracy. Instead, it continues to repeat older patterns of labor relations" (Silverman and Yanowitch 1997: 134–135).

It was economic crisis, not politics, that shifted the balance of power to the reformists and ended credit subsidies. Throughout 1994, inflation was spiraling out of control, while RCB credits were financing over two-thirds of the budget deficit, a level that both domestic and international investors considered unsustainable. On "Black Tuesday," October 11, 1994, the ruble collapsed. Public criticism of Garashchenko enabled Yeltsin to replace the populist central bank head with reformist Tatyana Paramonova and pass legislation disciplining public credit allocation.

Although the bankers' lobby eventually got rid of Paramonova, the April 1995 amendments to the Law on Banking prohibited the RCB from funding the deficit through credit allocation and limited commercial banks from loaning more than 20 percent of portfolio to shareholders. They also required bank liabilities to consist entirely of consumer deposits by 1999, in order to end dependence on central bank outlays (McCoy 1997: 115–117). While the end of credit subsidies rapidly improved Russia's fiscal performance, it triggered a national banking crisis. In March 1995 alone, RCB credits toward the deficit declined by over 30 percent and continued plummeting. The result was a sudden and severe credit crunch that threatened many dependent banks with insolvency (Deliagin 1996: 85–86).

But what the government took away by tightening credit, it gave back by creating a remarkably lucrative financial instrument that restored profitability and eliminated risk. Without recourse to the printing press to fund the deficit, the Yeltsin administration turned once again to financial reform. It created Russian government securities, known as GKOs, maintaining that their sale in public auctions would allow the market to determine the interest rate at which the government borrowed.

In practice, however, the state restricted competition and allowed large banks to collude. The FIGs lobbied successfully to limit foreign participation in the treasury bill market. The state even made several large banks official

GKO dealers. "As a result, the state allowed the biggest Russian banks to earn extraordinarily high returns" (Johnson 1997: 353). In 1996, banks were enjoying a 200 percent return on GKOs. High and volatile inflation contributed to astronomical yields, yet even when a pegged exchange rate lowered inflation from triple digits to stable levels, GKOs continued to offer extremely attractive real returns (Korhonen 1997: 17–19).

In early 1995, most banking assets were in hard currency. By 1997, over two-thirds were in securities, mostly T-bills. "With most other sources of profits vanishing, the market for state securities has offered commercial banks a particularly important opportunity for investment" (*OECD Observer*, February–March 1998: 46). As a former economic advisor to Russia put it, "The Russian government salvaged the banks by devising and offering very profitable treasury bills" (Aslund 1996: 497). By 1997, after the government had committed untold billions to cover interest payments on GKOs, the RCB brought down the yield to below 20 percent, "wiping out the windfall which covered most of the banking sector's other financial sins" (*The Banker*, September 1997: 84). Only then were foreigners allowed into the GKO market.

### Privatizing State Assets

As in many developing countries undergoing liberalization, Russia's privatization program transferred extremely valuable public assets to a small economic elite for fire sale prices. What makes the Russian case interesting is that much of this process was carried out as a footnote to what was supposed to be a straightforward government borrowing operation. The notorious "Loans for Shares" program allowed the largest banks to take control of some of Russia's most profitable firms in exchange for forgiveness on government loans worth only a small fraction of their actual value.

At the end of 1995, Finance Minister Vladimir Potanin, who also happened to be chairman of Uneximbank, orchestrated a $2 billion loan to the government from a consortium of large banks. The collateral was management of the shares of several large public companies. The lending terms stipulated that when the loans came due, if the government was unwilling or unable to liquidate its obligations, the banks would sell the shares in an open auction to private bidders. The government would receive 70 percent of proceeds, with the banks pocketing the rest.

It came as no surprise that the cash-strapped Yeltsin administration never repaid. However, what raised eyebrows even among Russians long accustomed to shady business-government deals was the audacious manner in which the public properties were liquidated. In each case of privatization, the banks that controlled the shares sold the firms to themselves in auctions that they were permitted to organize. The sale was clearly made possible by government cooperation (Johnson 1997: 355). Extensive collusion among bidders prevented competitive bidding, and the government received only a fraction of its expected revenue. "The loans-for-shares auctions were clearly rigged. Not only were foreigners barred from participating, but many Russian banks were kept out of the charmed circle" (*Forbes*, December 1, 1997: 150).

For less than $800 million, a handful of banks kept eight of Russia's largest companies, including Aeroflot and Norilsk Nickel, the world's largest nickel producer. A few years after the sale, market values were typically ten to twenty times the bidding price. The privatization program thus enabled the country's largest banks to become major stakeholders in other economic sectors virtually overnight. "The shares-for-loans auctions catalyzed the bank-led FIGs' leap from important players in the Russian economy to dominant financial-industrial conglomerates" (Johnson 1997: 352).

Notwithstanding the breathtaking level of corruption involved in rigging the auctions, the Loans for Shares program can be understood as a viable policy response to the economic and political constraints facing the government in the mid-1990s. For some, even a flagrant giveaway was preferable to keeping valuable property in the hands of the state. Characterizing the reprivatization process as "not very egalitarian," European economic analyst Rory McFarmer maintained that "the government was doing nothing with these companies, and most of the companies were suffering from heavy debt and tax arrears. Putting them into the hands of profit maximizers was probably a good idea for the given economic environment" (*Russia Review*, November 3, 1997: 9).

Even more importantly, and quite ironically, the Loans for Shares swindle dramatically bolstered the position of the country's most likely champions of market reform. Russia's most prestigious reformist technocrat, private entrepreneur and public administrator Anatoli Chubais, claims that he did not cooperate in the privatization scheme because he thought it was a good idea. Rather, after taking stock of the political interests arrayed against a transparent auction, he pragmatically gave his assent to the deal in order to strengthen the financial "oligarchy," the only group that he perceived as capable of defeating the opposition's efforts to halt economic liberalization. According to Chubais, because of the lingering Communist threat, "We did not have the choice between socialism and ideal capitalism" (*Forbes*, February 23, 1998: 90).

Loans for Shares was only the most publicized of a series of dubious privatization schemes that have gradually transferred a large proportion of Russia's extractive and productive resources to a small number of financial-industrial groups. According to Alexander Zourabov, president of Bank Menatep, "In Moscow you can hardly find a company that is visible on the market that is not under the control, directly or indirectly, by one of the major banking institutions" (*Russia Review*, November 3, 1997: 10). Indeed, bankers have come to dominate industry not by lending, but rather by acquiring.

### Filling the Political Vacuum

Post-Soviet politics became a symbiotic relationship between the government and private sector. However, unlike the South Korean case, this relationship did not involve either the delivery of investment opportunities or economic growth. Rather, the state depended on financial-industrial groups for political support of the reform agenda and for defense against a Communist comeback. The FIGs, in turn, relied on state institutions and policies to accumulate vast amounts of wealth, which in turn made them ever more powerful political allies.

Over time, this dynamic has turned Russia's political environment into a battlefield in which private firms struggle for wealth, power, and influence and in which civil society passively observes from the sidelines. The so-called 'Banker's War' reveals the extent to which narrow and particularistic interests dominate the country's political agenda. In the summer of 1997, the FIGs could not agree over who would win the bid to acquire telecom giant Svyazinvest. The result was a mud-slinging battle in which financial leaders publicly accused each other of graft, resulting in a number of high profile dismissals and official corruption charges. Significantly, popular mobilization was not a factor. As a financial reporter remarked about the increasing level of conflict among the banking elite, "Whoever is right or wrong, the leading financial houses have laid bare their continued dependence on dubious backroom political favours, which could be withdrawn at any shift in the Byzantine Kremlin winds" (*The Banker*, September 1997: 84).

Those winds began to blow cold following the August 1998 ruble meltdown. After the devaluation, the bankers managed to convince Yeltsin to fire Prime Minister Sergei Kiriyenko, fearing that the reformist official would attempt to liquidate some of their assets under bankruptcy laws. However, their hopes of installing the more pliable Viktor Chernomyrdin were dashed by an intransigent Communist-led duma, which twice vetoed his nomination. Eventually, to avert a full-scale political crisis, Yeltsin caved in and nominated former KGB head Yevgeny Primakov, a critic of reform who was hardly known for his sympathy toward the business community. Suddenly, the bankers were confronting a more hostile government and struggling to hold on to the properties they had amassed (Fairlamb 1998). Although the financial "oligarchy" is likely to be a permanent fixture of Russian politics, its future is hardly assured.

The vulnerability of Russia's financial elite indicates that there are limits to private power, especially in the wake of an economic disaster. However, the bankers were not humbled by social mobilization to limit their power, but rather as the result of power plays among a very small group of political actors. Victory and defeat in Moscow are defined in the narrowest of terms; most citizens do not breathe the rarified air of Russian politics and assume that those who do are simply competing for formal rights to plunder the country.

Some observers have discerned a semblance of political stability in the midst of this seeming chaos. Characterizing the conflictual relationship among the FIGs as a "clan system," Tom Graham, a former U.S. diplomat in Russia, argues that the oligarchy provides "a framework for competition that does not threaten the integrity of the system, as long as no one clan becomes capable of dominating a coalition of all the others" (1995). As long as Russia's citizenry continues to be fragmented and atomized, that political stability is likely to be based on a mutual understanding among particularistic and self-serving actors.

The cases of Mexico and South Korea suggest that stable governments undertaking economic change, in the effort to preserve political settlements, are likely to manipulate the reform agenda to channel benefits to powerful social groups. The case of Russia, however, suggests something more disturbing: Weak governments operating within an unorganized social environment may have great incentives to provide rent-seeking opportunities for narrow and particularistic private groups. While financial policy is by no means the only vehicle for delivering such benefits, it is probably one of the most effective, particularly when fiscal expansion is not an option.

## NOTES

1. The concept of political settlement was developed most fully in the extensive literature on Europe's adjustment to economic change. Przeworski (1985) developed the idea of "class compromise" in his assessment of European social democracy. In his pioneering international comparison of national adaptation to global economic change, Zysman (1983) argued that different national financial systems, which affect economic performance, were largely the product of political settlements.

2. The degree of liberalization can be overstated. For example, notwithstanding formal deregulation, the state continued to manipulate interest rates through informal "window guidance." (Amsden and Euh 1993: 381–382; *Euromoney*, September 1995: 378).

3. This argument has been extended to the Asian crisis countries in general (Dean 1998; Bosworth 1998). Interestingly, the Korean government contributed to the excessive unbalanced maturity structure of foreign debt by requiring burdensome information requirements and Finance Ministry approval for long-term obligations, but not short term. In addition, given that Korea's gradual financial liberalization was expected to bring down foreign interest rates eventually, many

borrowers apparently adopted a "wait and see" attitude by repeatedly rolling over short-term debts (Yoo, Chang and Park 1998: 739).

4. While foreign debt precipitated the crisis, in fact it was only the tip of the iceberg. Korean companies owed domestic banks over $300 billion, with 50 and 75 percent of that sum being short term. See Stephanie Strom, "Korea's Other Big Problem," *New York Times*, February 19, 1998, p. A1.

5. Of course, most developing countries facing security threats have not grown steadily for thirty years. Korea also enjoyed a highly developed educational system, as well as unprecedented levels of U.S. economic aid. Moreover, Japanese colonization prior to World War II not only planted the seeds of early industrialization, but also destroyed the authority of Korea's traditional elite and paved the way for a smoother economic transformation following independence.

6. Paul Krugman has argued that, far from being a "miracle," Asian growth was the mundane result of adding labor and capital inputs, not increases in productivity (1994). While that view has been hotly debated, Korean manufacturers have found it much more difficult to thrive in the world's highest value-added sectors.

7. The effects of Russia's own economic mismanagement were compounded in the late 1990s by external shocks beyond the government's control. The East Asian crisis led to a "global repricing of risk" among investors, and probably accelerated the pace of capital flight from the Russian financial market, while the collapse of oil prices deprived Russia of billions of dollars of foreign exchange earnings (Slay 1999).

8. In 1994, the government increased capitalization requirements to about $1 million. By that time, however, the financial system was saturated with tiny, undercapitalized banks created to channel credit to specific enterprises.

9. For a detailed analysis of how industrial directors and workers were able to hijack the reform agenda and defeat repeated reformist attempts to reduce credit subsidies, see McFaul (1995: 231–237).

# 7

## Conclusion: Domestic Politics, Global Markets, and Economic Reform

Moments after the Mexican peso was pounded by capital flight, Stanford economist Ronald McKinnon laid much of the blame for the devaluation on "the major institutions of international finance—banks in New York, Tokyo and London as well as stock and bond mutual funds (mainly on Wall Street)—which have a lemming-like bent to overlend in emerging markets" (*New York Times*, January 20, 1995: A29). McKinnon, who pioneered the case for financial liberalization in developing countries, maintained that Mexico's impressive reform efforts made the country a "target for mutual funds."

Three years later, in the midst of Asia's collapse, an exasperated Jagdish Bhagwati complained that "the idea and ideology of free trade and its benefits . . . have, in effect, been hijacked by the proponents of capital mobility. They have been used to bamboozle us into celebrating the new world of trillions of dollars moving about daily in a borderless world." The typically reflective Columbia economics professor railed against the "Wall Street-Treasury Complex," an ideological alliance among American policy makers and investment banking lobbyists that was largely responsible for the misguided advice that developing countries indiscriminately eliminate all restrictions to capital movements. Sounding more like a frustrated Marxist than a tireless proponent of market liberalization, Bhagwati concluded, "There is, in the sense of power elite a la C. Wright Mills, a definite network of like-minded businessmen among the powerful institutions—Wall Street, the Treasury Department, the State Department, the IMF and the World Bank" (1998: 11).

However, a year after the Asian debacle, the champions of free market capitalism were marching to a different drummer. Even the IMF, which had long maintained a zero-tolerance position for capital restrictions, had accepted the potential efficacy of regulations to stem inflows of short-term capital. The *Financial Times* maintained that "banks are disastrous vehicles for large scale capital flows across frontiers." The editors of one of the world's great bastions of capitalism concluded, "Unchecked international bank lending must be consigned to the past" (March 6, 1998: 17).

Has a "paradigm shift" occurred in the field of economics? Probably not. The laws of comparative advantage and the belief that open economies fare better than closed ones have not been challenged. However, following Mexico's fall into financial oblivion and subsequent meltdowns in East Asia and Russia, one of the central pillars of the consensus for market reform—financial opening—is in retreat. While not all critics see capital mobility in the same conspiratorial terms as Bhagwati, many of the leading proponents of economic liberalization now openly support restricting capital flows into developing countries.

## WEAK FINANCIAL SYSTEMS

Virtually all the cases of financial collapse in emerging markets during the 1990s were preceded by huge inflows of foreign capital, which created a strong and sustained credit boom throughout the region. While domestic corruption is blamed for much of the debacle, "without the influx of foreign funds . . . domestic crony capitalism alone could not have fed a boom and bubble of such proportions" (Lim 1998: 28). Moreover, given that the East Asian countries hit by devaluation are all characterized by long-standing close ties between business and government, it is difficult to explain how this corruption *simultaneously* turned two decades of remarkable growth into financial disaster.

Much of the foreign capital inflow took the form of portfolio investment, such as stocks and bonds (Riedel 1997: 7–10). While commercial banks dominated international lending during the 1970s and 1980s, providing huge loans for developing countries that would eventually totter on bankruptcy, by the 1990s mutual and hedge funds, money management firms, and life insurance companies became major players in global lending.

Changing international economic incentives, highly responsive capital markets, and a vastly improved economic outlook in developing countries contributed to this shift (Calvo et al. 1996; Fernández-Arias and Montiel 1996). Low interest rates in the early 1990s and a pervasive economic funk among the world's major economies made high-yield emerging market investments far more attractive. At the same time, improved creditor relations, macroeconomic stability and robust growth in East Asia gave foreign investors the confidence to move into new financial territory.

One of the reasons for growth, of course, was a freer financial system. Initial reform measures typically included interest rate deregulation, giving bankers greater incentive to lend. But governments also lowered or eliminated reserve requirements, ended mandatory credit allocation, and eased restrictions on foreign borrowing. Thus bankers not only had more control over their own capital, but they also had greater freedom to acquire more capital from external sources. In short, financial liberalization provided bankers with access to unprecedented amounts of capital to lend to the private sector.

What was dangerous about the quantity of loans that liberalization generated was the quality of the financial systems through which that capital passed. One of the major lessons learned from the Asian crisis is that high foreign capital inflows facilitate risky or excessive lending practices: "The rising volume of short-term flows was largely intermediated by the poorly regulated and ill-supervised domestic banking sector. Indeed, the over-lending and asset-price cycles in [East Asia] in the 1990s are reminiscent of the cycles that followed financial liberalization in many Latin American countries" (Kaminsky and Reinhart 1998: 447).

When foreign capital inundates a smaller economy, asset prices can take off, causing temporary euphoria and bubbles in nonproductive sectors such as real estate and stock markets. Domestic banks, in turn, with the opportunity to make lucrative loans in a booming economy, have greater incentive to borrow large sums of capital in foreign markets (Fernández-Arias and Montiel 1996: 56–57). They often lend this money for questionable investments, accepting assets with artificially inflated value as collateral. Not only does this extend the credit boom, but also makes domestic banks highly vulnerable to exchange rate devaluation and asset price collapse. Reflecting on the experiences of the euphoric and misguided investments preceding the Mexican and Asian crises, many economists lost faith in the discipline of open capital markets.

It is important to ensure that the inflow of funds is directed toward productive investment; allowing too much [foreign capital] to drain off on the stock exchange and consumption of imported goods will create bubbles and imbalances that are unsustainable. . . . If productive capacity reacts slowly or with a lag and domestic financial markets remain incomplete and poorly supervised, additional resources cannot be absorbed efficiently. (Ffrench-Davis 1998: 36, 38)

The Asian economies were widely considered more stable than that of Mexico prior to its devaluation. The structural weakness of Mexico's growth model was that most foreign capital went to finance consumption and inputs, which led to prolonged and unsustainable current account deficits that could only be financed with ever more foreign capital. East Asia was different: Trade was relatively balanced, and foreign capital inflows went primarily toward investment, not consumption (Khatkhate 1998: 964). This assured investors that Mexico's experience would not be repeated.

The flaw in their logic was the implicit assumption that all investments generate profit and growth. However, allocating capital to unviable productive ventures is no more likely to lead to stability than excessive consumption. In Asia, most foreign capital went through domestic banks and producers taking advantage of cheaper global interest rates, and much of it ended up in domestic assets, such as stocks and real estate. Given Asia's remarkable growth, "it was relatively easy for bankers to justify financing the rapidly expanding needs for new office space, leisure centers, golf courses and recreational residences" (Kregel 1998: 8). The problem was that the returns on those investments depended on the uninterrupted continuation of growth in the real economy.

A consensus is emerging among economists and policy makers that before foreign capital freely crosses a border, the domestic financial system should be developed and well regulated (Kawai 1998: 170; Bosworth 1998: 8). Laws must ensure accounting transparency and maintain adequate levels of capitalization; banks must be able to conduct credit risk assessment; while regulators must have the capacity to monitor banks activities and sanction violations. As the World Bank reported, "Today, the issue is not deregulation but finding the appropriate regulatory structure" (1999: 93).

Governments can implement good regulations and prudent standards. But bankers and regulators in virtually all emerging markets lack the experience to make them effective. This is understandable; before economic reforms, banks in most developing countries were creatures of the state, allocating capital to developmental or political priorities designated by national leaders. Even before the Asian crisis broke out, a team of Bank for International Settlements (BIS) economists worried that "bank credit managers reared in an earlier controlled financial environment may not have the expertise to evaluate new sources of credit and market risk" (Goldstein and Turner 1996: 17). Regulatory talent is equally scarce, and given modest public sector salaries, perhaps even harder to create. According to a leading expert on global financial reform, "experienced supervisors estimate that it could take many countries between five and ten years of substantial training before their supervisors' skills would be near the capacity found in industrial countries" (Caprio 1997: 115).

The recognition of pervasively weak financial institutions has given rise to remarkably iconoclastic ideas within mainstream economics: Restrictions on capital might be an appropriate policy. Indeed, the consensus that developing countries should open all markets has quickly given way to a new conventional wisdom among economists: The capital account is special, and the domestic banking system is problematic. In Bhagwati's view, "only an untutored economist will argue that . . . free trade in widgets and life insurance policies is the same as free capital mobility" (Bhagwati 1998: 8). Even the IMF concurs that capital restrictions could help slow excessive foreign capital inflows. In its 1995 International Capital Markets report, it concluded that emerging markets lacking a high developed regulatory structure, targeted controls such as taxation, and reserve requirements on foreign investment could be used effectively (Montgomery 1996: 101–102).[1]

## RE-EVALUATING GLOBAL INVESTMENT BEHAVIOR

As investors stared in shock at the financial collapse of what had been four of the world's most promising emerging markets—South Korea, Thailand, Indonesia, and Malaysia—many asked how the global policy community, along with the leading financial institutions and ratings agencies, could have missed such glaring economic problems. When the fallout of the Asian devaluations spread and intensified throughout 1998, threatening political stability and sending foreign capital stampeding out of emerging markets everywhere, many began to ask if something fundamental had changed in the global economy. The aftermath of the Mexican and Asian crises was so severe that economists began to fundamentally re-evaluate the behavior of international capital markets.

Did Mexico's current account deficit and an overvalued currency really merit such a steep devaluation and such a lengthy and devastating recession? In the opinion of a former World Bank advisor, "What is new and was dramatically illustrated by the Mexican crisis is how unforgiving the international financial system has become to unsound economic policies. . . . This has more to do with the profound transformations in the international financial system in the past two decades than with Mexico's policy mistakes" (Naím 1995: 122).

The reasons for the crash had as much to do with the unpredictable psychology of the global investment community and its reaction to changing information as with Mexico's economy. Two economists argue that capital markets in the 1990s became "sensitive . . . to the arrival of news that may not be directly related to the fundamentals driving asset returns . . . global investors may be susceptible to 'herding' behavior" (Calvo and Mendoza 1996: 173).[2] As a senior economist at Brookings wrote, "Investors are seeking to allocate a stock of wealth globally among national assets that are increasingly substitutable with one another. When news or the pressure of events causes investors to reallocate their assets, the resulting short-term demands on a country's foreign exchange reserves far exceed anything envisioned in the old regime of limited capital mobility" (Bosworth 1998: 7).

Moreover, this kind of decision making need not be irrational. In the context of myriad investment opportunities and capital mobility, investors confronting the "trade-off between diversification and costly information gathering" may simply choose to exit. In other words, as investors react sharply to even minor fluctuations in a county's economic performance, they become increasingly indifferent to the reasons underlying those changes. "Thus, diversification encourages ignorance, and in this environment even

frivolous rumors may trigger massive capital flows that are seemingly inconsistent with a country's 'fundamentals'" (Calvo and Mendoza 1996: 174).

Similarly, many economists believe that the reaction of investors in Asia
was based more on hysteria than analysis. As Jeffrey Sachs argued, "What we
have experienced is massive inflows based on high optimism about [Asia]
followed by massive outflows that one can only characterize as a panic.
While it is fashionable to talk about the myths of East Asian economic performance, I believe that—while those weaknesses are real—they cannot begin to account for the collapse" (quoted in Chanda 1998: 48). A *Wall Street
Journal* report on the "flight to quality" tried to explain why investors were
abandoning emerging markets.

In theory, a currency's value mirrors the fundamental strength of its underlying
economy, relative to other economies. But in the current white-knuckled climate,
traders and lenders are trying to guess what every other trader thinks. While traders
use the most modern communications, they act by fight-or-flee instincts. . . . It isn't
just economics at work now; it's a psychology that at times borders on panic. (August
24, 1998: A4)

Following the Mexican crisis, the international financial community
claimed it had learned hard lessons for the future. In July 1995, a professor
of international management wrote that one of the salubrious results of the
"tequila effect" was a more circumspect investment community:

In general, a closer scrutiny of the risk-return trade-offs of portfolio investment in
developing economies has replaced the exuberant approach of the pre-crisis era.
The unquestioned golden opportunities of the past are now regarded in a different
light, with the recognition that careful monitoring of macroeconomic conditions
in those markets is indispensable in order to avoid the excessive optimism of the
past and a repetition of the Mexico case. (Espana 1995: 47)

Yet the investment flowing into emerging markets during the 1990s was
controlled largely by money managers with very little knowledge of those
countries. Economic sustainability was not a relevant criterion for investment. In retrospect, it is clear that spectacular economic growth served as a
financial Trojan horse. Lenders all over the world gladly accepted the gift of
high returns and disregarded the well-known weaknesses in emerging market financial systems. "Good times are bad times for learning about creditworthiness of borrowers. . . . It's only when the system as a whole can no
longer roll over and expand debt that there is an actual test of loan quality"
(Smalhout 1998: 67).

In an environment of high growth and mass euphoria, a skeptical fund
manager could hardly be expected to defend the decision *not* to invest in
stocks or bonds earning several times the mundane rates offered in the
United States and other developed countries. Even those investors who had

done their homework and questioned the viability of certain emerging markets could scarcely opt out of such lucrative short-term opportunities. As the director of Dresdner Bank AG in Germany confessed, "All banks are under certain competitive pressure. If the market is attractive you go with the herd. Even if you have doubts you don't stop lending" (Chanda 1998: 47).

That razor cuts both ways. Investors who were more sanguine about the long-term prospects of more stable markets, such as Argentina in 1995, or Mexico in 1998, found it difficult to justify keeping their money in those markets when others were taking billions out every day. Because an information-poor investment community lacked the incentive and knowledge to distinguish among different countries, their behavior made massive and widespread capital flight a routine response to area-specific setbacks in emerging markets. As international financier George Soros wrote shortly after the Asian collapse, "Markets cannot be left to correct their mistakes, because they are likely to over-react and to behave in an indiscriminate fashion" (1998).

An analysis of global financial instability based on information and uncertainty reorients the debate over the effects of liberalization. Rather than lay responsibility for crisis upon short-sighted investors, as McKinnon does at the beginning of this chapter, those who call for changes in the world's financial architecture assume that integrated capital markets provide *systematic* incentives to increase volatility and promote dangerous boom and bust cycles. Put somewhat differently, while capital flight was the proximate cause of financial crisis in emerging markets, it is pointless to blame global capitalists for behaving like global capitalists.

The central argument of the information-based critique of global finance is that if international capital were less mobile, emerging markets would be less vulnerable to the whims and vagaries of impressionable money managers. Its focus on the global financial community, as opposed to weak national financial systems, is valid. After all, emerging markets that are unprepared to absorb massive inflows of foreign capital do not command high levels of global lending. Restricting capital movements would save developing countries from investors and would save investors from themselves.

While the movement in favor of appropriate capital controls has been largely validated by experience and theory, it should also be tempered by two considerations. First, just as political interests can distort deregulation, they can also influence re-regulation. During the 1970s and 1980s, governments used restrictions on capital and other forms of financial intervention for satisfying domestic constituencies more than for achieving stability and growth.

Second, high capital mobility is a necessary, but not sufficient, condition for financial crisis in emerging markets. Critics eagerly explain how volatile foreign capital flows undermine economic stability but do not explain why many liberalizing emerging markets do not experience financial collapse.

The global environment alone does not explain variation in the maturity periods of foreign debt, or why some countries received huge influxes of capital, at times between 5 and 10 percent of GDP, while others received only a modest amount. Why doesn't the international financial system destabilize all developing economies, and why does it undermine some countries with varying intensity and at different times?

The answer is that emerging markets do not offer equal opportunities for profit. Global savings do not fall from the sky. They cross borders when certain conditions are met. First, investors want to see growth, or at least high growth prospects. Second, the macroeconomic environment should be stable, with inflation under control and a reasonably balanced budget. Third, the flow of investment is likely to pick up when the government implements measures designed to prevent future policy reversals. Giving the central bank formal monetary autonomy or establishing a currency board are becoming increasingly common. On the other hand, pegging the exchange rate to a hard currency, which ensures the value of locally denominated assets, has fallen into relative disfavor. As the December 1998 collapse of the Brazilian *real* demonstrated, investors now routinely evaluate the sustainability of fixed currencies in terms of macroeconomic congruence.

Each of these conditions is an important factor in determining foreign capital movements into emerging markets, but they all presuppose the most important condition of all: the act of financial liberalization. Sustained foreign capital inflows cannot occur without laws that permit them, institutions that receive them, and inducements that encourage them. The dramatic surge in portfolio investment in East Asia during the early 1990s "required deregulation of capital markets in order for it to continue" (Henderson 1998: 20). Optimism may explode into euphoria, but the basic decision to invest requires an incentive. While incentives are often shaped by changing opportunities in global markets, they are also produced by *domestic* policy choices.

## TAKING DOMESTIC POLITICS SERIOUSLY

This book has asked what motivates national leaders to adopt inconsistent and unsustainable financial policies, even as they move toward reform measures such as trade reform and fiscal discipline. In the case of Mexico, and in other key emerging markets, a major part of that answer was domestic politics.

This is not to deny that governments of developing countries react to international pressure. The advanced countries and the global financial institutions they control routinely demand financial opening in exchange for greater access to their markets. Yet many of the countries that experienced financial crises during the 1990s opened their capital markets without great external pressure to do so and far more quickly than they needed to comply with market integration. Indeed, several successfully resisted foreign pressure to open their domestic banking system, belying the proposition that liberalization was simply a concession to foreign demands.

The success of national politicians ultimately depends on satisfying domestic, not global, constituencies. This basic premise has led scholars of economic policy making to explain government intervention and protectionism as the outcome of political decision. Traditionally, governments relied on fiscal policy to confer benefits upon social groups whose support they sought. Increased public spending, subsidies, credit allocation, and public sector employment represent highly visible and direct ways in which politicians can gain favor with critical constituencies. Not surprisingly, a high degree of state intervention has typically led to problematic economic performance: unsustainably high budget deficits, rampant inflation, and low productivity.

Students of economic reform have long recognized that social mobilization and electoral opposition can lead political leaders to adopt economic policies whose purpose has more to do with keeping them in power than with fulfilling development objectives. Even though the failure of economic *dirigisme* may be readily apparent and the need for reform impossible to ignore, the difficult reality of economic restructuring creates opportunities for the rise and expansion of political opposition, which caters to influential groups suffering from the reform process. In other words, leaders contemplating major economic reform face the dilemma that such policies will create the conditions for their eventual removal.

Virtually any developing country undertaking liberal reform must impose painful economic measures. Reductions in public spending, employment services and subsidies; the selling of public enterprises; a more burdensome (or at least more accountable) tax system; and, of course, international competition inflict social cost in the short term, while the fruits of restructuring tend to come much later, if ever.

Consequently, when economic liberalization has been achieved, it has typically been interpreted as a triumph of reason over politics. The logic is straightforward, if flawed: If catering to the demands of particular constituencies was the reason governments had traditionally intervened in the economy, then the implementation of reform was evidence that the state was no longer constrained by such forces. One venerable explanation for the change is that a "strong state" was able to ignore social pressures against reform. The question is thus refined: What makes certain governments durable enough to withstand the protest and opposition that are likely to result from reform? Extensive corporatist links to organized social groups, a strong and stable party system, a highly insulated bureaucracy, and repression enable governments to adopt the longer-term perspective required to make real economic reform possible.

Another explanation attributes more power to domestic actors, focusing on their changing policy preferences rather than state autonomy. In this perspective, repeated failures of state intervention in the past were so disastrous that they eventually reversed the traditional resistance to economic opening among major interest groups. The recognition that protectionism and state-led development had caused perennial instability and poor growth made key constituencies willing to endure the pain of market transition and convinced even well-entrenched, self-serving political interests to accept a radical new approach to economic growth.

These approaches go a long way toward explaining the move toward trade liberalization, fiscal discipline, and the demise of the state-owned enterprise. However, the episodes of financial turmoil in Mexico, Korea, and Russia suggest that market reform can be just as politically motivated as state intervention and, more ominously, that political considerations can limit and distort genuine liberalization programs. Particularly when deficit spending is not an option, the finance sector may be the most important remaining policy instrument that governments can manipulate for political benefit.

The dilemma of liberalization for the developing world is that political constraints may make comprehensive and coherent economic reform difficult to implement. If international lending institutions and economists have only recently begun to address regulatory obstacles to effective liberalization, they still largely ignore the domestic pressures on national leaders to pursue policies that undermine or contradict typical reform efforts. Politicians may attempt to appease social opposition stirred up by restructuring by turning to policy options that are fundamentally inconsistent with the larger transformation project. Given the potentially disastrous consequences of partial or incongruent liberalization, the social and electoral pressures facing most governmental reformers should receive far more attention from the international financial community.

## POLICY LESSONS FOR REFORMERS

Shortly before the outbreak of the East Asian financial crisis, economist James Riedel pondered the effects of capital mobility in that region. While recognizing that foreign capital flows can be destabilizing, he concluded in favor of capital market integration. Recalling the irresponsible public sector borrowing that characterized the 1970s and 1980, he maintained, "If the borrowing is by the private sector, the problem [of bad investment] should be self-correcting, as unwise borrowers can generally be counted on to put themselves out of business" (Riedel 1997: 17).

The optimistic assessment was not realized because national leaders confronting change rely on political advisors more than economics textbooks. There is a strong theoretical case that a tremendous amount of inefficient activity could be eliminated, if only politicians would leave the free market alone. Since even the most reformist of leaders do not, however, another approach seems in order. Members of the international policy-making community know that politics are complicated and that the leaders they advise face real pressures. However, the basic tool kit of economics was created to maximize the public good in the long term. It offers little in the way of addressing narrower demands in the short term—apart from admonishing leaders to simply reject them.

A political approach to reform in countries undergoing a "dual transition" suggests important policy implications. As authoritarian governments become more democratic, their plans to free the economy from generations of state intervention may collide with the need to win or preserve valued constituencies. The most powerful and well-organized vested interests are likely to make policy demands that reduce their exposure to the difficult transition to open markets. At the same time, politicians may be pressured to provide benefits for less organized groups with real voting power.

From the experiences of Mexico, South Korea, and Russia, we can derive two general propositions about developing countries that are making their way to democracy and markets. First, no matter how committed and indoctrinated government officials are to market principles, politics comes first. Leaders who know they can be replaced may be able to carry out significant reform measures, but they are also likely to shape policies to maintain or expand their social support base. Moreover, as the Russian case suggests, the less organized the civil society, the narrower the benefits to influential interests are likely to be. Second, largely as a consequence of the political imperative, the transition will not be seamless. The reform process is necessarily step by step, which means that certain economic sectors will be liberalized more quickly than others. This unevenness, in turn, will have serious implications for economic performance and stability.

We cannot easily generalize about the most appropriate areas of liberalization or policy reform sequence in all developing countries because there are so many areas in which states can warp or stall reform. The lesson of Mexico and Russia is not necessarily that the banking sector will inevitably be manipulated by every transitional government—although it is probably a good candidate in many!—but rather that the most serious distortions are likely to occur in policy areas that affect the most crucial constituents.

The economic disasters of promising emerging markets in the 1990s are not, as many critics have maintained, evidence of the failure of economic liberalization. On the contrary, this study suggests that those collapses were largely the result of governmental distortion and institutional incapacity. These traumatic experiences with financial markets, however, should not lead us to the conclusion that politics makes effective economic reform impossible. Rather, they should help policy reformers shape liberalization programs in ways that anticipate the manipulation and distortion of markets.

Because governments confronting political obstacles to economic restructuring may be tempted to allocate off-budget benefits to strategic constituencies, the implementation of comprehensive and consistent market reforms is unlikely. Given this political reality, policy makers should dedicate more effort to figuring out the best way to implement what must necessarily be *partial* liberalization. They should consider the implications of piecemeal reform measures, the pace of those reforms, and how combinations of liberal and nonliberal policies are likely to affect economic performance.

Orthodox policy makers might be tempted to use the Mexican case to argue that their theories and models were right all along. They could insist that what developing countries really need to do is free all their markets at once. That would be unfortunate. Rather, the gate-keepers of economic reform would do a much greater service to their profession and the countries they advise by studying the political limitations to liberalization. This approach will not bring about market utopia. However, it is much more likely to lead to the adoption of consistent and sustainable reforms than abstract models of economic efficiency.

## NOTES

1. One widely publicized case is Chile, which had previously opened its capital account in the 1980s and suffered catastrophic capital flight. Beginning in 1990, even as Chile deepened its commitment to macroeconomic reforms, the government imposed new restrictions on foreign capital: Thirty percent of portfolio investment had to remain in non-interest bearing accounts at the central bank; foreign-denominated loans were taxed 1.2 percent; and even venture capital for production investments had to stay at least one year. Chile subsequently enjoyed years of financial stability and high growth, undercutting the case of those who argued that capital restriction would either stifle the economy or be easily circumvented. "Statements about the ineffectiveness of controls on capital are highly exaggerated. Capital flow regulation tends to be effective as long as it is oriented to the predominance of midterm forces over short-term fluctuations in domestic markets" (Ffrench-Davis 1998: 38).

2. For a revealing account of how new information turned three historic credit booms into global panics, see Spotton (1997).

# Bibliography

Aguilar, Alonso, Fernando Carmona, Arturo Gullén, and Ignacio Hernández. 1983. *La Nacionalización de la banca y la crisis de los monopolios*. México, D.F.: Editorial Nuestro Tiempo.

Alexander, Arthur J. 1998. "Asia's Financial Crisis: Linked to Its Economic Miracle?" *JEI Report*, no. 19A (May 15), 1–13.

Amador, Lucy, and Enrique Quintana. 1992. "Inversión estadunidense: Menos riesgos, más impacto." *Este País* 14 (May), 3–6.

AMB (Asociación Mexicana de Bancos). 1991. "La banca mexicana en transición: Retos y perpectivos." *Comercio Exterior* 41:2, 1–44.

AMCB (Asociación Mexicana de Casas de Bolsa). 1991. *Mexico: Your Partner for Growth*. Mexico City: Mexican Investment Board.

AMDB (Academia Mexicana de Derecho Bursátil). 1990. "Actualización sobre las adiciones a las leyes del mercado de valores y sociedades de inversión." México, D.F.: Auditorio Telmex.

Amsden, Alice H. 1993. "East Asian Financial Markets: Why So Much (And Fairly Effective) Government Intervention?" In *Finance and the Real Economy: Issues and Case Studies in Developing Countries*, ed. Yilmaz Akyüz and Günther Held. United Nations University, World Institute for Development Economics Research, ECLAC, UNCTAD.

———. 1989. *Asia's Next Giant: South Korea and Late Industrialization*. New York: Oxford University Press.

Amsden, Alice H., and Yoon-Dae Euh. 1993. "South Korea's 1980s Financial Reforms: Good-bye Financial Repression (Maybe), Hello New Institutional Restraints." *World Development* 21:3, 379–390.

Aslund, Anders. 1996. "Russian Banking: Crisis or Rent-Seeking?" *Post-Soviet Geography and Economics* 37:8, 495–502.

Aspe, Pedro. 1993. *Economic Transformation the Mexican Way*. Cambridge: MIT Press.

———. 1992. "Macroeconomic Stabilization and Structural Change in Mexico." *European Economic Review*, 36.

Bailey, John J. 1986. "The Impact of Major Groups on Policy-making Trends in Government-Business Relations in Mexico." In *Mexico's Political Stability: The Next Five Years*, ed. Roderic A. Camp. Boulder, CO: Westview Press.

Baker, Carol Louise. 1993. "Three Aspects of Financial Markets in Mexico: The Exchange Rate, Inflation Rate and the Stock Market." Ph.D. diss., University of Wisconsin, Madison.

Bald, Joachim, and Jim Nielsen. 1998. "Developing Efficient Financial Institutions in Russia." *Communist Economies & Economic Transformation* 10:1.

Banco de México. 1993. *The Mexican Economy: 1993.* Mexico City.

Barnes García, Guillermo. 1989. "Una perspectiva sobre el sistema financiero." In *Mexico al Filo del Año 2000.* Mexico, D.F: Instituto Tecnológico Autónomo de México.

Basañez, Miguel. 1990. *El Pulso de los Sexenios: 20 Años de Crisis en México.* Mexico City: Siglo Veiniuno.

Bazdresch, Carlos, and Santiago Levy. 1991. "Populism and Economic Policy in Mexico, 1970–82." In *The Macroeconomics of Populism in Latin America*, ed. Rudiger Dornbusch and Sebastian Edwards. Chicago: University of Chicago Press.

Bencivenga, Valerie R., and Bruce D. Smith. 1991. "Financial Intermediation and Endogenous Growth." *Review of Economic Studies* 58, 195–209.

Bernard, Mitchell, and John Ravenhill. 1995. "Beyond Product Cycles and Flying Geese: Regionalization, Hierarchy, and the Industrialization of East Asia." *World Politics* 47, 171–209.

Bhagwati, Jagdish. 1998. "The Capital Myth: The Difference Between Trade in Widgets and Dollars." *Foreign Affairs* 77 (May–June), 7–120.

Bhatt, V. V. 1989. "Financial Innovation and Credit Market Development." Working Paper WPS 52, The World Bank, August.

Bosworth, Barry. 1998. "The Asian Financial Crisis: What Happened and What Can We Learn From It?" *Brookings Review* 16:3, 6–9.

Brannon, Jeff. 1986. "The Nationalization of Mexico's Private Banking System: Some Potential Effects on the Structure and Performance of the Financial System." In *Mexico: A Country in Crisis*, ed. Jerry R. Ladman. El Paso, TX: Western Press.

Bruhn, Kathleen. 1996. "Social Spending and Political Support: The 'Lessons' of the National Solidarity Program in Mexico." *Comparative Politics* 28:2, 151–177.

Buffie, Edward F. 1990. "Economic Policy and Foreign Debt in Mexico." In *Developing Country Debt and Economic Performance*, ed. Jeffrey D. Sachs. Chicago: University of Chicago Press.

Calvo, Guillermo A., and Enrique G. Mendoza. 1996. "Petty Crime and Cruel Punishment: Lessons from the Mexican Debacle." *American Economic Review* 86:2, 170–175.

Calvo, Guillermo A., Leonardo Leiderman, and Carmen M. Reinhart. 1996. "Inflows of Capital to Developing Countries in the 1990s." *Journal of Economic Perspectives* 10:2, 123–139.

Camp, Roderic A. 1993. *Politics in Mexico.* New York: Oxford University Press.

———. 1989. *Entrepreneurs and Politics in Twentieth Century Mexico.* New York: Oxford University Press.

Campos, Ricardo. 1993. *El Fondo Monetario Internacional y la deuda externa mexicana: Crisis y estabilización.* México, D.F.: Plaza y Valdes Editores.

Canavan, Chris, and Manuel Pastor, Jr. 1990. "What Every Buyer Should Know." *LatinFinance* 21.

Caplen, Brian. 1998. "A House Built on Sand." *Euromoney* no. 351 (July), 44–47.

Caprio, Gerard. 1997. "Bank Regulation: The Case of the Missing Model." In *Sequencing?: Financial Strategies for Developing Countries,* ed. Alison Harwood and Bruce L. R. Smith. Washington, D.C.: Brookings Institution Press.

Cardero, María Elena, and José Manuel Quijano. 1983. "Expansión y estrangulamiento financiero, 1978–81." In *La Banca: Pasado y Presente,* ed. José Manuel Quijano. Mexico, D.F.: Centro de Investigación y Docencia Económica.

Carlsen, Laura. 1993. "La Bolsa Mexicana de Valores." *El Cotidiano* no. 59.

*Carpeta Mexico.* 1993. Mexico, D.F.: Comisión Nacional de Valores. Secretaria de Hacienda y Credito Público.

Carstens, Agustín. 1994. "Foreign Exchange and Monetary Policy in Mexico." *Columbia Journal of World Business,* 29:2 (Summer), 72–77.

Casar, María Amparo. 1992. "Empresarios y estado en el gobierno de Miguel de la Madrid: En busca de un nuevo acuerdo." In *México: Auge, crisis y ajuste,* ed. Carlos Bazdresch, Nisso Bucay, Soledad Loaeza, Nora Lustig. México, D.F.: Fondo de Cultura Económica.

Castaneda, Gonzalo Albert. 1988. "Macroeconomic Consequences of the 1986–1987 Boom in the Mexican Stock Market and Treasury Bills Market." Ph.D. diss., Cornell University.

Centeno, Miguel Angel. 1994. *Democracy Within Reason: Technocratic Revolution in Mexico.* University Park: Pennsylvania State University Press.

Centeno, Miguel Angel, and Sylvia Maxfield. 1992. "The Marriage of Finance and Order: Changes in the Mexican Political Elite." *Journal of Latin American Studies* 24, 57–85.

Cerny, Philip G. 1988. "Financial Market Deregulation and the Competition State." Paper presented at Meeting of American Political Science Association, September, Washington, D.C.

Chanda, Nayan. 1998. "Rebuilding Asia." *Far Eastern Economic Review* 161 (February 12), 46–50.

Chang, Ha-joon. 1998. "Korea: The Misunderstood Crisis." *World Development* 26:8, 1555–1561.

Cho, Dong-sung. 1998. "Korea's Economic Crisis: Causes, Significance and Agenda for Recovery." *Korea Focus* 6 (January–February), 15–26.

Cho, Jae Ho. 1995. "External Debt and Policy Controversy in Korea." *Southern Economic Journal* 62:2, 467–480.

Cho, Yoon-je. 1998. "Direction for Structural Reform of Korean Economy." *Korea Focus* 6 (January–February), 27–40.

Clifford, Mark. 1990. "Seoul-mates again." *Far Eastern Economic Review* 147 (March 1), 46–50.

CNB (Comisión Nacional Bancaria). 1992. *Guía del Consejero.* México, D.F.

CNV (Comisión Nacional de Valores). 1993. *Annual Report.* México, D.F.

Cockcroft, James D. 1983. *Mexico: Class Formation, Capital Accumulation and the State.* New York: Monthly Review Press.

Collier, Ruth Berins. 1992. *The Contradictory Alliance: State-Labor Relations and Regime Change in Mexico.* Berkeley, CA: International and Area Studies.

Collier, Ruth Berins, and David Collier. 1991. *Shaping the Political Arena: Critical Junctures, the Labor Movement, and Regime Dynamics in Latin America.* Princeton, NJ: Princeton University Press.

Colmenares, David, Luis Angeles, and Carlos Ramírez. 1982. *La nacionalización de la banca.* México, D.F.: Editorial Terra Nueva.

Conger, Lucy. 1995. "Power to the Plutocrats." *Institutional Investor* 20 (February), 28–37.

Contreras, Oscar, and Vivienne Bennett. 1994. "National Solidarity in the Northern Borderlands" Social Participation and Community Leadership." In *Transforming State-Society Relations in Mexico: The National Solidarity Strategy,* ed. Wayne A. Cornelius, Ann L. Craig, and Jonathan Fox. San Diego, CA: Center for U.S.-Mexican Studies.

Coorey, Sharmini. 1992. "Mexico's External Debt Policies, 1982–1990." In *Mexico: The Strategy to Achieve Sustained Economic Growth,* ed. Claudio Loser and Eliot Kalter. Washington, D.C.: International Monetary Fund.

Córdoba Montoya, José. 1992. "Los retos del mercado de valores en los años noventa." *Ejecutivos de Finanzas* (June).

———. 1991. "Diez lecciones de la reforma económica en México." *Nexos* 14:158.

Cornelius, Wayne A. 1973. "Nation-Building, Participation and Distribution: The Politics of Social Reform under Cárdenas." In *Crisis, Choice and Change: Historical Studies of Political Development,* ed. Gabriel Almond, Scott Flanagan, Robert Mundt. Boston: Little, Brown and Company.

Cornelius, Wayne A., Ann L. Craig, and Jonathan Fox. 1994. "Mexico's National Solidarity Program: An Overview." In *Transforming State-Society Relations in Mexico: The National Solidarity Strategy,* ed. Wayne A. Cornelius, Ann L. Craig, and Jonathan Fox. San Diego, CA: Center for U.S.-Mexican Studies.

Cornelius, Wayne A., Judith Gentleman, and Peter H. Smith. 1989. "The Dynamics of Political Change in Mexico." In *Mexico's Alternative Political Futures,* ed. Wayne A. Cornelius, Judith Gentleman, and Peter H. Smith. San Diego, CA: Center for U.S.-Mexican Studies.

Crespo, José Antonio. 1992. "Crisis económica: Crisis de legitimidad." In *México: Auge, Crisis y Ajuste,* ed. Carlos Bazdresch, Nisso Bucay, Soledad Loaeza, and Nora Lustig. México, D.F.: Fondo de Cultura Económica.

Cypher, James M. 1990. *State and Capital in Mexico: Development Policy Since 1940.* Boulder, CO: Westview Press.

Dávila Aldás, Francisco. 1995. *Del milagro a la crisis: La ilusión, el miedo y la nueva esperanza: análisis de la política económica mexicana 1954–1994.* Mexico, D.F.: Distribuciones Fontamara.

Dávila Flores, Alejandro. 1990. "La bolsa mexicana de valores: ¿Alternativas para el financiamiento de la inversión productiva?" In *Testimonios de la Crisis: Los Saldos del Sexenio 1982–1988,* ed. Esthela Gutiérrez Garza. México, D.F.: Siglo Veintiuno Editores.

Davis, Diane E. 1992. "Mexico's New Politics: Changing Perspectives on Free Trade." *World Policy Journal* 9:4, 655–671.

Dean, James. 1998. "Why Left-Wing Moralists and Right-Wing Academics Are Wrong about Asia." *Challenge* 41 (March–April), 44–60.

Dee, Philippa S. 1986. *Financial Markets and Economic Development: The Economic and Politics of Korean Financial Reform.* Tubingen, Germany: Institut fur Weltwirtschaft an der Universitat Kiel. J.C.B. Mohr.

Deliagin, M. 1996. "The Banking Crisis in Light of Basic Tendencies of Economic Development in Russia." *Problems of Economic Transition* 39:3, 84–95.

Demirors, Uhran. 1994. "Credibility of Exchange-Rate Policy Wins Foreign Investors Favor in Latin America." *Latin American Money Markets* (January–February), supplement to *LatinFinance.*

Doh, Myung-Guk. 1996. "Recent Development of Financial Market Liberalization and Its Perspectives in Korea." *Business Korea* (June), 55–61.

Dornbusch, Rudiger. 1997. "A Thai-Mexico Primer: Lessons for Outmaneuvering a Financial Meltdown." *The International Economy* 11 (September–October), 20–23.

Dornbusch, Rudiger, and Alejandro Werner. 1994. "Mexico: Stabilization, Reform and No Growth." *Brookings Papers on Economic Activity* no. 1, 253–315.

Dresser, Denise. 1998. "Mexico after the July 6 Election: Neither Heaven nor Hell." *Current History* 97 (February), 55–60.

———. 1991. *Neopopulist Solutions to Neoliberal Problems: Mexico's National Solidarity Program.* San Diego, CA: Center for U.S.-Mexican Studies.

Ejea, Guillermo M., and Cristian G. Leriche. 1991. "Hipótesis acerca del auge bursátil." *El Cotidiano* no. 41.

Ejea, Guillermo M., Celso Garrido, Cristian Leriche, Enrique Quintana. 1991. *Mercado de valores: Crisis y nuevos circuitos financieros en México, 1970–1990.* México, D.F.: Casa Abierta al Tiempo.

Elizondo, Carlos. 1994. "In Search of Revenue: Tax Reform in Mexico under the Administrations of Echeverría and Salinas." *Journal of Latin American Studies* 26, 159–190.

———. 1992. "Property Rights in Mexico: Government and Business after the 1982 Bank Nationalization." Ph.D. diss., Nuffield College, Oxford University.

Espana, Juan R. 1995. "The Mexican Peso Crisis: Impact on NAFTA and Emerging Markets." *Business Economics* 30:3 (July), 45–50.

Estudillo Rendón, Joel. 1998. "The Learning Process." *Business Mexico* (June), 20.

Evans, Peter. 1995. *Embedded Autonomy: States and Industrial Transformation.* Princeton, NJ: Princeton University Press.

Fairlamb, David. 1998. "Reigning in the Oligarchs." *Institutional Investor* (November), 28–34.

Fernández-Arias, Eduardo, and Peter J. Motiel. 1996. "The Surge in Capital Inflows to Developing Countries: An Analytical Overview." *The World Bank Economic Review* 10:1, 51–77.

Fernández Hurtado, Ernesto. 1975. "El sistema bancario y la coyuntura financiera actual." *Ejecutivos de Finanzas* (January).

Ffrench-Davis, Ricardo. 1998. "Policy Implications of the Tequila Effect." *Challenge* 41 (March–April), 15–43.

Fitzgerald, E.V.K. 1985. "The Financial Constraint on Relative Autonomy: The State and Capital Accumulation in Mexico, 1940–82." In *The State and Capital Accumulation in Latin America, Volume 1,* ed. Christian Anglade and Carlos Fortin. London: Macmillan.

Fox, Jonathan. 1994a. "The Difficult Transition from Clientalism to Citizenship: Lessons from Mexico." *World Politics* 46, 151–184.

————. 1994b. "Political Change in Mexico's New Peasant Economy." In *The Politics of Economic Restructuring: State-Society Relations and Regime Change in Mexico*, ed. María Lorena Cook, Kevin J. Middlebrook, and Juan Molinar Horcasitas. San Diego, CA: Center for U.S.-Mexican Studies.

Frieden, Jeffry A. 1991. "Invested Interests: The Politics of National Economic Policies in a World of Global Finance." *International Organization* 45:4, 425–451.

Garrido, Celso. 1994. "National Private Groups in Mexico: 1987–1993." *Cepal Review* no. 53, 159–176.

de la Garza Toledo, Enrique. 1994. "The Restructuring of State-Labor Relations in Mexico." In *The Politics of Economic Restructuring: State-Society Relations and Regime Change in Mexico*, ed. María Lorena Cook, Kevin J. Middlebrook, and Juan Molinar Horcasitas. San Diego, CA: Center for U.S.-Mexican Studies.

Gavito, Javier. 1991. "México ante la apertura de servicios financieros." *Ejecutivos de Finanzas*, (March).

Gavito, Javier, and Ignacio Trigueros. 1994. "Los efectos del TLC sobre las entidades financieras." In *Lo Negociado del TLC*, ed. Geogina Kessel. Mexico City: McGraw-Hill.

Geyer, Anne. 1991. "Credit Card Surge." *Business Mexico* (June).

Gibson, Edward L. 1992. "Conservative Electoral Movements and Democratic Politics: Core Constituencies, Coalition Building and the Latin American Electoral Right." In *The Right and Democracy in Latin America*, ed. Douglas Chalmers, Maria do Carmo, Campello de Souza, and Atilo A. Boron. New York: Praeger.

Gil Díaz, Francisco. 1984. "Mexico's Path from Stability to Inflation." In *World Economic Growth*, ed. Arnold C. Harberger. San Francisco: Institute for Contemporary Studies.

Girón, Alicia. 1994. "La banca comercial de México frente al TLC." *Comercio Exterior* 44:12, 1068–1074.

Goldstein, Morris, and Philip Turner. 1996. "Banking Crisis in Emerging Economies: Origins and Policy Options." *BIS Economic Papers*, no. 46. Basel, Switzerland: Bank for International Settlements.

González Turbicio, Enrique. 1994. "Social Reform in Mexico: Six Theses on the National Solidarity Program." In *Transforming State-Society Relations in Mexico: The National Solidarity Strategy*, ed. Wayne A. Cornelius, Ann L. Craig, and Jonathan Fox. San Diego, CA: Center for U.S.-Mexican Studies.

Goodman, John B., and Louis W. Pauly. 1993. "The Obsolescence of Capital Controls? Economic Management in an Age of Global Markets." *World Politics* 46, 50–82.

Goulet, Denis. 1983. *Mexico: Development Strategies for the Future*. Notre Dame, IN: University of Notre Dame Press.

Graham, Thomas. 1995. "Russia's New Regime." *Nezavisimaya Gazeta* (November 23).

Green, Rosario. 1981. *Estado y Banca Transnacional en México*. Mexico, D.F.: Editorial Nueva Imagen.

Gruben, William C., John H. Welch, and Jeffrey W. Gunther. 1993. "U.S. Banks, Competition and the Mexican Banking System: How Much Will NAFTA Matter?" *Financial Industry Studies* (October). Federal Reserve Bank of Dallas.

Guillén López, Tonatiuh. 1989. "The Social Bases of the PRI." In *Mexico's Alternative Political Futures*, ed. Wayne A. Cornelius, Judith Gentleman, and Peter H. Smith. San Diego, CA: Center for U.S.-Mexican Studies.

Guillén Romo, Héctor. 1990. *El sexenio de crecimiento cero: Contra los defensores de las finanzas.* México, D.F.: Ediciones Era.

Gurría Treviño, José Angel. 1994. *Flujos de capital: El caso de México.* Santiago, Chile: Economic Commission for Latin America and the Caribbean.

Gutiérrez, Roberto. 1992. "El endeudamiento externo del sector privado de México, 1971–1991." *Comercio Exterior* 42:9, 852–864.

Gutiérrez Pérez, Antonio, and Ignacio Perrotini. 1994. "Liberalización financiera y estabilización macroeconómica en México: Dasafíos y perspectivas." *Investigación Económica* 209, 77–106.

Haggard, Stephan, and Sylvia Maxfield. 1993. "The Political Economy of Capital Account Liberalization." In *Financial Opening: Policy Issues and Experiences in Developing Countries,* ed. Helmut Reisen and Bernard Fischer. Paris, France: OECD.

Hakim-Simon, Miguel. 1988. "The Efficiency of the Mexican Stock Market." Ph.D. diss., Claremont Graduate School.

Hale, David. 1998. "What the Asia Crisis Is All About." *The International Economy* 12 (January–February), 18–23.

Hamilton, Nora. 1986. "State-Class Alliances and Conflicts: Issues and Actors in the Mexican Economic Crisis." In *Modern Mexico: State, Economy and Social Conflict,* ed. Nora Hamilton and Timothy F. Harding. London: Sage Publications.

Hanke, Steve H., and Sir Alan Walters. 1994. "The Wobbly Peso." *Forbes* (July 4), 161.

Hansen, Roger D. 1971. *The Politics of Mexican Development.* Baltimore, MD: Johns Hopkins University Press.

Helleiner, Eric. 1994. *States and the Reemergence of Global Finance.* Ithaca, NY: Cornell University Press.

Hellman, Judith Adler. 1983. *Mexico in Crisis.* (2nd ed.). New York: Holmes & Meier Publishers.

Henderson, Callum. 1998. *Asia Falling: Making Sense of the Asian Crisis and its Aftermath.* New York: BusinessWeek Books.

Heredia, Blanca. 1994. "Making Economic Reform Politically Viable: The Mexican Experience." In *Democracy, Markets and Structural Reform in Latin America,* ed. William Smith, Carlos H. Acuña, and Eduardo A. Gamarra. Miami, FL: North-South Center Press.

Heyman, Timothy. 1991. "Euphoria on Reforma: Mexico's Stock Market is Posting Dazzling Numbers and There Is More to Come." *LatinFinance* no. 28.

Hoskins, W. Lee, and James W. Coons. 1995. "Mexico: Policy Failure, Moral Hazard, and Market Solutions." *Policy Analysis,* no. 243.

House, Richard. 1994. "Masters of the Game." *Institutional Investor* 28 (March 1994), 53–62.

Huhne, Christopher. 1998. "How the Rating Agencies Blew It on Korea." *The International Economy* 12 (May–June), 46–63.

Ibarra, David. 1988. "Comments on the Mexican Financial System." In *Financial Liberalization and the Internal Structure of Capital Markets in Asia and Latin America,* ed. Miguel Urrutia. Tokyo, Japan: The United Nations University.

Ihlwan, Moon. 1998. "Letter from Seoul: A Nation on the Edge." *The Washington Quarterly* 21:2 (Spring), 99–104.

Jacobs, Eduardo. 1981. "La evolución reciente de los grupos de capital privado nacional." *Economía Mexicana* no. 3.

Jacobs, Eduardo, and Wilson Peres Núñez. 1982. "Las grandes empresas y el crecimiento acelerado." *Economía Mexicana* no. 4.

Johnson, Juliet. 1997. "Russia's Emerging Financial-Industrial Groups." *Post-Soviet Affairs* 13:4, 333–365.

———. 1996. "Banking in Russia: Shadows of the Past." *Problems of Post-Communism* 43 (May–June), 49–59.

Kaminsky, Graciela L., and Carmen M. Reinhart. 1998. "Financial Crises in Asia and Latin America: Then and Now." *American Economic Review* 88:2, 444–448.

Kang, Peter K. 1988. "Political and Corporate Group Interests in South Korea's Political Economy." *Asian Profile* 16:3 (June), 209–223.

Kaufman, Robert R., Carlos Bazdresch, and Blanca Heredia. 1992. "The Politics of the Economic Solidarity Pact in Mexico: December 1987 to December 1988." Prepared for the World Bank Project on the Political Economy of Economic Reform, July 29, Washington, D.C.

Kawai, Masahiro. 1998. "The East Asian Currency Crisis: Causes and Lessons." *Contemporary Economic Policy* 16, 157–172.

Khatkhate, Deena. 1998. "East Asian Financial Crisis and the IMF: Chasing Shadows." *Economic and Political Weekly* (April 25), 963–969.

Kim, Chung-soo. 1998. "How the Chaebol Can Survive." *Korea Focus* 6 (January–February), 41–54.

Kim, Duk-choong, and Dongsuk Suh. 1998. "Financial Liberalization and Korean Corporations' Financing Policy for Globalization." *Journal of Asian Economics* 9:1, 31–66.

Kim, Eun Mee. 1997. *Big Business, Strong State: Collusion and Conflict in South Korean Development 1960–1990.* Albany: State University of New York Press.

Kim, Hyuk-rae. 1998. "Family Capitalism and Corporate Structure in Korea." *Korea Focus* 6 (January–February), 55–67.

Kim, Sunhyuk. 1997. "State and Civil Society in South Korea's Democratic Consolidation: Is the Battle Really Over?" *Asian Survey* 37 (December), 1135–1144.

Klesner, Joseph L. 1997. "Democratic Transition? The 1997 Mexican Elections." *PS: Political Science & Politics* 30:4 (December), 703–711.

Korhonen, Iikka. 1997. "A Brief Assessment of Russia's Treasury Bill Market." *Review of Economies in Transition* no. 3, 15–22.

Kregal, J. A. 1998. "East Asia Is Not Mexico: The Difference Between Balance of Payments Crises and Debt Deflations." Working Paper no. 235. Blithewood, NY: The Jerome Levy Economics Institute.

Krugman, Paul. 1999. "The Return of Depression Economics." *Foreign Affairs* 78:1, 56–74.

———. 1994. "The Myth of Asia's Miracle." *Foreign Affairs* 73:6, 3–10.

Lamdany, Ruben. 1993. *Russia: The Banking System During Transition.* Washington, D.C.: The World Bank.

Lee, Charles S. 1997. "Not a Pretty Picture." *Far Eastern Economic Review* (September 25).

Levin, Baron F. 1995a. "The Power of Patience: Why UDIs Need More Time to Kick In." *Business Mexico* (September), 51.

———. 1995b. "Working through the web with UDIs." *Business Mexico* (June), 22–26.

Lim, Linda Y. C. 1998. "Whose 'Model' Failed? Implications of the Asian Economic Crisis." *The Washington Quarterly* 21:3 (Summer), 25–36.

Lindau, Juan D. 1992. "Schisms in the Mexican Political Elite and the Techno-cratic/Politician Typology." *Mexican Studies/Estudios Mexicanos* 8:2, 217–236.

Lissakers, Karin, and Julio Zamora. 1989. "The Financial Sector in Mexico's Economic Reform. (Part II: The Capital Markets)." Conference Paper no. 13. Presented at conference, Mexico: Contrasting Visions. Columbia University and New York University Consortium. April 1989, New York City.

Loaeza, Soledad. 1992a. "The Role of the Right in Political Change in Mexico 1982–88." In *The Right and Democracy in Latin America*, ed. Douglas Chalmers, Maria do Carmo, Campello de Souza, and Atilo A. Boron. New York: Praeger.

———. 1992b. "Delamadridismo: La segunda modernización mexicana." In *México: Auge, crisis y ajuste*, ed. Carlos Bazdresch, Nisso Bucay, Soledad Loaeza, and Nora Lustig. México, D.F.: Fondo de Cultura Económica.

Loaeza, Soledad, and Claudio Stern. 1990. *Las clases medias en la coyuntura actual.* Mexico, D.F.: Centro de Estudios Sociales. Colegio de México.

López Portillo, José. 1988. *Mis tiempos: Biografía y testimonio político.* México, D.F.: Fernández Editores.

Low, Ann M. L. 1992. "Slip-Sliding Away: Financial Markets Subside After a Spectacular High Tide." *Business Mexico* (October).

Luna, Matilde, Ricardo Tirado, and Francisco Valdés. 1987. "Businessmen and Politics in Mexico, 1982–1986." In *Government and Private Sector in Contemporary Mexico*, ed. Sylvia Maxfield and Ricardo Anzaldún Montoya. La Jolla, CA: Center for U.S.-Mexican Studies.

Lustig, Nora. 1992. *Mexico: The Remaking of an Economy.* Washington, D.C.: The Brookings Institution.

Madariaga Lomelí, José. 1990. "Perspectivas de la bolsa ante la liberación de servicios financieros." *Ejecutivos de Finanzas* (August 1990).

Mallaby, Sebastian. 1997. "Paper Tiger: Korea's Collapse, Made in Japan." *The New Republic* (December 22), 12–13.

Manchaca Trejo, Mauricio. 1989. "Seis años de banca nacionalizada." *Alto Nivel* (January).

Mansell, Catherine. 1994a. "De represión financiera a las operaciones de mercado abierto." In *Reformas y reestructuración de los sistemas financieros en los países de América Latina.* México, D.F.: Centro de Estudios Monetarios Latinoamericanos.

———. 1994b. "The Internationalization of the Mexican Financial System." Discussion paper presented at Conference on The Global and Comparative Analysis of Financial Institutions, May 9–13, Bellagio, Italy.

———. 1993. "The Impact of the Mexican Bank Reprivatizations." Paper prepared for Conference on Privatization in Latin America, Institute of the Americas, January 28–29, La Jolla, California.

———. 1992. *Las Nuevas Finanzas en México.* México, D.F.: Editorial Milenio S.A. de C.V. Instituto Tecnológico Autónomo de México.

Marichal, Carlos. 1997. "The Rapid Rise of the Neobanqueros: Mexico's New Financial Elite." *NACLA Report on the Americas* 30:6.

Márquez, Javier. 1987. *La Banca Mexicana: Septiembre de 1982–Junio de 1985.* México, D.F.: Centro de Estudios Monetarios Latinoamericanos.

Marray, Michael. 1992. "Growing Pains." *Euromoney* (September), 147–152.

Marriott, Cherie. 1997. "Chaebol: Misfits of Global Finance." *Global Finance* (March), 34–37.

Maxfield, Sylvia. 1990. *Governing Capital: International Finance and Mexican Politics.* Ithaca, NY: Cornell University Press.

———. 1989. "International Economic Opening and Government-Business Relations." In *Mexico's Alternative Political Futures,* ed. Wayne A. Cornelius, Judith Gentleman, and Peter H. Smith. San Diego, CA: Center for U.S.-Mexican Studies.

McComb, Robert P., William C. Gruben, and John H. Welch. 1994. "Privatization and Performance in the Mexican Financial Services Industry." *Quarterly Review of Economic and Finance* 34 (Special Issue), 217–235.

McCoy, Patricia A. 1997. "Levers of Law Reform: Public Goods and Russian Banking." *Cornell International Law Journal* 30:1, 45–137.

McFaul, Michael. 1995. "State Power, Institutional Change, and the Politics of Russian Privatization." *World Politics* 47, 210–243.

McGill, Peter. 1995. "Joining the Club." *Euromoney* (September), 373–382.

Mejía Barquera, Fernando. 1985. *Televisa: El quinto poder.* México, D.F.: Claves Latinoamericanas.

Meyer, Lorenzo. 1983. "Mexico: The Political Problems of Economic Stabilization." In *Mexico's Economic Crisis: Challenges and Opportunities,* ed. Donald L. Wyman. San Diego, CA: Center for U.S.-Mexican Studies.

Meyer, Michael C., and William L. Sherman. 1987. *The Course of Mexican History.* New York: Oxford University Press.

Molinar, Juan Horcasitas, and Jeffrey Weldon. 1990. "Elecciones de 1988 en Mexico: Crisis del autoritarismo." *Revista Mexicana de Sociología* 52:4.

Molinar Horcasitas, Juan, and Jeffrey A. Weldon. 1994. "Electoral Determinants and Consequences of National Solidarity." In *Transforming State-Society Relations in Mexico: The National Solidarity Strategy,* ed. Wayne A. Cornelius, Ann L. Craig, and Jonathan Fox. San Diego, CA: Center for U.S.-Mexican Studies.

Montgomery, John D. 1996. "Recent Turbulence in Emerging Markets: Lessons for Financial Policy." *Social and Economic Studies* 45, 89–107.

Moore, Robert R. 1993. "The Government Budget Deficit and the Banking System: The Case of Mexico." *Financial Industry Studies* (October). Federal Reserve Bank of Dallas, 27–36.

Morris, Stephen D. 1995. *Political Reformism in Mexico.* Boulder, CO: Lynne Rienner Publishers.

Mosk, Sanford A. 1950. *Industrial Revolution in Mexico.* Berkeley: University of California Press.

Musalem, Alberto, Dimitri Vittas, and Asli Demirgüç-Kunt. 1993. "North American Free Trade Agreement: Issues on Trade in Financial Services for Mexico." Washington, D.C.: The World Bank.

Naím, Moises. 1995. "Mexico's Larger Story." *Foreign Policy* 99 (Summer), 112–130.

Nakarmi, Laxmi. 1995. "Seoul Yanks the *Chaebol*'s Leash" *Business Week* (October 30), 58.

NCD (National Commission for Democracy). 1995. "U.S. aid package to Mexico is band-aid for failed global economic policies and a threat to peoples of both countries." Press release (January 25).

Newell, Roberto, and Luis Rubio. 1984. *Mexico's Dilemma: The Political Origins of Economic Crisis.* Boulder, CO: Westview Press.

O'Brien, Courtney. 1996. "Institutionalizing Reform in the Russian Banking System." *World Outlook* 22 (Summer), 31–52.

Orme, William A. 1989. "Wiping the Ledger Clean: How Mexican Companies Eliminated Billions in Debt and Got Back into Business." *LatinFinance* no. 12.

Ortiz, Guillermo Martínez. 1994. *La reforma financiera y la desincorporación bancaria.* México, D.F.: Fondo de Cultura Económica.

Palencia Gomez, José-Ramon. 1992. "Evolution of the Mexican Financial System Towards a Universal Bank." *Money Affairs* 5:1, 33–41.

Park, Won-Am. 1996. "Financial Liberalization: The Korean Experience." In *Financial Deregulation and Integration in East Asia,* ed. Takatoshi Ito and Anne O. Krueger. Chicago: University of Chicago Press.

Park, Yung Chul. 1998. "Investment Boom, Financial Bust." *Brookings Review* 16:3, 14–17.

Payne, Douglas W. 1995. "Wall Street Blues." *New Republic* (March 13), 22.

Pazos, Luis. 1986. "The False Austerity Policies of the Mexican Government." In *Crisis and Response: A Roundtable on Mexico.* New York: International Security Council.

Peritore, N. Patrick, and Ana Karina Peritore. 1993. "Cleavage and Polarization in Mexico's Ruling Party." *Journal of Developing Areas* 28:1, 67–88.

Pineda, Alfredo. 1991. "El nuevo sistema financiero mexicano." *Alto Nivel* (May 1991).

Poniatowska, Elena. 1971. *La noche de Tlatelolco: Testimonios de historia oral.* México, D.F.: Ediciones Era.

Przeworski, Adam. 1985. *Capitalism and Social Democracy.* New York: Cambridge University Press.

Purcell, Susan Kaufman, and John F. H. Purcell. 1980. "State and Society in Mexico: Must a Stable Polity be Institutionalized?" *World Politics* 32:2, 194–227.

Quijano, José Manuel. 1983. "La banca nacionalizada: Antecedentes y consecuencias." In *La Banca: Pasado y presente,* ed. José Manuel Quijano. México, D.F.: Centro de Investigación y Docencia Económica.

———. 1981. *México: Estado y banca privada.* México, D.F.: Centro de Investigación y Docencia Económica.

Quintana, Enrique, Carlos Leriche, and Pedro Bustos. 1987. "La bolsa de valores y la agonía financiera." *El Cotidiano* no. 16.

Ramírez, Miguel D. 1989. *Mexico's Economic Crisis: Its Origins and Consequences.* New York: Praeger.

Reding, Andrew. 1989. "Mexico under Salinas: A Façade of Reform." *World Policy Journal* 6:4, 685–729.

Riedel, James. 1997. "Capital Market Integration in Developing Asia." *World Economy* 20:1, 1–19.

Riner, Deborah L. 1989. "Ficorca: A Success Story." *LatinFinance* no. 12.

Rodríguez San Martín, José Arnulfo. 1990. "Financiamiento y formación de capital durante la crisis mexicana." *Ejecutivos de Finanzas* (April 1990).

Rubio, Luis. 1990. "El sector privado en el pasado y en el futuro de México." In *Industria y trabajo en México,* ed. James W. Wilkie and Jesús Reyes Heroles. Azcapotzalco: Universidad Autónoma Metropolitana.

Rubtsov, Boris, and Michael Tucker. 1995. "Russian Financial Institutions in an Emerging Free Market Economy." *Business & the Contemporary World* 7:1, 67–76.

Ruiz Durán, Clemente. 1989. "Moneda y crédito." In *México: Informe sobre la crisis (1982–1986)*, ed. Carlos Tello. México, D.F.: Centro de Investigaciones Interdisciplinarias en Humanidades. UNAM.

Rumer, Boris. 1991. "New Capitalists in the U.S.S.R." *Challenge* (May–June), 19–22.

Salinas de Gortari, Carlos. 1994. *Sexto Informe de Gobierno.*

Scherlen, Renee G. 1998. "Lessons to Build On: The 1994 Mexican Presidential Election." *Journal of Internamerican Studies and World Affairs* 40:1, 19–38.

Schmidt, Samuel. 1991. *The Deterioration of the Mexican Presidency: The Years of Luis Echeverría.* Tuscon, AZ: University of Arizona Press.

Schwartz, Anna J. 1998. "Time to Terminate the ESF and the IMF." *Cato Foreign Policy Briefing*, no. 48.

Sender, Henny. 1998. "Money Isn't Everything." *Far Eastern Economic Review* 161 (February 12), 56–59.

Shadlen, Ken. 1997. "Corporatism and the Associative Logics of Business: Small Industry and the State in Post-Revolutionary Mexico." Ph.D. diss. University of California, Berkeley.

Sikkink, Kathryn. 1991. *Ideas and Institutions: Developmentalism in Brazil and Argentina.* Ithaca, NY: Cornell University Press.

Silverman, Bertram, and Murray Yanowitch. 1997. *New Rich, New Poor, New Russia: Winners and Losers on the Russian Road to Capitalism.* Armonk, NY: M. E. Sharpe.

*Sistema financiero Mexicano: Alternativas para el futuro.* 1990. México, D.F.: Centro de Investigación Para el Desarrollo.

Slay, Ben. 1999. "An Interpretation of the Russian Financial Crisis." *Post-Soviet Geography and Economics* 40:3, 206–214.

Smalhout, James H. 1998. "Mexico East: Lessons—Right and Wrong—For Asia from the Peso Crisis." *Barron's* 78 (May 4), 67.

Smith, Geri. 1996. "Tossing a Lifeline to Mexico's Biggest Banks." *Business Week* (January 22), 80.

Smith, Geri, and Wendy Zellner. 1993. "The Gringo Banks Are Drooling." *Business Week* (September 13), 84–85.

Smith, Peter. 1986. "Leadership and Change: Intellectuals and Technocrats in Mexico." In *Mexico's Political Stability: The Next Five Years*, ed. Roderic Camp. Boulder, CO: Westview Press.

Solís, Leopoldo. 1981. *Economic Policy Reform in Mexico: A Case Study for Developing Countries.* New York: Pergamon Press.

Soros, George. 1998. "Toward a Global Open Society." *Atlantic Monthly* 281:1 (January), 20–33.

Sosa, José Luis. 1990. "Perversiones en la economía nacional." *El Cotidiano* no. 38.

Spotton, Brenda. 1997. "Financial Instability Reconsidered: Orthodox Theories versus Historical Facts." *Journal of Economic Issues* 31:1, 175–195.

Stein Velasco, Luis F. 1988. "Menor carga financiera." *Alto Nivel* (November).

Stevens, Evelyn P. 1974. *Protest and Response in Mexico.* Cambidge: MIT Press.

Story, Dale. 1987. "The PAN, the Private Sector, and the Future of the Mexican Opposition." In *Mexican Politics in Transition*, ed. Judith Gentleman. Boulder, CO: Westview Press.

———. 1986. *Industry, the State and Public Policy in Mexico.* Austin: University of Texas Press.

Strom, Stephanie. 1998. "Korea's Other Big Problem." *New York Times*, February 19, A1.

Su, Zhan, and Jean-Christophe Loubet Del Bayle. 1996. "Restructuring of Korean Chaebols: An Evolution Toward a Type of Japanese Keiretsu?" *Asian Profile* 24:6.

Suárez Dávila, Francisco. 1994. "Liberación, regulación y supervisión del sistema bancario mexicano." *Comercio Exterior* 44:12, 1049–1053.

Suárez Gaona, Enrique. 1987. *¿Legitimación revolucionaria del poder en México? Los presidentes, 1910–1982*. México, D.F.: Siglo Veintiuno Editores.

Szymczak, Philippe. 1992. "Mexico's Return to Voluntary International Capital Market Financing." In *Mexico: The Strategy to Achieve Sustained Economic Growth*, ed. Claudio Loser and Eliot Kalter. Washington, D.C.: International Monetary Fund.

Tello, Carlos. 1984. *La nacionalización de la banca en México*. México, D.F.: Siglo Veintiuno Editores.

———. 1979. *La política económica en México: 1970–1976*. Mexico, D.F.: Siglo Veintiuno Editores.

Ten Kate, Adriaan. 1992. "Trade Liberalization and Economic Stabilization in Mexico: Lessons and Experience." *World Development* 20:5, 659–672.

Ungson, Gerardo R., Richard M. Steers, and Seung-Ho Park. 1997. *Korean Enterprise: The Quest for Globalization*. Boston: Harvard Business School Press.

Valdés Ugalde, Francisco. 1994. "From Bank Nationalization to State Reform: Business and the New Mexican Order." In *The Politics of Economic Restructuring: State-Society Relations and Regime Change in Mexico*, ed. María Lorena Cook, Kevin J. Middlebrook, and Juan Molinar Horcasitas. La Jolla, CA: Center for U.S.-Mexican Studies.

Vargas Medina, Agustín. 1998. "Las cifras resultan escalofriantes." *Época* (June 22).

Vega Cánovas, Gustavo. 1995. "NAFTA and Financial Services." In *The Politics of Free Trade in North America*, ed. Gustavo del Castillo and Gustavo Vega. Ottowa: Centre for Trade and Policy Law.

Vidal, Gregorio. 1994. "Reforma económica, mecanismos de financiamiento y procesos de inversión." *Comercio Exterior* 44:12, 1083–1092.

Villegas, H. Eduardo, and Rosa Ortega O. 1991. *El nuevo sistema financiero mexicano*. México, D.F.: Editorial PAC, S.A. de C.V.

Vogel, Steven K. 1996. *Freer Markets, More Rules: Regulatory Reform in Advanced Industrial Countries*. Ithaca, NY: Cornell University Press.

Wade, Robert. 1998. "The Asian Debt-and-Development Crisis of 1997–?: Causes and Consequences." *World Development* 26:8, 1535–1553.

———. 1990. *Governing the Market: Economic Theory and the Tole of Government in East Asian Industrialization*. Princeton, NJ: Princeton University Press.

White, Russell N. 1992. *State, Class, and the Nationalization of the Mexican Banks*. New York: Crane Russak.

Willoughby, Jack, and Lucy Conger. 1998. "Under the Volcano." *Institutional Investor* 23 (June), 97–98.

World Bank. 1999. *Knowledge for Development 1998/99*. New York: Oxford University Press.

Yavlinsky, Grigory. 1998. "Russia's Phony Capitalism." *Foreign Affairs* 77 (May–June), 67–79.

Yoo, Chul Gyue, Ha-Joon Chang, and Hong-Jae Park. 1998. "Interpreting the Korean Crisis: Financial Liberalisation, Industrial Policy and Corporate Governance." *Cambridge Journal of Economics* 22, 735–746.

Zedillo, Ernesto. 1987. "Mexico." In *Capital Flight and Third World Debt*, ed. Donald R. Lessard and John Williamson. Washington, D.C.: Institute for World Economics.

———. 1986. "Mexico's Recent Balance-of-Payments Experience and Prospects for Growth." *World Development* 14:8, 963–991.

Zysman, John. 1983. *Governments, Markets and Growth: Financial Systems and the Politics of Industrial Change*. Ithaca, NY: Cornell University Press.

# Index

## About the Author

TIMOTHY P. KESSLER is a Social Science Consultant with the World Bank. Since completing his graduate work, Dr. Kessler has held positions as a professor of political science, legislative fellow in the U.S. House of Representatives and as a resident associate at the Carnegie Endowment for International Peace. His articles on policy issues have appeared in *World Politics* and *The Journal of Commerce* among other scholarly publications.

ISBN 0-275-96568-6

HARDCOVER BAR CODE